WHAT PEOPLE

Reclaimin

This is a very interesting discussion ⌐⌐   ⌐
the current world, and indeed of all history, which puᴛ⌐ ⌐ ⌐r
scrutiny a number of common assumptions which are seldom
examined.
Ronald Hutton, Professor of History, Bristol University

Brendan Myers is that rarest of creatures, a philosopher who
writes in a style that is eminently readable, refreshingly jargon-
free, not remotely patronising and, what's more, genuinely
engaging. Rather than a dry, academic text, reading this gives one
the feeling of sitting with the author in a warm room, probably
with a glass of wine or a decent pint of real ale, and listening to
him expound his ideas with pleasure and enthusiasm. In this
case, those ideas are all about civilisation, asking what it is, if it is
a good thing, and how we can make it better. Given the daily
dose of depression drip-fed to us on every news bulletin, these
are perhaps the most pressing questions of our age. In seeking to
answer them, Myers demonstrates a remarkable breadth of
knowledge of prehistory, history, politics and philosophy, from
the earliest stirrings of humanity to the present day. That he can
analyse with such clarity the seemingly chaotic mess we as a
species have got ourselves into is remarkable in itself. Even
moreso is that he is able to untangle the chaos sufficiently to
draw from it causes for optimism and a plan for the future that
might just see us thrive rather than merely survive. Anyone
running for political office should not be allowed to do so until
they have read this book. If this were done, the world would
undoubtedly be a better, safer, saner place.
Philip Shallcrass, Founder and Chief of the British Druid Order

Brendan Myers is one of the most creative and exciting of contemporary Pagan philosophers whose new book *Reclaiming Civilization* is filled with arresting insights and closes with a fascinating discussion of virtue ethics' relationship with life's "immensities." There is good food here for the mind and the soul.
Gus DiZerega, Political scientist with the Atlas Economic Research Foundation, author of *Fault Lines* and *Persuasion, Power, and Polity*

Reclaiming Civilization

A Case for Optimism for the Future of Humanity

Reclaiming Civilization

A Case for Optimism for the Future
of Humanity

Brendan Myers

Winchester, UK
Washington, USA

First published by Moon Books, 2017
Moon Books is an imprint of John Hunt Publishing Ltd., Laurel House, Station Approach,
Alresford, Hants, SO24 9JH, UK
office1@jhpbooks.net
www.johnhuntpublishing.com
www.moon-books.net

For distributor details and how to order please visit the 'Ordering' section on our website.

Text copyright: Brendan Myers 2016

ISBN: 978 1 78535 565 3
978 1 78535 566 0 (ebook)
Library of Congress Control Number: 2016949322

A CIP catalogue record for this book is available from the British Library.

Design: Stuart Davies

Printed and bound by CPI Group (UK) Ltd, Croydon, CR0 4YY, UK

We operate a distinctive and ethical publishing philosophy in all
areas of our business, from our global network of authors to
production and worldwide distribution.

CONTENTS

Preface, Acknowledgements, and Dedication

I wrote this book because I am angry. The practice of civilization, its customs and institutions and power-relations, and even the language by which we speak of it, has been hijacked by some profoundly evil people. I wish to wrest it back from them, so that everyone of every political culture may see it for what it is, and then pass their own judgment upon it.

I also wrote this book because I am frustrated. Many good and beautiful people of my acquaintance have lost hope for the future of humanity. I am very aware that many of them have endured abuse, violence, poverty, chronic illness, systematic racism and sexism and homophobia, long-term trauma symptoms from those experiences, as well as *the apathy of the comfortable*, for long stretches of their lives. I do not fault them for their condition; I can see how various forces in our society, controlled by everyone and by no one, have beaten the hope out of them. It breaks my heart to see good people give up. They could be heroes; able to see the world for what it is and for what it could otherwise be; able to change our cultures and our planet into something more wonderful. But instead they struggle only to survive, one day at a time, and often because their situation leaves them little other choice.

But my disposition is not all storm clouds and rain. I am also fascinated by the ways and reasons people use the word 'civilization'. (This part of the text is inspired by Sid Meier's famous video game.) It's one of those words which, in ordinary language, has no precise definition: it means something both glamorous and at the same time vague and fuzzy. The only consistent thing that can be said of its ordinary usage is that we tend to utter it in the mode of judgment. We say that a given society, historical or present-day, has reached a peak of

1

civilization, or that its state of civilization is declining. We rank societies by how civilized they are relative to each other. Or we say certain foreign customs, such as honor killings, are uncivilized. We say that this person is civilized and that person is not. We tell our children to act in a civilized manner.

My purpose in writing this book, then, is to understand the essence of civilization properly. I want to understand why it fails so many people, and what we should do about that. I would like to see a civilization that empowers as many people as possible to pursue a demystified and deliberate relationship with reality. It is my hypothesis that from the many thousands, the many millions, of those relationships, hope and optimism and other beautiful things will arise and persevere.

Alas, one of my conclusions, if I may give it away in advance, is that civilization is not an unambiguously good thing. The 'shining city on the hill' is a mirage. It lessens the suffering of one group by entrenching the suffering of others; and it promises things to the protected and the privileged that it can never entirely deliver. Nevertheless, civilization may yet be a salvageable enterprise. We certainly *can* dispel the kind of suffering that civilization exports to the people at its margins. And that is a worthy task.

This book is the third of three (originally planned) books in the series A Study of the Sacred. I had in mind to cover the idea of the sacred from an individual view (in *Loneliness and Revelation,* 2010), and next from an interpersonal view (*Circles of Meaning, Labyrinths of Fear,* 2012), and now in this book from a social-political view. Though this book builds on the work of those previous titles, I hope it is complete enough to be understood by readers who haven't seen the previous books. Where necessary, concepts carried on from those previous books are explained in the endnotes.

I am grateful to the people of Křeničná, in Central Bohemia, Czech Republic, who in July of 2015 graciously let me share in their village life while I explored the ideas laid out in this book. I'm grateful to the Reidinger family, who gave me their home for all of that month and made me feel most welcome, and to their neighbors who invited me into their lives for a little while. (I changed some of their names in the text, to protect their privacy.) I'm also grateful to the many people who responded to my informal surveys, and to colleagues of mine at Cégep Heritage College who gave some helpful comments on the text, especially Pat Moran. Early drafts of the first and second movements of this text were inflicted on students in my World Views class, and I'm grateful for their comments and their patience as I re-wrote their 'required' text on the fly. Most of all, I'm especially grateful to Melinda Reidinger, who fed me a steady diet of classic anthropology texts during my stay, and who later provided valuable commentary on the nearly finished text. Without her friendly criticisms and factual corrections, this book would have been very different.

With gratitude and with respect I dedicate this one to the many professors who mentored me, or who influenced me in less formal ways, through my years of university life, especially those who have now gone into the west:

Brian Wetstein
Jay Newman
Jean Harvey
Thomas Duddy

Overture: A Meditation Upon a Lake

§ 1. Why Should I Return to the City?

I've cycled seven kilometers through the forested hills, which begin near my front door and continue northwards for what looks like forever. The story in my tourist's map says my destination is a lookout platform above Pink Lake, in Gatineau Hills national park: a lake with no oxygen in its lowest depths, and therefore home to a unique and fragile ecosystem. The story in my mind, however, says that my destination is the climax of a hero's quest: a tower in the midst of a deep dark wood, near a magical lake. The treasure I hope to find at the end of this adventure is the answer to a question: why, if at all, should I go back to the city?

This question is, of course, a symbol for a deeper one. Let me attempt to convey what it stands for. Behind me on this bicycle path is the route back to my house. Were I to return there, I could take up again my share of the gains of civilization. There's clean water in my kitchen and bathroom. Electricity in the walls to power my computer and other machines. Libraries and museums to enrich my mind. Food that is safe and healthy to eat. Telephones and computer networks to keep me in touch with the rest of the human world. Hospitals to care for me if I am ill or injured. Police to protect me from criminals, armies to protect me from other armies. Every few years there's an invitation to vote for the people who will take charge of all these things.

With these gains come debts and responsibilities. I must find a job, and pay my bills, and respect the law. Outstanding among my responsibilities is the unwritten requirement to ignore, or sometimes to participate in, something I know to be entirely absurd. For instance, when I vote, I might find that all the candidates are incompetent or corrupt. Maybe their talents lie – so to speak – in their ability to hide their true intentions. The laws I'm bound to obey might prevent me from doing something that harms no one, or they might oblige me to do something that harms myself and others. They might punish people who don't deserve punishment, or reward people who didn't earn their reward. The books I read or the films I watch might stupefy me, instead of enlighten me. When I spend money, I might be indirectly helping to exploit or enslave the worker who made what I just bought. Or, my money might help to destroy an irreplaceable natural environment, from which the raw materials came. I might find that other people whom I depend on, be they business people, administrators, or even my friends and lovers, regularly deceive and manipulate me in order to protect their reputations or assert their influence. In the course of professing commitment to religion or politics, I might attack people who profess different religions or different politics, and I might call that violence my demonstration of piety, loyalty, and integrity.

I arrive at the lookout platform. I lock my bike to a fence post and search for a quiet place to breathe. Suddenly I discover I'm sitting on the threshold of three immensities: the city behind me, the lake before me, the sky above me. Here in this liminal place, the question, *Why should I go back to the city?*, becomes the question of why, if at all, I should put up with these absurdities. Why, if at all, I should turn around and rejoin civilization?

Civilization! A word like no other, in any language. It announces every society's highest and deepest values: it's the name we give for the most enduring and most glorious of humanity's monuments and cultural achievements. It speaks of that which a nation may share in common with other nations. In a previous study, I said the sacred is, 'That which acts as your partner in your search for the highest and deepest things: the real, the true, the good, and the beautiful.'[1] Civilization is a name for the sum of all those partnerships; perhaps it follows that civilization is the sum of all that is sacred; or to put it another way, it is the most sacred of all sacred things. Or, so it might be for those who live in a 'civilized' society.

Yet the word also speaks of the conquests, colonizations, and oppressions which make that enduring glory possible. It lifts up one society by putting down another; it demands the capture and taming of wild lands and animals; it summons flag-waving believers to war. An informant of mine described her impression of Strasbourg Cathedral, in France, one of the finest examples of high Gothic architecture, as, 'Pure terror...reflecting in its beauty a thousand years of war and horrors.' (A. Valkyrie, activist) Yet without civilization, there would be no Beethoven, no Shakespeare, no Einstein. Without it, we would not drink wine, nor read books after dark by electric light, nor would anyone have walked on the moon. How can civilization be all these things, both wonderful and terrible, at the same time? What is the *essence* of civilization – if it has one, at all? This book is about one possible answer to those questions, and it's the story of how I found it.

An essence, we philosophers sometimes say, is 'that which something ultimately *is*' – or, to make the concept easier to grasp, an essence is 'the *statement* which expresses that which something ultimately is'. As we shall soon see, the quest shall take us not only through the usual halls of economics and politics, but also to some of the muddiest fields of ecology, the highest hills of metaphysics, and the deepest caves of human nature. I find such questions inherently interesting, and for me that's reason enough to ask them. But the absurdities may lead me to some dark conclusions. What if civilization is a machine for crushing people? What if it's a machine that must inevitably break down? To consider these things is to consider *metaphysical* perils to human life. For it's not only the destruction of individual people's lives at stake. It's also the destruction of everything we point to as proof of the significance of our existence: art, literature, architecture, music, knowledge, the whole inheritance of history, and the very possibility of a legacy for the future.

Without the sense of significance that comes from those things, life seems unbearable. The question, *Why should I go back to the city?*, is also the question, *Why, if at all, should I have hope for the future of humanity?*

This is the sort of question that every social or political activist, every politician, every captain of industry and finance, every human being who loves another human being, must ask. Along the way to an answer, I'll consider many theories of civilization, and I'll discuss their logical merits and flaws. But I don't want to produce a mere technical report, of interest only to other technicians. I want to build a foundation for optimism, for everyone – if one can be built at all. And if it should turn out that there is no hope for the future: well that, too, would be a discovery, even if an unhappy one. Then I should find some way to hold on to my soul while I immerse myself in the absurdity.

§ 2. How Deep do the Absurdities Go?

Practical examples of the absurdities of modern society are easy to find. I asked a few of my friends to name their favorites. Here are some of their replies:

- Wealthy people who praise the value of the 'rustic' and 'simple' life, and who claim to want such a life, but without replicating the real toils and burdens of such a life. Marie Antoinette running her own hobby farm at Chateau Versailles, for example.
- Precocious displays of social status and prominence: rich teenagers photographing themselves in bathtubs full of Perrier water.
- Dozens of people sharing a city bus, but none of them sharing a conversation with each other.
- Religions whose doctrines promote peace, charity, and neighborly love, but whose practitioners' behavior involves violence, racism, and unquestioning obedience.

7

- Consumer products that save no one any time or work, which create no new possibilities for human life and action, and which are designed to be thrown out after very few uses. Shaving cream, for example: a totally pointless product; all you need is hot water.
- Food that is saturated with processed sugar, but does not actually taste sweet; sugar being added to give the food a superficial texture, a 'weight'.
- The huge variety of pre-packaged or frozen food available in grocery stores, which are not in fact a variety of real food choices, but are only a variety of brand names, packaging graphics, and minor differences among the additives.
- The entire 'war on terror', in which the United States and its allies fight an enemy they accidentally and perhaps indirectly created.
- Plentiful government money for war-fighting and for monuments to commemorate past wars, but not enough to care for wounded, dismembered, or psychologically traumatized soldiers returning from the wars.
- Political slogans or jargon words that mean the very opposite of what a first-glance, plain-language impression would suggest. 'Right to life', for instance, is not a blanket obligation on all persons to abstain from murder. It actually means government regulation of a woman's use of her own reproductive organs. 'Right to work', as another example, doesn't oblige employers to hire anyone, but does prevent workers from going on strike to protest their badly-paid, insecure, health-destroying, and mind-numbing jobs.
- The anarchist punk rock band, The Sex Pistols, licensed artwork and graphics related to their brand for use by a line of credit cards.[2]
- Bherlin Gildo, a Swedish man standing trial in Britain for terrorism, had the charges against him dropped when it

was revealed that British intelligence agencies were supporting the same force Mr. Gildo was accused of joining. In the words of his defense lawyer: 'If it is the case that HM government was actively involved in supporting armed resistance to the Assad regime [in Syria] at a time when the defendant was present in Syria and himself participating in such resistance it would be unconscionable to allow the prosecution to continue.'[3]

- In June of 2015 a terrorist, bearing the flags of Rhodesia and apartheid South Africa stitched on his clothing, entered a church in South Carolina and murdered nine black people. Nevertheless the governor of the state, Nikki Haley, declared that, 'We'll never understand what motivates anyone to enter one of our places of worship and take the life of another.'[4]

- Investigative journalist Trevor Aaronson discovered that the United States FBI, an agency responsible for domestic counter-terrorism, is in fact 'the organization responsible for more terror plots over the last decade than any other'. The FBI uses sting operations to equip individuals they suspect might commit terrorist crimes, in order to arrest them in the act. But, as Aaronson told a CBC reporter: 'The FBI provided everything these men needed. They provided the weapons, the transportation and in some cases even the idea itself.'[5]

- Modern society offers a great abundance of opportunity, wealth, comfort, political freedom, widely available education and medicine and (let us admit it) distraction. Yet many people find that suicide is a preferable alternative. In the year 2011, 2,728 Canadians took their own lives.[6] By contrast in low-tech, pre-industrial societies, suicide is less common, and more 'altruistic'; for instance elderly persons might take their lives to spare others the burden of caring for them.[7]

These examples perhaps say as much about the priorities of the people I polled, as they do about modern society. But I'm sure you see the point. Life in an urban, organized, technologically-intensive society involves accepting and even making private peace with seemingly incoherent, unintentionally comic, and self-contradicting situations like these. I might accept them if I imagine I will benefit from them, or if I fear that others who benefit from them will retaliate against their critics. Or, perhaps people accept them using a kind of personal cost-benefit analysis. They're willing to put up with a city mayor who regularly gets drunk in public, utters racist slurs, and who ignores a police investigation against himself, so long as he cuts taxes.[8]

Let us take this question a step further. For the absurdities of modern society might go deeper. Instead of threatening one group or another, be they large or small, they may appear to threaten *all of civilization itself*. That could not possibly happen, could it? Despite all its problems and contradictions, civilization is 'too big to fail', isn't it?

No, it's not. There are many ways that civilization could falter or collapse entirely, and we have plenty of examples from history.

A civilization could be threatened by the growing economic power of a rival society. *The Economist* magazine, that intellectual vanguard of Western capitalism, predicted in 2015 that Western corporations would lose their position of global dominance within only ten years.[9] But a conquered society is only the most theatrical example; it is not nearly the most interesting.

A very popular, but often very poorly expressed, belief holds that civilization may collapse due to overpopulation. In 2015 The United Nations reported that the human population grew to 7.3 billion people, and predicted that there will be 9.7 billion of us around the year 2050, and 11.2 billion in 2100. India will be more populous than China, and Nigeria will be more populous than the United States.[10] The potential danger of overpopulation is, in my view, rather exaggerated; I also dislike how it is also regularly used as a basis for punishing poor people for having children.[11] But a civilization certainly can damage itself through its habits of planetary resource consumption. A growth period, for instance, could prompt unrestrained consumption of the resources of the earth, to the point where we become dependent on a certain natural resource at precisely the moment that resource runs out. Scientists estimate that the world will run out of readily-accessible petroleum on or about the year 2048.[12] And two-thirds of the human race has not enough fresh water, or no water at all.[13] A report by the World Economic Forum rated water scarcity as one of the top three biggest risks to people and economies, alongside failure to adapt to climate change, and weapons of mass destruction.[14] Economists at the University of Maryland and University of Minnesota created a mathematical model of a civilization's 'through-put' from nature's regeneration rate to different kinds of human consumers, in search of a general theory for why societies collapse, independent of particular circumstances like history, technology, or natural disaster. They discovered that collapse is inevitable when there is excessive resource depletion and excessive class inequality. In the summary of their findings, they wrote:

> ...either one of the two features apparent in historical societal collapses – over-exploitation of natural resources and strong economic stratification – can independently result in a complete collapse. Given economic stratification, collapse is very difficult to avoid and requires major policy changes, including major reductions in inequality and population growth rates. Even in the absence of economic stratification, collapse can still occur if depletion per capita is too high.[15]

Economic inequality in contemporary Western civilization is very severe right now, and getting worse. In Canada, the wealth of the richest 10 per cent of Canadians grew by 42 per cent in the past ten years; at the same time the wealth of the poorest 10 per cent of Canadians shrank by 150 per cent.[16] A study by Oxfam, the international charity organization, found that half of the entire world's wealth is owned by only 62 individuals.[17] Economics, then, may be civilization's best friend and its worst enemy: it could lift a people up only to throw them down again.

Of all the conceivable threats to the future of humanity, the threats emerging from climate change, global warming, resource depletion, air and water pollution, seem to me the most immediately dangerous. The overwhelming majority of qualified scientists agree that those dangers are caused by human activity, especially industrial pollution and the burning of fossil fuels. Indeed, the study of climate change and global warming draws from the work of thousands of scientists all over the world, in every field of science; it's no exaggeration to say that the study of climate change is probably the largest collective scientific endeavor in all of human history. The organization that co-ordinates much (though not all) of this effort is a United Nations agency called the International Panel on Climate Change. In its fifth Assessment Report (2013), the IPCC considered every kind of climate-affecting force, from natural events like volcanic eruptions and solar radiation, to human-created greenhouse gases. It concluded that: 'This evidence for human influence has grown since AR4 [the previous report, seven years earlier]. It is *extremely likely* that human influence has been the dominant cause of the observed warming since the mid-20th century.'[18] For example, the IPCC found that the contribution of solar radiation to climate change was less than the margin of error for the calculation of the contribution of greenhouse gases like carbon dioxide and methane. (*ibid*, figure SPM.5, pg. 14) The report also describes, with high confidence, that humanity's disruption of the global climate system will lead to higher 'risk of death, injury, ill-health, or disrupted livelihoods', and higher risk of 'breakdown of infrastructure networks and critical services such as electricity, water supply, and health and emergency services'.[19] It's also worth noting that over the past 20 years, the actual impacts always turned out worse than the IPCC's predictions.[20]

Humanity's collective impact on the global ecosystem is now so pervasive that some scientists have declared we are living in a new geological era, the Anthropocene. Here's how a scientific journal recently described it:

> We suggest that the modern biosphere differs significantly from these previous stages and shows early signs of a new, third stage of biosphere evolution characterized by: (1) global homogenization of flora and fauna; (2) a single species (*Homo sapiens*) commandeering 25–40% of net primary production and also mining fossil net primary production (fossil fuels) to break through the photosynthetic energy barrier; (3) human-directed evolution of other species; and (4) increasing inter-action of the biosphere with the technosphere (the global emergent system that includes humans, technological artifacts, and associated social and technological networks). These unique features of today's biosphere may herald a new era in the planet's history that could persist over geological timescales.[21]

The effects of the Anthropocene are global, and serious. To choose just one example: we produce so much pollution and waste that geologists can now identify distinct layers in the earth's crust made of waste aluminum and plastic, as well as materials from nuclear test explosions.[22] And we may end up drowning in our waste. A study published by the Organization for Economic Cooperation and Development predicted that from now to the year 2060, between six million and nine million people will die as a result of global air pollution.[23]

Some people believe that a civilization's collapse can be prevented by advanced technology. For instance, we might be 'saved' by the introduction of electric cars, or home 3D printing. But this need not be the case: for example, technological development might make us more energy-efficient, but can also increase total resource extraction and throughput, enough to negate the energy-efficiency gains.[24] It's also possible that technological development and progress might some day advance to the point where people are no longer able to control their own machines. Some scientists have predicted a day when computers will be fast enough and complex enough to exceed the limits of human intelligence. On that occasion, which some futurists call the Singularity, our robots might turn on us, enslave us, or destroy us, or pacify and 'farm' us, in order to preserve themselves. Some observers, including Oxford philosopher Nick Bostrom, believe that artificial intelligence is a greater threat to civilization than climate change.[25] Artificially intelligent military robots don't yet exist, but their likely predecessors do. Some wealthy countries are already equipping their armies with computerized weapons programmed to automatically detect targets and fire on them without a human command. Prominent scientists and industry leaders are already calling for these weapons to be banned.[26]

Finally, and least theatrically, but perhaps most philosophically, a civilization might end because its people become bored with it. In this scenario, civilizations do not fall; rather, they exhaust themselves. The glamour fades from their myths and legends. For instance, a society might attempt to sell its ideas to other societies, but find that no one's buying. Back in 1989, most people in the West thought their values had triumphed over the world: the Soviet Union and its Communist bloc in Eastern Europe had just crumbled, and China opened its economy to international capitalism. But while the West's economic system seemed to take root around the world, its political and moral values did not. A 2015 editorial in *The New York Times* said: 'Couple the tightening of Chinese authoritarianism with Russia's turn toward revanchism and dictatorship, and then add the rise of radical Islam, and the grand victory of Western liberalism can seem hollow, its values under threat even within its own societies.'[27] British historian and filmmaker Niall Ferguson argued that the prominence of the West might be about to end, partially because other societies have adopted certain Western values especially including science, consumerism, and competition, but mainly because people in the West have lost confidence in their own values.[28] By the way, Ferguson took no pleasure in this conclusion; part of his aim was to encourage Westerners to re-capture their dominant position in the world.

Suppose a collapse of civilization isn't inevitable: just probable, and perhaps avoidable. In that case another question can arise: is civilization a good thing? Is it worth saving? Some activists in my acquaintance think that the answer is 'no', because the idea of civilization has justified too many crimes against humanity. Here in Canada, the most visible example of this is the forcible assimilation of the many nations of Indigenous people. A Truth and Reconciliation Commission was established to document the role of the residential schools in the assimilation effort, and it released its final report in 2015. The Commission's mandate was to 'reveal to Canadians the complex truth about the history and the ongoing legacy of the church-run residential schools'.[29] The report made it clear that the schools were justified by an imperialist notion of civilization:

Numerous arguments were advanced to justify such extravagant interventions into the lands and lives of other peoples. These were largely elaborations on two basic concepts: 1) the Christian god had given the Christian nations the right to colonize the lands they 'discovered' as long as they converted the Indigenous populations; and 2) the Europeans were bringing the benefits of civilization (a concept that was intertwined with Christianity) to the 'heathen'. In short, it was contended that people were being colonized for their own benefit, either in this world or the next.[30]

But the 'civilizing' program of the residential schools certainly did not benefit Aboriginal people. The first page of the report described Canada's 'civilizing' effort as *cultural genocide*, and defined it as follows:

> ...the destruction of those structures and practices that allow the group to continue as a group. States that engage in cultural genocide set out to destroy the political and social institutions of the targeted group. Land is seized, and populations are forcibly transferred and their movement is restricted. Languages are banned. Spiritual leaders are persecuted, spiritual practices are forbidden, and objects of spiritual value are confiscated and destroyed. And, most significantly to the issue at hand, families are disrupted to prevent the transmission of cultural values and identity from one generation to the next.[31]

In cultural genocide, as contrasted to physical genocide, most of the people live on, and so do their descendants. But almost everything that made the people unique and autonomous is destroyed. The commission also described how the loss of identity and culture contributed to making Aboriginal people's lives disproportionally worse-off in nearly every measurable way: rates of educational attainment and income are lower; rates of substance abuse, prison time, apprehension of children by child-welfare agencies, and suicide, are higher. The effects were also multigenerational: children who were abused in the schools went on to become parents who abused their own children. It was all that they knew. (*ibid* pp.183-228) While working on a report for the Aboriginal Policing Directorate, I personally interviewed several Elders who were victims of the residential school system. They described to me horrific beatings as punishment for even the smallest infraction of the rules, including violent punishments for telling the truth about teachers who had sexually assaulted them. One man told me how, on his second day at the school, his clothing and hair was forcibly cut from his body, heaped in a pile in front of him, and set on fire. According to one meaning of the word civilization, which we will see later in these meditations, there's nothing civilized about this violence. But according to another meaning of the word, that kind of violence certainly is a civilized act, and we should therefore find civilization a terrible thing.

Is there a way to have civilization without cultural genocide, without similar forms of oppression, and without irreversibly damaging the planet and ourselves along with it? Any answer, whether 'yes' or 'no', would lead to an intellectual discovery, although one kind of answer would find that civilization's greatness lies in humanity's ability to conquer and murder and destroy – a deeply repugnant conclusion.

The idea that civilizations fall, and indeed the thought that perhaps they *necessarily* fall, whether by nature or by design, can lead to a kind of existential crisis. Its implication is that everything we do, all the art, literature, music, family-making, monument-building, scientific discovery, technological advance, and so on, is ultimately for nothing. In the face of the absurdities that come with civilization, or the crimes and disasters perpetrated in the name of civilization, it may look as if no amount of reform, or protest, or activism, nor even passive resistance, will help to change or save the world. Similarly, all the features of civilization's greatness: all those monuments, all that art and poetry and drama, all those battles and victories and tragedies, the plumbing of the seas and the rockets to the stars, the glorious exultations of the many holy names of God – all the desperate sounds of civilization – are finally about *nothing*, nothing whatever, nothing at all. And into this nothing, my own endeavors fall.

Ahead of me on this bicycle-path, there is what suddenly looks like an attractive alternative. There's land, lake, and sky, stretching from where I stand all the way to the Arctic ocean, thousands of kilometers ahead. We've given many names to this realm: nature, creation, the wilderness, the countryside, the frontier. For its rocky roughness, and forbiddingly cold and stormy winters, some of the first Europeans to explore my part of the world called it 'the land God gave to Cain'. There are people here, of course: towns, mines, logging camps, and First Nations reserves. But these settlements are few, and small, and far-scattered: they sit like islands in a sea of trees. Yet in this un-citied land I might find everything I need to survive and to flourish, if I knew what to look for and how to use it. There are animals I might hunt and plants I might harvest to make my dinner every day. There are trees I might use to build a shelter, or to make firewood to cook my food and to stay warm at night. There are rocky cliffs and wild storms to test my strength, and flowing rivers and lakes to drink, to wash in, and to play in – assuming they haven't been polluted already. There's the sun and moon to light my way, and stars to fill my mind. The question, *Why go back to the city?*, becomes a question about which way of life is better: my urban, sophisticated, high-tech, and socially intensive life, or a rural, simple, low-tech, and socially relaxed life? Both lives require specialized skills; both are highly demanding and risky; both offer their own personal and social rewards. But if I thought that one of them was too full of absurdities, I might find the other appealing, even if for no other reason than to escape cognitive dissonance. The two options by which I finished my last meditation are now three: to stay and accept the absurdities of civilization; to protest against them; or to keep cycling north and leave them all behind.

§ 3. What Questions to Ask?

Good philosophy begins with a good question. It finds a problem in the world that no one else, or very few others, will admit actually exists. Then it stares that problem in the face, directly and bravely and honestly, and then reasons about what the best answer might be.

My initial question, *Why go back to the city?*, cannot be answered until I address three other, more precisely phrased questions, which I shall call the 'root questions of civilization'. The first of them is: *What is it?* What is civilization?

I want to know because, whatever civilization might be, I'm living in one. It's all around me, it works both for me and against me, and I appear to be part of it. Even at my meditation-place overlooking the lake, almost everything I can see around me is in some way a product of civilization: the asphalt-paved road and the bicycle that brought me here, the synthetic fibers in my clothes, the machine-cut posts and planks in the viewing platform, the aircraft contrails in the sky above. The very fact that the forest and lake still exist in their present 'natural' state is also, curiously, a product of civilization. For I am in the domain of a national park that civilization (represented by certain government agencies) designates and manages as a nature preserve. This wasn't always the case: there were farms here once, and a logging industry, and on the other side of the lake there's an abandoned mica mine. Now the nearby signs of civilization are different, but no less human: interpretive centers, marked trails, paved roads, and, because I'm ten kilometers from my country's capital, several government conference facilities. Somewhere in here, but not marked on the maps, is the prime minister's holiday cottage. So while it looks like I've escaped civilization, I've actually come close to one of its centers of power. I cycled out here to escape it for a while, but it appears the city followed me. So to ask the first of my root questions, '*What is civilization?*' is also to ask, 'What's going on? Why won't the city let me go? Is there no escape?'

I already have one partial answer to my first root question: civilization, whatever else it may be, is a manufacturer of absurdities. This partial answer prompts in me more questions. How far do the absurdities go? Why does civilization produce so many of them? Where do they come from? More seriously: why does civilization produce so many terrors, oppressions, and depravations for so many people? To make these questions philosophical: are the absurdities of civilization only matters of *accident*, which could in theory be fixed with improved laws or advanced technology? Or do they emerge from the *essence* of civilization, and therefore perhaps cannot be escaped? To be more simple about it: my second root question of civilization is, *What's wrong with it?*

There's an urgent, practical, and ethical reason to ask this. If enough people believe that civilization is inevitably bound for self-destruction, they might steer the body politic in a certain way, such as to postpone the end, or to hasten it. Prophecies of the end come from all sides of the political spectrum. The left wing says we are threatened by climate change, global warming, the patriarchy, or the internal contradictions of capitalism. From the right, it's socialism, atheism, feminism, foreign immigration, or same-sex marriage. Or it's the famous 'clash of civilizations', the phrase certain politicians use whenever they talk about war between 'the West', and the communists in Russia or Vietnam, or the Muslims in the Middle East, or any number of other peoples in many other places.

Given how closely civilization supports me, might I be under a moral duty to preserve it from whichever of those threats are real? Or, given how civilization also grasps me, might I be obliged to escape from it before it pulls me down? These problems can be gathered to form the third of my root questions: *What, if anything, should be done for civilization?* If we discover that the faults of civilization emerge from its essence, then what, if anything, can give us realistic hope for the future?

This third root question is vague, and must remain so until I have a complete answer to the second. For only then will I know the nature of the problem that I should do something about. I'm not the first to pose these questions, and among specialists there is no generally accepted universal answer. There are, instead, a multitude of competing answers. Any or all of them might be wrong. I will have to pose my own answers. And they, too, might be wrong. Let's give it a try anyway. Here we go!

First Movement: What is Civilization?

§ 4. Some Academic Views

Attempts to define the meaning of the word civilization almost always begin with a complaint about how hard that is to do. In 1935, for instance, Arnold Toynbee wrote that: 'Civilizations are institutions of the highest order—institutions, that is, which comprehend without being comprehended.' (I: 455) Here's historian Shepard Clough, writing in 1951: 'Many authors who have addressed themselves to the question of civilization have shied away from an attempt to define civilization and hence have failed to make clear what forces contribute to upward or downward trends of achievement.'[32] Here's historian Felipe Fernández-Armesto, writing only fifteen years ago: 'Civilization has meant so many different things to different people that it will be hard to retrieve it from abuse and restore useful meaning to it.'[33] This is perhaps another absurdity of civilization: hundreds of writers have published thousands of books, and perhaps spent millions of hours researching and thinking about what civilization is, and yet we still don't know.

What most scholars who study civilization say about it in common is this much: it's a society that develops, changes, grows more complex and powerful over time – in short it's a society that evolves. This is a trivially true conclusion, for *all* societies evolve, including the least technologically advanced bands and tribes. We owe this idea of social evolution not to Darwin, as you may expect, but to another Englishman of the 19th century: Herbert Spencer, and an essay he published in 1857 called *Progress: Its Law and Cause*. Here in Spencer's text is the first appearance of the word in its present meaning:

The advance from the simple to the complex, through a process of successive differentiations, is seen alike in the earliest changes of the Universe to which we can reason our way back, and in the earliest changes which we can inductively establish; it is seen in the geologic and climatic evolution of the Earth; it is seen in the unfolding of every single organism on its surface, and in the multiplication of kinds of organisms; it is seen in the evolution of Humanity, whether contemplated in the civilized individual, or in the aggregate of races...[34]

It's mainly, although not exclusively, from Spencer that we get the idea that societies pass through developmental stages: to follow Spencer's own plan, societies begin as 'simple' nomadic hunter-gatherers, then they progress to 'compound' organized villages with identifiable leaders, 'doubly-compound' large societies with institutions like churches and state-level governments, and finally 'trebly-compound' world-spanning empires like his own Victorian Britain. This idea influences Darwin, who didn't include the word 'evolution' in his *Origin of Species* until the sixth edition (1872). It influences other sociologists like Edward Tylor, from whom we get the better-known narrative of a society's natural progress from 'savagery' to 'barbarism' to 'civilization'. It may have influenced Karl Marx and Friedrich Engels, as they argued for a sequence from primitive communism to feudalism to mercantilism to capitalism to communism.[35]

In the study of civilization, three big names almost always appear on top of the reading list: Edward Gibbon, Oswald Spengler, and Arnold Toynbee. Instead of studying one event or one movement, one society, one era, and its influences, which many historians had done before, these three were the first to look at human history *sub specie aeternitatis*, 'under the aspect of eternity'. They tried to see all of history in a single glance, in search of larger, higher, deeper patterns. And of these big names, Toynbee is the biggest. Between 1935 and 1961 he published a twelve-volume monsterwork entitled *A Study of History*. There he studied no less than 28 societies, seeking a common narrative. He thought he found one in the idea that a civilization is a kind of super-organism (a word also coined by Spencer), with five definite stages of life: genesis, growth, troubles, universal state, and finally disintegration. The nearest that he gave to a direct definition of 'civilization' is this difficult, but expressive, paragraph from early in the text:

> An essential difference between civilizations and primitive societies *as we know them*...is the direction taken by mimesis or imitation... In primitive societies, as we know them, mimesis is directed towards the older generation and towards dead ancestors who stand, unseen but not unfelt, at the back of the living elders, reinforcing their prestige. In a society where mimesis is thus directed backward towards the past, custom rules and society remains static. On the other hand, in societies in process of civilization, mimesis is directed towards creative personalities who commanded a following because they are pioneers.[36]

I think that what Toynbee has in mind here is that civilizations are distinguished from other societies by the direction in time where they look for their inspiration. Civilizations look ahead; the so-called 'primitive' societies look back. Toynbee is also specific about what events prompt or summon a society to look forward: a two-fold challenge that stimulates its 'pioneers' to action. One challenge is 'a human challenge inherent in the disintegration of the antecedent civilizations from which they sprang'. The other is 'the challenges of the physical environment',[37] including the challenges involved in food production and survival (what he calls 'hard lands'), and also the threat of enemy violence. These challenges must be neither too easy nor too hard. Indeed, according to Toynbee there is 'a golden mean' between an easy challenge, which leaves the people idle and stagnated, and an impossible challenge, which can never be overcome.

Toynbee's idea that civilization is a future-looking, progressive, and especially pioneer-directed society, remains enormously powerful. For instance, it influenced Alfred Kroeber, the American cultural anthropologist, whose theory of 'cultural configurations' sought to explain the appearance in history of individuals of great genius. Kroeber compiled a long list of 'individuals recognized as superior' in art, literature, science, philosophy, and so on; he found that 'culturally productive individuals appear in history, on the whole, prevailingly in clusters. This makes their appearance a function of sociocultural events. If it were not so, they should appear more evenly spaced out...'[38] Kroeber's point is that that genius emerges from culture and not from 'race' or genetic dispositions. The idea also certainly influenced Kenneth Clark, the art historian, director of Britain's National Gallery, BBC television presenter, and dearly lovable upper-class twit. In his thirteen-part documentary series *Civilisation: A Personal View* (1969), he regarded civilization as always prompted forward by the 'energy' of 'men of genius'. In a discussion of Montaigne and Shakespeare he said '...the first requisites of civilisation are intellectual energy, freedom of mind, a sense of beauty and a craving for immortality...one of the first ways in which I would justify a civilisation is that it can produce a genius on this scale.'[39] Civilizations fail, or various civilizing movements end, according to Clark, when that energy exhausts itself.[40] Clark also clarified Kroeber's thoughts about the emergence of cultural geniuses: 'Nearly all the steps upward in civilisation have been made in periods of internationalism.'[41] That is to say: when there's a free and peaceful movement of persons and ideas across national borders, the best minds and people will tend to appear. Again, the unstated message is that the emergence of genius has nothing to do with race.

We need not restrict ourselves to the academics to see the reach of Toynbee's idea. It's also behind the remark made by

Larry Page, co-founder of Google and one of the richest technology entrepreneurs in the world, that in his last will and testament he would not leave his fortune to charity. Instead he would give it to Elon Musk, another super-wealthy technology entrepreneur, who plans to build human colonies on the planet Mars.[42] Similarly, it's the idea behind Mark Zuckerberg's transfer of billions of dollars to a quasi-charitable business venture, The Chan Zuckerberg Initiative, which aims 'to join people across the world to advance human potential and promote equality for all children in the next generation'.[43] In all these cases, it's assumed that civilization advances (let the notion of 'advance' remain broad here) not through the work of mass movements nor social forces, nor the luck of nearness to strategic resources, but rather it advances through the influence of exceptional individuals.

It's an interesting idea, and there's no shortage of historical examples to support it. But we have cause for serious concern here. We might worry about what kind of people Toynbee's 'pioneers' are. I've no reason to doubt the philanthropic intentions of men like Musk, Page, and Zuckerberg, even if their big projects are not truly 'philanthropic' in the narrow sense of being purely selfless. Nevertheless, we might wonder whether some of history's most murderous tyrants could also be counted among Toynbee's pioneers. The emphasis on individual pioneers could also obscure the contributions of the many millions of ordinary people, whose names are never recorded by posterity. Their daily labor in the fields, factories, schools, hospitals, churches, ships, dockyards, and nurseries – their daily slog in the messy furrows and alleys of human life – almost certainly does more to improve the life of more people than any warrior-king's victories or merchant-king's investments. To paraphrase another famous pioneer: it's in the salt of the earth where we see the light of the stars. (Matt. 4:13-16)

Toynbee's other idea, that civilizations are super-organisms, living things in their own way, lends itself to the idea that civilizations may die, just as all mortal creatures die. Gibbon might have thought similarly: he named his comprehensive chronicle of Roman history 'The decline and fall'. Observe that this text was published the same year as the foundation of the United States of America. Perhaps Gibbon was warning his readers that nations with big ambitions are still things that end, just like everything else. Gibbon identified four main forces that brought Rome down: 'The injuries of time and nature,' 'The hostile attacks of the barbarians and Christians,' 'The use and abuse of the materials,' and finally, 'The domestic quarrels of the Romans.'[44] Intellectuals ever since have built cottage industries for themselves applying Gibbon's checklist to their own societies, or drawing up similar checklists of their own. In 2012, for instance, the American political magazine *Salon* published '8 striking parallels between the U.S. and the Roman Empire'. Its parallels included: political careerism as a path to personal wealth (i.e. corruption), perpetual warfare, income inequality, and 'loss of the spirit of compromise'.[45] Historian Cullen Murphy wrote a book-length treatment of the analogy: *Are We Rome?* (2007). His short answer was 'No – but we're getting there.'

This organic side to Toynbee's idea was actually inherited from his predecessor Oswald Spengler; and when Spengler speaks of the end phase of civilization, he really rings funeral bells at Christmas. In his book *The Decline of the West* (1918) – notice a title which, like Gibbon's title, emphasizes entropy – he wrote that all great societies pass through three definite stages: Primitive Culture, High Culture, and finally Civilization. The 'organic-logical sequel, fulfillment, and finale of a Culture' is to become a Civilization. But to him that meant the same thing as to become a stagnated and calcified failure:

The Civilization is the inevitable *destiny* of the Culture... Civilizations are the most external and artificial states of which a species of developed humanity is capable. They are a conclusion, the thing-become succeeding the thing-becoming, death following life, rigidity following expansion, intellectual age and the stone-built, petrifying world-city following mother-earth and the spiritual childhood of Doric and Gothic. They are an end, irrevocable, yet by inward necessity reached again and again.[46]

Kroeber, by the way, also proposed a theory of civilizations' rises and falls, connected to his theory of genius and greatness. Here's anthropologist D.K. Simonton summarizing Kroeber's view:

...the growth of a given *cultural pattern* is characterized by a formative period of pioneers and precursors who represent the culture's birth; these are then followed by the great creators who mark a Golden Age, who are themselves succeeded by a less distinguished cohort of the Silver Age; the latter are themselves followed by *epigones* who display the unfortunate features of *pattern exhaustion,* the whole historical sequence concluding with the descent into a Dark Age.[47]

Notice the reappearance in Kroeber of Toynbee's pioneers; notice also the claim that some kind of Dark Age must follow logically, if not directly, after a Golden Age. Civilization, so held the prevailing views of the time, was a thing that necessarily falls. This view still holds strong in the imagination today. The popularity and profitability of disaster films and home-invasion horror films attest to this.

A gloomy idea – and as if to ease that gloom, the next wave of academics to study civilization leaned away from general visions like those, and defined civilization by making checklists of 'civilized' features, the possession of which renders a society a civilization. Thus in 1951 Shepard Clough said that the concept of civilization 'refers to achievements in such aesthetic and intellectual pursuits as architecture, painting, literature, sculpture, music, philosophy, and science and to the success which a people has in establishing control over its human and physical environment.'[48] Similarly, archaeologist Vere Gordon Childe, across two books *What Happened in History* (1942) and *Man Makes Himself* (1951) created what has come to be the definitive list of properties that a society must possess to be truly civilized:

- Cities;
- State-level government;
- Specialization of labor;
- Concentration of surplus resources;
- A class structured society;
- Monumental public works;
- Long-distance trade;
- Standardized monumental artwork;
- Literacy;
- The sciences.

These ten traits are not all equally important. Archeologist Charles Redman, for instance, noted that the first five traits are major organizational and economic principles, while the last five tend to be by-products of the first. Nor do all civilizations have all of these qualities equally: some might lack a few of them, or emphasize some over others. Christopher Scarre and Brian Fagan reduced the list of necessary features down to three: a city with a population numbered at least in the thousands; specialization and interdependence with the surrounding rural hinterland, such that the city provides certain services for the villages and also relies on those villages for food; and third, a degree of organizational complexity, expressed in various forms such as centralized institutions and monumental architecture.[49]

Just because it's fun, let's include among the list-makers Sid Meier, the computer game designer who made the award-winning *Civilization* series. For the game's third edition, published in 2002, he wrote that five main 'impulses' drive the urge to civilization: exploration, economics, knowledge, conquest, and culture. The game also lists five character-defining 'qualities', which may distinguish one society from another: commercial, expansionist, industrious, militaristic, religious, and scientific.[50] Every 'civ' in the game is distinguished by possessing an unique combination of two of these qualities. One could say that the game defines civilization *ex hypothesi*, as a society that pursues those five interests, using some combination of those six qualities. More interesting than this list, to me, is the way the items on the list were chosen: a combination of the developer's academic research, and comments from the game's players and fans. It's like the designers 'crowd-source' the philosophical and scientific world view for each edition of the game. The game could thus be treated as a picture of a loose consensus in pop culture concerning what civilization is all about, such as it was when each edition of the game was published.

The most recent checklist-maker (as of the moment I write this chapter) is probably American historian Ian Morris, who invented a statistical indicator to measure the developmental progress of any given society, and so determine how civilized it is compared to other societies. He called his indicator the Social Development Index, and derived it from these four main observations:

- Energy capture, in kilocalories per capita per day;
- Social organization: the population and the political complexity of the largest city in the region;
- Information technology: the reach of the best available means of communication;
- War-making capacity.

Of these four, Morris says that energy capture is the most important. It covers everything from the food on our plates to the fuel in our cars, from sails on sailboats to nuclear power plants. History itself is a matter of accounting for which society captures more energy faster than other societies, and so puts itself on top of the world. Indeed Morris imagines a Great Chain of Energy, as a substitute for the mediaeval concept of the Great Chain of Being; the chain of energy starts with gravity, moves down next to the nuclear reactions inside stars, next to the radiation from those stars which is collected by plants on earth. It then goes into the food webs described by ecologists until it reaches the muscles of people and animals, 'and that determines everything else'.[51] Social development, according to Morris, is a matter of 'scrambling up the Great Chain of Energy', in order to capture more energy, and to capture it closer to the top of the chain. Here's Morris' best expression of what he has in mind:

> This process of scrambling up the Great Chain of Energy is the foundation of what, following Naroll in the 1950s, I will call social development – basically a group's ability to master its physical and intellectual environment to get things done. Putting it more formally, social development is the bundle of technological, subsistence, organizational, and cultural accomplishments through which people feed, clothe, house, and reproduce themselves, explain the world around them, resolve disputes within their communities, extend their power at the expense of other communities, and defend themselves against others' attempts to extend power.[52]

Morris' idea is that we should be as objective as possible about what constitutes a civilization; and that a mathematically quantifiable standard, such as energy capture, is the best way to be objective. He states that his measure of social development 'is not a method for passing moral judgment on different communities' (ibid pg. 144). His idea certainly makes no distinction between capitalist or socialist or communist economies, present or historical; and no distinction between democratic or dictatorial states. In that way his work could be compared to the Kardashev Scale, which measures a society's level of civilization in terms of energy-consumption.[53] But Morris also says that measuring a society by the quality of its literature, the beauty of its art, or the inspiration of its philosophy, and so on, is unacceptable because it is too 'notoriously culture-bound' (pg. 145).

Having said all that: drawing up checklists might not tell us much. Any list might make it appear as if all you need to 'succeed' as a civilization, whatever 'success' might mean, is to possess the right cultural values. Jared Diamond, in *Guns, Germs, and Steel* (1997) argued that the dominance of the West, and later of Asia, had nothing to do with intellectual or cultural values. It had much more to do with the good luck of being near to strategic resources, such as navigable inland waterways, and animals that are easy to domesticate. Fernández-Armesto argued that just about every item on any checklist could actually be struck off, because they are '...so obviously plucked *a parti pris* from the social environments of the men who have proposed them as to be unworthy of consideration. Most societies have them, and can rejoice or repine in mixed measures. But there is nothing particularly civilized about any of them.'[54] In other words, Fernández-Armesto accuses all the list-makers of being too deeply immersed in observer bias. From another culture's point of view, energy capture as a measure of civilization might look equally as 'notoriously culture-bound' as a study of art and literature. Indian philosopher Ananda Coomaraswamy, for instance, wrote that: 'In a true civilization, *laborare est orare*. But industrialism – 'the mammon of in-justice' – and civilization are incompatible.'[55] Notice his use of the Latin motto from the Rule of St. Benedict: 'To work is to pray'; it hints at what Coomaraswamy thinks 'true' civilization is really about. Had he lived to read Morris' book, he might say that it's wrong to measure a society by how completely it masters its environment and gets things done; rather, we should measure it by the kind and the quality of things done.

Curiously few of these checklists mentioned religion, which most historians tend to agree is a major part of the workings of any society that could be called a civilization. A popular college history textbook says that religion 'was the central force' in the earliest civilizations, and that religion 'provided satisfying explanations for the workings of nature, helped ease the fear of death, and justified traditional rules of morality... Religion united people in the common enterprises needed for survival.'[56] I cite a college textbook here not because it's especially noteworthy, but rather because it's a sample of a commonplace idea; and a sample of what the next generation will grow up believing. However, at least one recent American scholar, Samuel Huntington, gave great prestige to religion in his study of civilization. In an essay published in 1993 he described civilization as 'the highest cultural grouping of people and the broadest level of cultural identity people have short of that which distinguishes humans from other species.'[57] Of all the reasons why people might identify with these super-large cultural groupings, religion is the most important: religion, he says, 'provides a basis for identity and commitment that transcends national boundaries...' (*ibid.*) Following this prescription, he estimated that there were about eight or nine active civilizations on earth at the time his essay was published. One could criticize his work by looking at which nations he grouped together with other nations, and why they wouldn't fit together well at all; Mongolia and Thailand, for instance, were pushed together as 'Buddhist Civilization'. But the deeper problem appears right in his title. It has to do with the way he says the world's different culture-groups are naturally or inevitably bound to war with each other:

> ...the fundamental source of conflict in this new world will
> not be primarily ideological or primarily economic. The great

divisions among humankind and the dominating source of conflict will be cultural. Nation states will remain the most powerful actors in world affairs, but the principal conflicts of global politics will occur between nations and groups of different civilizations. (*ibid.*)

This thesis is important more for its influence than for its logic. It was read with approval by some of the most powerful men in the administration of the United States government throughout George W Bush's presidency. Indeed, in retrospect, his definition seems deliberately engineered to explain both the existence of, and the supposed moral necessity of, the war America was fighting against Iraq at the time and which it would fight again less than ten years later.

Even with the solid descriptive (I do not say definitive) footing provided by the checklist makers, some academics refuse to define civilization at all. Alfred Kroeber, for instance, wrote: 'Like many anthropologists, I use the word civilization almost synonymously with the word culture. At any rate I try to put no weight on the distinction.'[58] Norbert Elias, the sociologist who did the most to study civilization as a behavioral norm, wrote that a successful civilization is a society that inserts its values into people's lives so intimately that those values become no longer a question, but instead a presupposed given. They become something people don't feel a need to talk about anymore:

> To a certain extent, the concept of civilization plays down the national differences between peoples; it emphasizes what is common to all human beings or – in the view of its bearers – should be. It expresses the self-assurance of peoples whose national boundaries and national identities have been so fully established that *they have ceased to be the subject of any particular discussion*, peoples which have long expanded outside their borders and colonized beyond them.[59]

The summary of the academic view is that there is no single academic view. Instead, there's a collection of overlapping, varying, and competing views. By studying them, the most we can logically conclude is that a civilization is just a peculiarly complicated kind of society. We can say with some confidence that it's a kingdom, a republic, or an empire, or the like. But it is not a tribe, a chiefdom, or a band. So long as our definition of civilization is only a description or only a checklist of features, then logically we can say no more. I need to go deeper in order to solve my root questions. For these scientific answers do not give us the *essence* of civilization. To find that essence, I need philosophy.

§ 5. The Big Picture: Cities and Monuments

A first attempt to answer this, the first of my root questions, can be drawn from the Latin word *civitas*: the ancient origin of modern English words including city, civic, civil, and indeed civilization itself. I think this basic beginning accords well with the way most people associate the word civilization with dreamy images of palaces, cathedrals, castles, and glass skyscrapers. To test this, I entered the word 'civilization' into a popular stock photography bank on the internet. Almost all the images that came up were works of architecture. So civilization, in the popular imagination, has something to do with *building things* – things like cities. This seems to me a good place to start looking for the essence of it. For if one is at a loss to define civilization in a single proposition, one might be able to recognize it in things like houses, roads, monuments, and public squares. Something as simple as a bus ticket is a sign of civilization. It implies a society that has attained the necessary threshold of population density, technological advancement, and political will, to require and to build a public transit system. What is more, with features like price, the nature or duration of service it grants, and the graphic design, a bus ticket is a pocket-sized sample of the city's unique identity. It's a visible piece of the essence of a city. Kenneth Clark recognized the essence of civilization in a similar way. In the first episode of his famous BBC television documentary 'Civilisation: A Personal View', Clark stood on the shore of the Seine river in Paris, across from Notre Dame cathedral, and said:

> What is civilisation? I do not know. I can't define it in abstract terms – yet. But I think I can recognise it when I see it: and I am looking at it now... If I had to say which was telling the truth about society, a speech by a minister of housing or the actual buildings put up in his time, I should believe the buildings.[60]

So let's take this as our starting place: civilization means life in a *built-up* environment; life in cities. This is already the view of various scientists: to take one example, anthropologist Philip Bagby:

> Civilization, let us agree then, is the culture of cities and cities we shall define as agglomerations of dwellings many (or to be more precise, a majority) of whose inhabitants are not engaged in producing food. A civilization will be a culture in which cities are found.[61]

Of course, this only takes the scientific description from my previous meditation and reduces the list down to just one item; as it happens, the very first item on V. Gordon Childe's list. And to say that the essence of civilization is city life leaves unanswered the question of what the essence of city life is. Robert Park, an early 20th century urban sociologist, moved away from a physical or geographical definition. He said:

> The city is, rather, a state of mind, a body of customs and traditions, and of the organized attitudes and sentiments that

inhere in these customs and are transmitted with this tradition. The city is not, in other words, merely a physical mechanism and an artificial construction. It is involved in the vital processes of the people who compose it; it is a product of nature and particularly of human nature.[62]

Historian Fernández-Armesto disliked both ways of thinking about cities. He observed that: 'No one has ever established a satisfactory way of distinguishing a city from other ways of organizing space to live in.'[63] Similarly, as noted by Karsten Harries, an American philosopher who specializes in the aesthetics of architecture and urban design:

What then is a city? A place where a multitude dwells together. But in what manner? There are no simple answers to such questions: 'city' might connote a sheltered place, whose walls promise security and peace, a refuge from the insecurity reigning outside; or it might connote a festal place, a place of joy welcoming weary travelers with unfamiliar delights, allowing them to forget the toil and pain of the everyday; or it might connote the residence of a ruler. Conceptions of what a city is and should be can be expected to change with time and place.[64]

Because of the shifting meaning of city life, we do not yet have the *essence* of civilization. But we are already a step closer to finding it. (Notice, as a passing aside, the reference to walls. More about that later.)

Whatever else they might be, it seems likely that cities shall be the centers of any future civilizations. Slightly more than half of all humanity now lives in cities: a United Nations estimate gave the world's urban population at 3.5 billion, and also estimated that by the year 2050 the world's urban population will grow by 2.5 to 3 billion more. The report also estimated that the number of people living in slums grew to 767 million people in the year 2000, up from 650 million in 1990.[65] At the moment I write this, the largest mass-migration of human beings ever undertaken in the history of the world is in progress: 250 million people moving from China's rural countryside into its cities.[66]

Could you have civilization without a city? I'll say more about that question later. But here I'd like to draw attention to the fact that even when you are far from a city, the signs of civilization can still surround you: crops and trees growing in straight lines, or aircraft trails in the sky, or the ruins of long abandoned houses and farms. Even in the most remote points of the ocean, thousands of miles from the nearest city, you can easily find one of civilization's most enduring and permanent signs: its garbage. All of earth's oceans now host fields of plastic particles and other debris, floating on or slightly beneath the surface; the largest of which is known as the 'Great Pacific Garbage Patch'.[67] Its size is hard to estimate; most reports say it's about as big as Texas. Easier to measure is its density, which has been calculated at 335,000 items and 5.1 kilograms of rubbish per square kilometer.[68] Here at my meditation-place, I can see seven fast-food wrappings and an unmatched sandal, all within a stone's throw of my seat. According to a report by the Conference Board of Canada, my country is the world's biggest per-capita producer of garbage.[69] The city itself may not be everywhere, but its footprint is wide indeed.

This separation between the urban and the wild leads me to the next meditation.

§ 6. The Small Picture: Etiquette, Manners, and Excellence

There's a second way to think about civilization. For we also use the word civilization to mean civilized behavior: rational, refined, moderate, polite, softened, cultured and cultivated; and, as one of my informants suggested, domesticated. We also speak of the process of growing up and becoming a civilized adult, according to some model of what it means to be grown up. One of the earliest appearance in print of this personal sense of the word appeared in the writings of Victor de Riqueti, Marquis de Mirabeau (better known as Mirabeau the Elder), some time in the 1760s, as follows:

> I marvel to see how our learned views, false on all points, are wrong on what we take to be civilization. If they were asked what civilization is, most people would answer: softening of manners, urbanity, politeness, and a dissemination of knowledge such that propriety is established in place of laws or detail; all that only presents me with the mask of virtue and not its face, and civilization does nothing for society if it does not give it both the form and the substance of virtue.[70]

What's interesting about this fragment is that it's critical, even openly hostile, to the notion of civilization; Mirabeau sees it as something superficial and fake. Note also his contrast between civilization and *virtue*, which (elsewhere in his text) he treats as a quality of the emerging middle class, and the moral world view of contemporaneous philosophers such as Kant and Rousseau. Civilization, by contrast, he associates with the established upper class. Norbert Elias, the scholar who did the most to chart the development of this behavioral notion of civilization, notes that in some languages the words *civilization* and *culture* are nearly interchangeable in this upper-class sense.

> *Civilisé*, like *cultivé*, *poli*, or *policé*, one of the many terms, often used almost as synonyms, by which the courtly people wished to designate, in a broad or narrow sense, the specific quality of their own behaviour, and by which they contrasted the refinement of their own special manners, their 'standard', to the manners of simpler and socially inferior people.[71]

So Mirabeau's use of the word 'civilization' is part of a general attack on the values of the aristocracy. But even as a social reformer's rallying cry, it is still an expression of the idea that civilization means something to do with personal behavior. To say that someone is civilized is to mark that person as a human being and not as an animal: someone who possesses things the animals are often believed to lack, such as education, and decorum. And finally, civilized behavior marks you as not just any human, but as a member of a sophisticated, advanced, evolved, and cultured society, instead of a member of an unsophisticated or an as-yet uncivilized predecessor society.

This brings us back to another feature of the scientific checklist: class stratification. So-called civilized behavior not only serves as the conspicuous sign of one's membership in a certain kind of society, but also a conspicuous sign of one's membership in that society's ruling class. Table manners, sexual courtship customs, taste in music or clothing or art, and even the ways we go to war, become increasingly interfused with complex and subtle conventions of words and gestures and practices, the purpose of which is to distinguish those who know them (having learned them in an upper-class world) from those who don't know them. The idea is to make it harder for lower class people to acquire them and so pass themselves off as members of the upper class. Yet the rituals of civilized behavior do, eventually, filter down to the middle and lower classes. As noted by Elias: '...much of what had originally been the specific and distinctive social character of the courtly aristocracy and then also of the courtly-bourgeois groups, became, in an ever widening movement and doubtless with some modification, the national character.'[72] That movement is not necessarily toward equality and democracy. For the upper classes can always find new ways to preserve their distinct identity. By the time a certain aristocratic custom has been taken up by the lower classes, the upper classes have already evolved new, even more complex and demanding habits by which to differentiate themselves. Paradoxically, this might involve adopting the 'folksy' arts and crafts of the working class or of foreign ethnic groups. It works for them as long as the standards of taste and the means of adoption remain under their power. As philosopher-sociologist Pierre Bourdieu said, 'The working class 'aesthetic' is a dominated aesthetic.'[73]

Though Elias didn't mention it, the knowledge of aristocratic manners is clearly only one kind of personal talent; could the 'small picture' of civilization also include other talents? We might find them if we consider distinctions between people that are not of social class, but of virtue, in the old classical sense of an *excellence*: a personal skill developed to a high degree of precision and subtlety and sophistication. These skills can belong to painting, dancing, architecture, jewelry making, cooking: any field of arts and handicrafts. In this respect, we could say it is more civilized to eat bread and drink wine than to eat raw nuts and drink water; more civilized to carve a lifelike statue in marble than to scratch a stick-figure on a wall. Yet it may not be the materials, nor even the craft, which matters here, but mastery and effort. In this respect the Chinese principle of *kung fu* (from the Cantonese root words *gong*: work, accomplishment, merit; and *fu*: a man) may be useful. Someone has *kung fu*, as philosopher Cheng Hao put it, after 'directing the whip toward the inner self' for many years; *kung fu* requires seriousness, discipline, devotion, and effort.[74] In the West the term *kung fu* is mostly associated with weaponless martial arts, but it can also refer to any activity that requires long years of education and practice to master: calligraphy, or gardening, for instance. It is thus comparable to the old Greek concept of *arete*, 'excellence'.

This dimension of 'small picture' civilization is potentially more accessible to more people because it has nothing to do with social class. This dimension also treats Toynbee's 'pioneers' and Clark's 'men of genius' as individuals who bring the big and small pictures of civilization together. They can come from any social or economic background, they can have any kind of artistic or scientific or technical talents; and their individual achievements eventually join the collection of 'the civilization you can look at' (to borrow Clark's words). I'm thinking of outstanding works of art, no less than cities and monuments and tall towers: Da Vinci's *Mona Lisa*, for example. Nearly everyone agrees it is an achievement of artistic *kung fu*, and as much a monument to humanity's greatness as the Pyramids of Giza or the many skyscrapers of Hong Kong. And, measuring 77cm by 53cm, it is definitely a 'small picture'! Of course, the achievements of working-class heroes might catch the attention of upper-class patrons, or make those working class heroes themselves shockingly rich, or both. Such was the case for Vincent Van Gogh, who was poor for most of his life, who chose working-class experiences for many of his subjects (think of works like *The Potato Eaters*, or *The Night Café*, or *The Sower*), and who wanted to make art to cheer the lives of other poor people around him. He is now regarded as one of the greatest artists of all time. His works are worth millions of dollars and are only visible to the public in elite galleries.

This skill-based version of the 'small picture' of civilization still admits of a hierarchy of sorts, since some people will be better at some talents than others, and some talents will be deemed more important than others. But, as there may be thousands of talents here, so there can also be thousands of hierarchy-vectors; and the vector of class becomes only one among many. In this sense, a single mother at home who makes a hearty stew for her children, and who insists they eat it at the same table together as a family, creates her own kind of civilization. Hers is of course very different than that of the lofty lord in his mansion eating an expensive meal cooked for him by his chef. But hers may be no less civilized for being merely different. Indeed on at least one important vector, hers may have the greater dignity: she created the meal with the work of her own hands. The lord, on the other hand, might have merely paid someone for it.

§ 7. The First House

The previous meditations gave us a summary of the scientific and historical views, along with some of their implications. I'd like to turn to a philosophical view now. But this turn is frustrated by the fact that the very word 'civilization' was not much used by philosophers until the 1700s. To find a history of the idea that dates back further in the past, I will have to invent it.

The word itself hints how that could be done. As noted, its root is in various Latin words for cities and urban life. Philosopher Jay Newman thought the way to understand the word is to look at the other half of its origin: the suffix -*zation*, which denotes a process. 'We speak of a particular civilization or of certain civilizations, but we should not forget that the term 'civilization' primarily signifies a process that something is undergoing or has undergone.'[75] We have already seen something like this in the 'big picture', where civilization means city life: the visible result of a process by which communities grow and complicate themselves. We also saw this in the 'small picture' where civilization means an individual person's mastery of various talents, including the talent for behavioral etiquette. Civilization, whatever else it might be, is not a 'thing': it is a time-extended activity, an event.

What else could it mean? There are several possibilities. To explore one of them, let's go back in time, and visit Marcus Vitruvius Pollio, who was a civil and military engineer in the service of Emperor Augustus Caesar of Rome. (You know his name; Leonardo da Vinci drew a diagram of him standing inside a circle and a square.) About 15 BCE, he presented his king with a manual on the theory and practice of architecture. In Book 2 of this ten-book masterwork, he imagined what life might have been like for 'the men of old', as he called them; people who lived before the invention of civilization. The text in which he imagines the construction of the first house is worth quoting at length:

> The men of old were born like the wild beasts, in the woods, caves, and groves, and lived on savage fare. As time went on, the thickly crowded trees in a certain place, tossed by storms and winds, and rubbing their branches against one another, caught fire, and so the inhabitants of the place were put to flight, being terrified by the furious flame. After it subsided, they drew near, and observing that they were very comfortable standing before the warm fire, they put on logs and, while thus keeping it alive, brought up other people to it, showing them by signs how much comfort they got from it. In that gathering of men, at a time when utterance of sound was purely individual, from daily habits they fixed upon articulate words just as these happened to come; then, from indicating by name things in common use, the result was that in this chance way they began to talk, and thus originated conversation with one another.
>
> Therefore it was the discovery of fire that originally gave rise to the coming together of men, to the deliberative assembly, and to social intercourse. And so, as they kept coming together in greater numbers into one place, finding themselves naturally gifted beyond the other animals in not being obliged to walk with faces to the ground, but upright and gazing upon the splendour of the starry firmament, and also in being able to do with ease whatever they chose with their hands and fingers, they began in that first assembly to construct shelters.[76]

There's a lot going on in these two paragraphs. Notice, for a start, words like 'savage' and 'wild beast' in the very first sentence: words for non-civilized and non-human ways of life. (Remember

44

this for later.) In the next sentence, there's the claim that these 'men of old' feared the natural forces of the world, especially fire. Vitruvius might have been hinting at Greek philosophers such as Lucretius and Petronius, who argued that the gods themselves were only creations of human fear.[77] But Vitruvius also says that somewhere in this prehistory, curiosity grew stronger than fear. With that curiosity people learned to capture and cultivate fire, and then they gathered around it, and formed the first small community. They learned to speak with words: and being able to speak, they no longer lived 'like wild beasts'. Vitruvius concludes that these transformations of consciousness empowered the people to build the first separations between the natural world and the human world: the first walls, not of cities, but of houses.

What interests me about Vitruvius' imagination here is the way these fictitious 'men of old' are portrayed as similar to animals, but also different: they are 'gifted beyond the other animals', especially in their ability to stand on two legs, so that they look up and contemplate the stars, again with curiosity instead of fear. That this transformation of consciousness is implied twice in these paragraphs seems to me significant. I shall explore it more deeply later. For now let me observe that Vitruvius describes it in order to say we build houses not only for meeting physical protection needs, but also to meet social needs.

This leads me to the account of the domestication of fire: Vitruvius treats the hearth as the centre of community life. What makes a hearth fire special? Its light and warmth give us a place where work may continue through the darkness of night. But, more importantly, it gives us a place where we may carry out work not directly related to immediate survival needs; presumably, most of those needs were met during the day. Thus the hearth fire is the place where we may cook food not only for health, but also for pleasure. Its flickering colors and shapes can become the inspiration for abstract thinking. Surrounded by friends and family who share its warmth, it is where we may hold conversations, tell stories, sing songs, and love each other.

As if participating an ancient tradition, some modern architects still consider the fireplace a central feature of dwelling places. For instance, here's 19th century German architect Gottfried Semper:

> Before men thought of erecting tents, fences, or huts, they gathered around the open flame, which kept them warm and dry and where they prepared their simple meals. The hearth is the germ, the embryo, of all social institutions. The first sign of gathering, of settlement and rest after long wanderings and the hardship of the chase [i.e. hunting], is still the set of the fire and the lighting of the crackling flame.[78]

Similarly, here's the famous American architect, Frank Lloyd Wright: in a discussion of house design, he argued for the abolition of attics and 'unwholesome' basements, but he stopped at the hearth. 'The *integral* fireplace became an important part of the building itself in the houses I was allowed to build out there on the prairie. It comforted me to see the fire burning deep in the solid masonry of the house itself. A feeling that came to stay.'[79]

The construction of a shelter and the lighting of the integral fire need not imply a conquest or an oppression of the natural world. It is humanity doing the same thing any animal does when building a home. Birds build nests; rabbits build warrens; beavers build dams; humans build houses. Perhaps this is why Vitruvius' description of the first house is little different from an animal shelter: 'At first they set up forked stakes connected by twigs and covered these walls with mud. Others made walls of lumps of dried mud, covering them with reeds and leaves to keep out the rain and the heat.'[80] So the dwelling centre distinguishes the human world from the wild world; it is definitive, without necessarily being antagonistic.

The simple shelter, one might argue, is not by itself a sign of civilization. But, by separating the human realm from the rest of the earth, the simple shelter is the first step on the *process* toward civilization. We have already seen Clark's declaration that 'civilised man must feel that he belongs somewhere in space and time'. Separating out a parcel of earth, to make a dwelling-place and a centre, is one way to establish that feeling. Another way to see the step to civilization was implied by Vitruvius, where he said:

> Then, taking courage and looking forward from the standpoint of higher ideas born of the multiplication of the arts, they [the first men] gave up huts and began to build houses with foundations, having brick or stone walls, and roofs of timber and tiles; next, observation and application led them from fluctuating and indefinite conceptions to definite rules of symmetry.[81]

The house, so deliberately constructed, and set apart from the rest of the earth, is no longer a 'natural' environment. (Be careful how you use the word 'nature', my friends; it is the most slippery of all fish.) It is, instead, an environment of artifice, of craft, of deliberate design, and of human dominance. From that observation emerges another way to look at the essence of civilization: it is the impulse, even the divine command, to: 'Be fruitful, and multiply, and replenish the earth, and subdue it: and have dominion over the fish of the sea, and over the fowl of the air, and over every living thing that moves upon the earth.' (Genesis 1:28) Civilization, in this way of thinking, is the capacity and the will to farm the land, to tame the animals, to shelter from the storm, and generally to master the earth. The first house, then, was a first step toward that mastery.

This view of civilization appears in some academic work I have not mentioned previously. 'Civilization is a way of distancing from nature, which is for our good, if it's used properly,' wrote archaeologist Georgio Buccellati.[82] Historian Felipe Fernández-Armesto wrote: 'I propose to define it [civilization] as a type of relationship: a relationship to the natural environment, recrafted, by the civilizing impulse, to meet human demands. By 'a civilization' I mean a society in such a relationship.'[83] Fernández-Armesto thought that command over nature was the only important criterion by which one can define civilization, and indeed it is the only measure by which we can call one society more civilized than another.

On the fringes of a city, like on my perch above this lake, the separation between the urban and the wild might be hard to pin down with precision. Gardens and farms can blend into meadows and forests; wildlife can come and go with ease. But when you're downtown, there's no mistaking that one is surrounded by the works and deeds of humankind. On the rare occasions when animals such as goats and deer somehow wind up in the centre of a city, the incident is so unusual that it makes the national news.[84] So the separation between the city and the countryside may always be a matter of degree, and never a matter of absolutes. The idea of mastery of the earth has been, of course, a flashpoint in environmental ethics debates since the beginning of the contemporary green movement. Economic systems, political world views, and religions have been accused of certifying humanity's mastery of the earth, to the detriment of the earth and all life upon her; a position severely condemned by Pope Francis, in his 2015 encyclical, *Laudato Si'*.

> We have come to see ourselves as her [earth's] lords and masters, entitled to plunder her at will... This is why the earth herself, burdened and laid waste, is among the most abandoned and maltreated of our poor.[85]

This notion of separation, and of entitlement to mastery, is taking me to another meditation.

§ 8. The Ancient Great Wall

We have seen that part of the essence of civilization lies in city life, and in aristocratic behavior, that is, the customs of the city's ruling class. Yet the essence of civilization appears not in just any kind of city: it appears in a *walled* city – a city that separates the human world from the natural world. The prestige and the history of the word civilization is such that it automatically invokes what is perhaps the oldest of all political categories: 'us' and 'them'. The historian Ralph Turner suggested that the recognition of 'in-group' and 'out-group' interests may in fact be older than cities: it might have been a mode of thinking that made urban life possible.[86] Civilization, following his argument, was perhaps invented accidentally, by people who built walls around their settlements to protect themselves from wild animals, bad weather, and especially from other people. In that respect, the construction of the first house, the spiritual centre marked off or carved out of the realm of nature, is more civilized than my previous meditation acknowledged. But in this new meditation let's imagine a cluster of houses, and perhaps a few public buildings among them such as a lord's palace or a market square or a temple. And let's build a wall around all them, and so transform an entire city into a house for an entire community.

City walls require a large and organized labor force to build. When they're finished they need watchmen to stand guard on them. Walls imply a politically organized community: if not yet a full-fledged city in the usual meaning of the word, then at least a community that's organized enough to envision a difference between their own members and everyone else, and then to enact a plan to separate them. The ancient Greek city of Sparta had no walls: the warriors believed they should be ferocious enough to not need them. But Sparta was also one of the most class-stratified of all the ancient Greek city states, with the ruling oligarchs on the top, several grades of middle class, and a working class on the bottom called the *helots*, whom one chronicler of the day said were 'slaves to the utmost'.[87] I wouldn't want to speculate about which came first, the social distinctions or the walls. If I had to guess, I'd say it was social distinctions. The smallest and least complex of human societies have them; so do our genetically nearest animal relations, the bonobos and chimpanzees. But walls would certainly have expanded their importance. As noted by historian and security analyst R.D. McCrie:

> To live within a walled community was a privilege to be earned with alacrity and retained with diligence. Walls expressed the power and promise of urban life. The word *urban* itself derives from the Latin *urbs*, or city; this was the center of civility, borrowed from the Latin *civis*, or citizen... When gates descended at sundown, no one could enter or leave. An early surveillance society imbued the walled city. Individuals who sought to stay within the walled compound overnight in some locations would have to have a current resident authorize their stay and take responsibility for their behavior while present.[88]

The word civilization, then, may originally have corresponded to what we today call a gated community. Of course, today it is no longer necessary for a city to have a physical wall to be a centre of civilization. But the city does need a means to distinguish and to separate members of the in-group from everyone else. The wall in a modern city might take the form of a small plastic card, to be kept in one's wallet, carrying information about one's identity such as a photograph, date of birth, and home address. The card might grant certain legal powers to its bearer, such as the right to drive a car, to purchase alcohol, or to cross an international border. The wall today could also involve electronic surveillance. In the words of world-renowned architect Richard Rogers, modern cities are intensely segregated and militarized. When you pass from no-go areas like the ghettos and enter the city's downtown business sector:

> ...TV cameras and security devices screen almost every
> passing pedestrian. At the touch of a button, access is blocked,
> bullet-proof screens are activated, bomb-proof shutters roll
> down. The appearance of the 'wrong sort of person' triggers a
> quiet panic. Video cameras turn on their mounts. Security
> guards adjust their belts. A new type of citadel has emerged
> which relies not only on physical boundedness, high fences,
> barbed wire and imposing gates but increasingly on invisible
> electronic hardware.[89]

Finally, the wall can also be entirely intangible: it can take the
form of citizenship laws, national or religious sentiments, a
common language (or a common regional dialect!), or any other
behavioral sign by which someone recognizes another as like-
unto-herself, and recognizes a third person as different from
herself. As the physical wall and its legal equivalents are the
distinctions between people in the big picture, so do rules of
etiquette and manners form the intangible distinctions between
people in the small picture. As one etiquette rulebook from 1879
explained it, etiquette 'is the barrier which society draws around
itself, a shield against the intrusion of the impertinent, the
improper, and the vulgar'.[90]

If the word for the in-group is 'civilized', then what are the
words for the out-groups? The word used by archaeologists is
faubourg: a neighborhood that springs up outside the city wall
and presses close to the gates. Faubourgs appear when there isn't
enough room inside the walls for everyone who wants to be part
of the city. The nearest equivalent word in modern English is
'suburb', although I suspect that most of the time a better modern
word would be 'favela' or 'shanty town': a neighborhood of
poverty, depravation, and perhaps the kind of angst that arises
from the ability to see the wealthy centre of a city and to know

you will never be invited in.

The words for uncivilized people tend to be the same as pejorative words for working class or poverty class people: older words like *simpleton, peasant, serf, wastrel, yob, country bumpkin,* and *local yokel;* newer words like *chav, redneck, welfare queen, white trash, mouth-breather,* and my favorite, *knuckle-dragging troglodyte.* Probably the oldest words for people without civilized manners are also the most judgmental and offensive: words like *primitives, barbarians,* and *savages.* Those three words have a long and ugly history. They are used not only to identify people who don't live in cities; they also identify those who, because they don't live in cities, *therefore don't count as full members of the human race.* This will require some explanation.

Let's look at each of those three horrible words in turn. The word *barbarian* comes to us from ancient Greek, and refers to societies that did not speak the Greek language. To those refined and petulant ears, the languages of the Celts or Germans sounded like nonsense syllables. The Bible itself deploys the word in reference to language, implying that those who do not understand each other are like barbarians to each other (1 Corinthians 14:11). The word also refers to behavior: the *Oxford English Dictionary* says a barbarian is a 'rude, wild, uncivilized person', an 'uncultured person'. We saw this already in the very first sentence of Vitruvius' account of the first house: 'The men of old were born like the wild beasts...and lived on savage fare.' Gibbon devotes an entire chapter to the 'State of the Barbaric World' (ch. XLII), in which, for example, he describes the society of a Celtic tribe called the Lombards, as follows: 'Fierce, beyond the example of the Germans, they delighted to propagate the tremendous belief that their heads were formed like the heads of dogs, and that they drank the blood of their enemies whom they vanquished in battle.'[91]

The word *primitive* comes from Old French and Late Middle English, and has to do with time and history. A primitive thing is the earliest or the original of its kind. It's rough and simple, possibly very effective for its purpose, and possibly possessing its own kind of dignity, but nonetheless old-fashioned, behind the times, and obsolete.

Finally, the word *savage* invokes impressions of perpetual violence, 'cruel or barbarous deeds', or even a style of life barely distinguishable from the life of wild animals.[92] As you can see, the language of civilization is encoded with the presupposed superiority of the civilized, and the presupposed inferiority of everyone else.

Against this point someone might say, is this too extreme? The reply is *no*. Toynbee, for instance, speaks of 'primitive' peoples as those who lack the enterprising and heroic spirit needed to get a new civilization up and running:

Primitive societies, as we know them by direct observation, may be likened to people lying torpid upon a ledge on a mountain-side, with a precipice below and a precipice above; civilizations may be likened to companions of these sleepers who have just risen to their feet and have started to climb up the face of the cliff above...[93]

Here, in Toynbee's account, the un-civilized are not inhuman, but neither are they 'awake'; they do not fully develop themselves, nor discharge the full extent of their human powers.

Going back in time a bit for another example: French *philosophes* such as Voltaire and Mirabeau, who first used the word in the modern way, deliberately opposed it to 'barbarism', right from the beginning.[94] Fernández-Armesto observed that this distinction between the civilized and the barbaric is part of the very 'process' of civilization: 'The word 'civilization' denotes a process of collective self-differentiation from a world characterized, implicitly or explicitly, as 'barbaric' or 'savage' or 'primitive'.' He called this usage of the word 'obviously unsatisfactory', but noted that that its usage:

> ...began in eighteenth-century Europe, where politesse and manners, sensibility and taste, rationality and refinement were values espoused by an elite anxious to repudiate the 'baser', 'coarser', 'grosser' nature of men. Progress was identified with the renunciation of nature; reversion to the wild was derogation.[95]

The distinction can appear even when the word 'civilization' is not mentioned. Early modern philosophers such as John Locke, for instance, could speak quite casually of 'the wild Indian who knows no enclosure',[96] in contrast to the European peasant farmer. Similarly, Voltaire said that reading Rousseau made him want 'to walk on all fours' and 'embark in search of the savages of Canada'.[97] The distinction also can be found in pre-modern world views. As noted by Elias:

> The decisive antithesis expressing the self-image of the West during the Middle Ages was that between Christianity and paganism or, more exactly, between devout, Roman-Latin Christianity, on the one hand, and paganism and heresy, including Greek and Eastern Christianity, on the other.[98]

Thus we can add another world to our lexicon of uncivilized epithets: *pagan*. The OED and other sources says the word comes from Roman Latin where it originally meant a civilian, in the sense of someone who was not a soldier. When early Christians called themselves *milites*, 'enrolled soldiers' for Christ, the ordinary everyday word for a non-soldier became a brand of contempt for those not so enrolled for Christ. The word also referred to people who lived in a rural countryside region, a *pagus*. And since Christianity was first preached in cities, the word stuck as an insult for country people who were merely late to hear the 'good news'; although some of these pagans wore the term proudly, as a sign of their cultural commitments.[99] The OED, in a religious zeal typical of the year it was first compiled, also defines 'pagan' as: 'One of a nation or community which does not worship the true God; a heathen'; it also mentions synonyms of a sexual character, like *paramour*, and *prostitute*.[100] This distinction between the civilized and the pagan remains strong today. For example, in November 2015 a religious fundamentalist group in Scotland called the Solas Centre for Public Christianity declared that a British pagan revivalist group, The Children of Artemis, constituted 'one of the biggest threats to Western civilization and the Christian values which underpin our society'.[101] All this, despite the fact that the very idea of civilization was invented by pagans, not only in the classical pre-Christian Mediterranean, but also non-Christians in India and China and Egypt and Arabia and Ireland and Thailand and Mongolia and Japan and Peru and Mexico and west Africa and – you get the idea.

Mind you, this is not necessarily a reason to be proud of the pagan accomplishment. For the idea of civilization is also an ideology of the superiority of a conqueror and the inferiority of the conquered. For instance, the 1st century CE Roman general Agricola wrote that he conquered the Celts of Britain with the 'enervating luxuries' of Roman trade goods and the Roman lifestyle. Civilization was, in effect, a weapon of assimilation and oppression. Here are his own words:

> The population was gradually led into the demoralizing temptations of arcades, baths, and sumptuous banquets. The unsuspecting Britons spoke of such novelties as 'civilisation', when in fact they were only a feature of their enslavement.[102]

Although the word 'barbarian' does not appear in this quotation, nonetheless you can smell the conceited superiority of his attitude. The wall was built high and wide in Europe's classical Pagan period, long before Christian soldiers added their watch-towers.

Perhaps the best place where one can see the presupposition of the superiority of civilization, and the alleged un-humanity of the uncivilized, is in documents from the period when Europeans first colonized the continent of Turtle Island (North America). These writings describe Aboriginal people in stunningly dehumanizing language. Words like 'savage' and 'primitive' occur frequently in sources like the *Jesuit Relations*. Further back, in the 10th century, Norsemen who attempted a colony on the island of Newfoundland referred to the Beothucks, the local indigenous people, as *skraelings,* an old Norse word for a barbarian.[103] Aboriginal people themselves, confronted with the way European colonists spoke of them, were deeply offended. Here's Tatanga Mani, of the Stoney nation, replying to the anti-civilized names applied to his people:

> You whites assumed we were savages. You didn't understand our prayers. You didn't try to understand. When we sang our praises to the sun or moon or wind, you said we were worshipping idols. Without understanding, you condemned us as lost souls just because our form of worship was different from yours. We saw the Great Spirit's work in almost every-thing: sun, moon, trees, wind, and mountains. Sometimes we approached him through these things. Was that so bad? I think we have a true belief in the supreme being, a stronger faith than that of most whites who have called us pagans... Indians living close to nature and nature's ruler are not living in darkness.[104]

Similarly, here's Chief Luther Standing Bear, of the Oglala Sioux nation, replying to the anti-civilized names applied to the landscape:

We did not think of the great open plains, the beautiful rolling hills, and winding streams with tangled growth, as 'wild'. Only to the white man was nature a 'wilderness', and only to him was the land 'infested' with 'wild' animals and 'savage' people. To us it was tame. Earth was bountiful and we were surrounded with the blessings of the Great Mystery. Not until the hairy man from the east came and with brutal frenzy heaped injustices upon us and the families we loved was it 'wild' for us. When the very animals of the forest began fleeing from his approach, then it was that for us the 'Wild West' began.[105]

Curiously, and also tellingly, the use of those words in many colonist's writings had nothing to do with the actual observed behavior of First Nations people. Here's an example, from the 17th century lawyer Marc Lescarbot, which describes the behavior of Mi'kmaq people in what is now the Canadian Maritimes: 'Our savages, though naked, are not void of those virtues that are found in civilized men, for every one has in him, even from his birth, the principles and seeds of virtue.'[106] Lescarbot then drew attention to the courage, honor, temperance, and generosity, of the Mi'kmaq people: qualities which, when found in a white man, everyone would call civilized. As another example: Nicolas Denys, a businessman from around the same time and place, wrote of the Mi'kmaq that:

The law which they observed in old times was this, to do to another only that which they wished to be done to them. They had no worship, all lived in good friendship and understanding. They refused nothing to one another, if one wigwam or family had not provisions enough, the neighbours supplied them... And in all other things it was the same. They lived pure lives; the wives were faithful to husbands, and the girls very chaste. (*ibid* pg. 595)

Notice the invocation of Christianity's Golden Rule, and the implicit critique of the behavior of white women, in Denys' account here. Without using the word, Denys suggests that Mi'kmaq culture was more civilized than the European. The abundance of evidence of the dignity and the honorable accord of the First Nations people, and the relative near-absence of evidence for the kind of behavior normally denoted by the words 'barbarous' and 'savage', except in self-defensive warfare, leads one to conclude, as historian Daniel Paul concluded, that:

> ...we must assume that the early writers used the term [savage] because of their belief in the superiority of their race. In other words they were racist. Their belief that European Christian civilization was the most superior in the world prevented them from forming unbiased opinions about civilizations that clearly had certain human values superior to their own.[107]

We may now add a second point to our preliminary answer to the first of my root questions. Whatever else civilization is, it involves an Ancient Great Wall, as I shall call it, which separates the in-group from the out-group. At its deepest level it distinguishes the civilized by elevating to the political realm a basic category of biology: 'human' and 'nonhuman'. From these two basic categories are derived yet more: 'citizen' and 'foreigner', 'friend' and 'stranger', or the bellicose version of the latter, 'friend' and 'enemy'.

But note the subtle point here. By invoking words like 'barbarian' and 'savage' as the words for the out-group, we are not necessarily describing the actual behavior of the out-group. We are more likely describing the myths and illusions that allow the in-group to feel superior. Keep this last observation in mind for a while; I might return to it in a later meditation.

§ 9. Thinking Shall Replace Killing

Now, to continue exploring this 'retroactive continuity' for the philosophy of civilization, let's go back in time again: to Athens, Greece, in the 6th century BCE. Here we find what is generally agreed to be the birthplace of Western civilization. Obviously there is not one single dramatic moment that definitively initiated Western civilization. It was a sequence of related yet distinct events in which one Greek community, Athens, transformed itself from an independent city-state, into the leader of a coalition of allied city-states called the Delian League. Then Athens transformed that coalition into an international empire. If we want to identify a single influential individual, a 'pioneer' in Toynbee's sense, who did the most to make this happen, and so make a very messy and complicated process look much simpler than it really is, that individual would be Pericles. He was the political leader of Athens from 461 BCE to 429 BCE, the general who won the most decisive battles of the period, and the orator who helped Athens discover its artistic and intellectual genius. Through his diplomatic work, various Greek cities entered into contracts with Athens, in which Athens would protect all of them from Persian attack. In return, Athens would receive a money tribute from all of the cities under its protection. But Pericles diverted some of the money away from the war effort and into architecture, sculpture, theatre, music and the arts. As noted a generation later by Plutarch, one of his biographers:

[Pericles] was also anxious that the unskilled masses, who had no military training, should not be debarred from benefiting from the national income, and yet should not be paid for sitting about and doing nothing. So he boldly laid before the people proposals for immense public works and plans for buildings, which would involve many different arts and industries and require long periods to complete, his object being that those who stayed at home, no less than those serving in the fleet or the army or on garrison duty, should be enabled to enjoy a share of the national wealth.[108]

Pericles also established competitive music and theatre festivals, and created for Athens a great reputation as a centre of the arts, which it held for many centuries. It is worth adding that, in Plutarch's account, Pericles transformed Athenian society this way not primarily by force of arms, but also by force of *words*. Even his opponents acknowledged his mastery of oratory and rhetoric. Reading between the lines of his biography one gets the impression he was a master psychological manipulator as well. Athens was a democracy, and Pericles had to be elected every year. But as Plutarch says, Pericles was re-elected for forty consecutive years. He preserved his position by creating a reputation as an honorable and selfless person, concerned with the glory of Athens as a whole and not just his own personal glory. This point was also noted by Thucydides in his account of Pericles' famous Funeral Oration. Plutarch also emphasized that Pericles was unmoved by bribery and never enriched himself personally from the public treasury.[109]

Plutarch's portrait of the man veritably drips with worshipful adoration. It's almost embarrassing to read it. But I think there is an important observation here. Athens, in the time of Pericles, became a society that held artistic and intellectual activity to be at least as culturally important as military victory. Thinking was beginning to replace killing as a social force. It's this shift in emphasis, this movement, that I want to draw attention to here.

It's not only in classical Greece where this movement emerges. It is, I suspect, an elemental idea, which anyone can discover, at any time and place. The phrase 'thinking shall replace killing', as I have used it here, comes not from the speeches of Pericles, but from the story of Deganawidah, the Great Peacemaker who established the Iroquois Confederacy. The birth of the Peacemaker was prophesied to his mother by a messenger from the Great Spirit;

and he was born to her while she was still a virgin.[110] He was surrounded by miraculous signs, such as a canoe made of solid stone that floated perfectly. But let's look at his meeting with the first person who accepted his message of peace: a woman who pressed him to describe how his peace message would translate from theory to practice. He answered by saying that the Great Peace:

'...will take the form of a longhouse,' replied Deganawidah, 'in which there are many fires, one for each family, yet all live as one household under one chief mother. Hereabouts are five nations, each with its own council fire, yet they shall live together as one household in peace. They shall be the Kanonsiónni, the Longhouse. They shall have one mind and live under one law. Thinking shall replace killing, and there shall be one commonwealth.'[111]

One of the Peacemaker's followers asked him what people who accepted the Great Peace would be like. The Peacemaker answered:

Reason brings Righteousness, and Reason is a power that works among all minds alike. When once Reason is established, all the minds of all mankind will be in a state of Health and Peace. It will be as if there were but a single person.[112]

There are many more instances of this elementary idea appearing in other places in the world. Consider this statement made by Njall Thorgeirsson, the leading figure of a 10th century Icelandic saga that bears his name: 'With law our land shall rise, but it will perish with lawlessness.'[113] Later in the story, the *Althing* or annual public assembly of Iceland gathered, however:

...many said that this was hardly worth it, for even cases

61

brought to the Thing were getting nowhere, – 'and we would rather,' they said, 'press our claims with point and blade.' 'That you must not do,' said Njal, 'for it will not do to be without law in the land.'[114]

Njal's preoccupation with law is an instance of the same movement we found in Pericles and in Deganawidah: that it is better to work out our problems with rationality, than with violence. The earliest example of this movement that I can think of appears in the Code of Hammurabi, circa 1700 BCE. In its preamble we find the assertion that the whole point of the Code is: 'to bring about the rule of righteousness in the land, to destroy the wicked and the evil-doers; *so that the strong should not harm the weak...*' and also 'to give the protection of right to the land' and bring about 'the well-being of the oppressed'.[115]

In the mythology of my own ancestors, the Irish Celts, there is a collection of stories that together are called *The Cycle of the Invasions*. They detail how Ireland was populated by a series of colonists, and describe the various problems they encountered. Most had to do with diseases, but some had to do with warfare against a tribe of possibly-indigenous monsters known as the Fomhoire. When the gods won the final battle against the Fomhoire, the peace was proclaimed by a goddess named *An Mhorrigán*, a name that in English means the Great Queen. It's curious that she is the one to proclaim the peace because as a goddess she specializes in warfare, and she is very capable of bloodthirsty violence, like any of the men of a tribal warrior society like the pre-Christian Celts. During the preparations for the battle, she promises: 'I have stood fast; I shall pursue what was watched; I will be able to kill; I will be able to destroy those who might be subdued.'[116] Yet after the battle is over, she proclaims peace. Here are her own words:

Peace to [as high as] the sky

sky to the earth
earth beneath sky
strength in everyone
a cup very full
a fullness of honey
honour enough
summer in winter
spear supported by shield
shields supported by forts
forts fierce eager for battle
'sod' [fleece] from sheep
woods grown with antler-tips [full of stags]
forever destructions have departed
mast [nuts] on trees
a branch drooping-down
drooping from growth...[117]

This is not the whole of the proclamation, but you have the general impression. I think this is a very interesting moment in the mythology of the Celtic people. The goddess who, until that moment, had been responsible for warfare, now also becomes responsible for peace. The poem refers to several culturally significant symbols that have little to do with war-fighting and more to do with the maintenance of a flourishing and cultured human society. We see, for example, the salmon, representing wisdom; the river Boyne and the monument of Newgrange, representing time and eternity; the woods full of stags, symbolizing fertility and kingship; the drooping tree branches heavy with nuts, representing prosperity. The warrior culture is not forgotten, since she does mention military things like the building of forts. But otherwise, this proclamation describes a society that delights in purposes other than (or in addition to) warfare. In this change, the iron-age Celtic people did not cease to be a warrior people. But I think they also began to recognize other values, such as art, justice, and peace.

What does all this have to do with civilization? It's this: civilization is the process by which a society shifts its priorities, from violence to intelligence, from conquest to culture. I've chosen examples from societies that had no contact with each other at the time when these statements were first uttered, in order to show that the movement from killing to thinking may very well be a universal idea. It is universal, not in the sense that every society adopts it a matter of historical destiny, but rather in the sense that the potential for discovering it is available to anyone, anywhere, at any time. In this transformation, a society does not give up its capacity for warfare. But I think it also gives to itself new, additional priorities, such as art, music, justice, education, trade, and peace.

That this process is a *rational* one is a well established proposition in the history of Western philosophy. One of the first people to write of civilization this way was Paul-Henri Thiry, Baron d'Holbach, in a 1773 text called *Système sociale*:

> There is nothing that places more obstacles in the way of public happiness, of the progress of human reason, of the entire civilization of men, than the continual wars into which thoughtless princes are drawn at every moment... Human reason is not yet sufficiently exercised; the civilization of peoples is not yet complete; obstacles without number have hitherto opposed the progress of useful knowledge, the advance of which can alone contribute to perfecting our government, our laws, our education, our institutions, and our morals.[118]

Note how d'Holbach uses the word to designate a process; one with obstacles to overcome; one which is 'not yet complete'. Nearly 150 years later, Albert Schweitzer could speak of civilization in broadly similar terms, as if the association between civilization and rationality was by then mostly settled:

> For a quite general definition we may say that civilization is progress, material and spiritual progress, on the part of individuals and of the mass. In what does it consist? First of all in a lessening of the strain imposed on individuals and on the mass by the struggle for existence. The establishment of as favourable conditions of living as possible for all is a demand which must be made partly for its own sake, *partly with a view to the spiritual and moral perfecting of individuals,* which is *the ultimate object of civilization.*[119]

Look closely at the last sentence in the quoted text. It means, as he explains, that 'both individuals and the mass let their willing be determined by the material and spiritual good of the whole and the individuals that compose it; that is to say, their actions are ethical. Ethical progress is, then, that which is truly of the essence of civilization...'[120] We began this meditation with the idea that civilization is a kind of process. Now we can say more precisely what *kind* of process: it's the development of rationality as an expanding circle of social, ethical, and political values.

The earliest reference to the idea of moral progress comes from the 1st century CE historian Plutarch, in a chapter of his *Moralia* called 'How a Man may be Sensible of his Progress in Virtue'.[121] But Plutarch's treatment of the topic is deeply individualist: he speaks of the development of *personal* habits, such as calmness, a preference for listening over speaking, and letting go of vanity and pride. As an *historical* phenomena, the idea of the expanding circle might arguably have first appeared in the Old Testament, for instance in passages like this one, where God instructs the people of Israel: 'Do not oppress a foreigner; you yourselves know how it feels to be foreigners, because you were foreigners in Egypt.' (Exodus 23:9) The first appearance of this idea on which we can put a definite date is in 1869, in a text called

History of European Morals, by Anglo-Irish philosopher William Edward Hartpole Lecky. Here's where the expression first appears:

> At one time the benevolent affections embrace merely the family, soon *the circle expanding* includes first a class, then a nation, then a coalition of nations, then all humanity, and finally, its influence is felt in the dealings of man with the animal world. In each of these stages a standard is formed, different from that of the preceding stage, but in each case the same tendency is recognized as virtue.[122]

The idea of an expanding circle was picked up with great enthusiasm by the environmental movement, where writers often express the hope that over time the circle would grow to include animals, landscapes, and the earth as a whole. Aldo Leopold, professor of forestry and widely regarded as among the first important promoters of environmental ethics, expressed that wish as follows:

> This extension of ethics, so far studied only by philosophers, is actually a process in ecological evolution... The thing [ethics] has its origin in the tendency of interdependent individuals or groups to evolve modes of co-operation. Politics and economics are advanced symbioses in which the original free-for-all competition has been replaced, in part, by cooperative mechanisms with an ethical content. The first ethics dealt with the relation between individuals; the Mosaic Decalogue [the Ten Commandments] is an example. Later accretions dealt with the relation between the individual and society...[123]

From there, he hoped that a third step would soon be taken: a step that 'enlarges the boundaries of the community to include soils, waters, plants, and animals, or collectively the land'. (*ibid* pg. 413)

Ecologists like Leopold tend not to make the connection between ethical progress and civilization. But other philosophers often do make the connection. Indeed, by the 20th century the connection between civilization and ethical progress was so well established that philosophers didn't need to argue for it anymore. All they had to do was describe and clarify it. We have already seen several of those examples, notably the example of Albert Schweitzer; three more should suffice to make the point:

- Sigmund Freud, in 1930: 'The word 'civilization' describes the whole sum of the achievements and the regulations which distinguish our lives from those of our animal ancestors and which serve two purposes – namely to protect men against nature and to adjust their mutual relations.'[124]
- Leo Strauss, in 1941: 'Civilization designates at once the process of making man a citizen, and not a slave; an inhabitant of cities, and not a rustic; a lover of peace, and not of war; a polite being, and not a ruffian.' Furthermore, the driver of this process is the combination of ethics and science: '...and both united. For science without morals degenerates into cynicism, and thus destroys the basis of the scientific effort itself; and morals without science degenerates into superstition and thus is apt to become fanatic cruelty.'[125]
- Jay Newman, in 1982: 'Civilization is the process of approximating or realizing, primarily by the use of reason, the greatest possible number of trans-cultural or universal human aspirations, both for oneself and for the greatest possible number of others.' Newman identifies rationality as the most important quality in this process: 'If we cannot reason with people, and if they cannot reason with each

other, then it is hard to regard them as civilized... I am not making a value judgment here: I am describing an observable phenomenon.' Reason, according to Newman, brings with it increasing respect for outsiders: ''Primitive men' do not see those outside the 'tribe' as having the rights that those inside the tribe have. As men become more civilized, they see more and more people outside the tribe as having rights.'[126]

These authors presented almost no arguments for these positions. To my mind, the omission of argument doesn't make their positions wrong, but rather it suggests that their positions were so well established they did not appear to need argumentation anymore. This is something which, as we have seen, Norbert Elias predicted: a civilization's most deeply held ideas are those that 'have ceased to be the subject of any particular discussion'.

If the process of civilization began with the construction of walls around cities, perhaps the process *advances* when those ancient walls are pulled down. In this respect it may be better to say that humanity's most important moment was not in Athens at the time of Pericles, but in China during the time of Confucius. While he was the Minister of Crime (a office akin to chief prose-cutor) in the State of Lu, cities in his care were so well managed that: '...vendors of lamb and pork stopped raising their prices. Men and women walked on different sides of the street, no one picked up anything lost on the road, and strangers coming to the city did not have to look for the officers in charge, for everyone made them welcome.'[127] In 498 BCE, perhaps feeling emboldened by this success, he persuaded his sovereign, Duke Deng of the Kingdom of Lu, to order the demolition of the walls surrounding the three cities Hou, Bi, and Cheng. Confucius believed that these three cities, unprotected by walls, would be forced to trust each other. Also, they'd be less likely to stir up rebellions against the duke.

Alas, the story did not end well for Confucius personally. The aristocratic families who ran those cities did not tear down their defenses. Duke Deng laid siege to them. The rebel leaders of Bi and Hou eventually relented, and their walls were taken down; the leaders of Cheng resisted, and Duke Deng was eventually forced to retreat. Confucius saw the way the political winds were blowing, so he resigned his post and fled into exile. He took a large group of students with him, and with their help he attempted to spread his ideas elsewhere. He did attain some partial success that way, and he eventually returned home some thirteen years later. But he never attained the degree of political power and influence he once enjoyed. On his deathbed, he thought himself a failure: his last words were: 'No intelligent monarch arises; there is not one in the kingdom that will make me his master. My time has come to die.' (*Li Chi* II,1,ii.20.) But perhaps he spoke too soon. Three centuries later a monarch did arise who took Confucius as his teacher: Emperor Gaozu, first of the Han dynasty. Persuaded by the Confucian scholar Lu Jia that the philosophy of Legalism (i.e. rule by force and terror) doesn't work, Gaozu made Confucianism the state's official policy. From there, Confucian ideas about interpersonal relations, about how to create a well-ordered and peaceful society, about how to lead a nation by setting a moral example, and I think especially his trust in people's basic good-heartedness,[128] turned out to illuminate all of Chinese history for many centuries, including up to the present day. Well, that's what victory looks like to me.

This meditation on progress in ethics and rationality has been, of course, only one way to create 'retroactive continuity' in the philosophical history of civilization. There may be others. But before I move on to them, let me pose a question.

§ 10. Walls and Circles

Civilization is an expanding circle; civilization is a rising wall. Which observation is the truth? Or, are both of them true? And if so, how can that be?

When the in-group thinks the wall is threatened by the expanding circle, they often invoke the language of civilization as a rallying cry to build the wall higher. In the 1980s, the Reagan administration referred to communism as a 'plague' spread by 'depraved opponents of civilization itself' in 'a return to barbarism in the modern age'.[129] Thirty years later American statesmen were still repeating the trope. US Secretary of State John Kerry used it in 2015, in a speech to French embassy staff following a terrorist attack in Paris. He portrayed the attack not as a clash between two different and incomparable civilizations (Huntington-style), but rather as a clash between all civilizations on one side and uncivilized barbarism on the other:

> Don't mistake what these attacks represent. This is not a clash of civilizations. These terrorists have declared war against all civilization. They kill Yezidis because they are Yezidis. They kill Christians because they are Christians. They kill Shia because they are Shia. And on. They rape and torture and pillage and call it the will of God. They are in fact psychopathic monsters, and there is nothing, nothing civilized about them. So this is not a case of one civilization pitted against another. This is a battle between civilization itself and barbarism, between civilization and medieval and modern fascism both at the same time.[130]

Two months later, following another violent attack in Paris, France, American presidential candidate Donald Trump proposed banning all Muslims in the entire world from entering the United States.[131]

To choose an example from my own country: in September of 2015, posters appeared on the campuses of three Toronto universities that invited people to join a club called 'Students for Western Civilization'. The poster called for a protest against a supposed bias against Western civilization in university education. The club's website claimed that students are indoctrinated by a 'neo-Marxism', which 'identifies white people as oppressors and everyone else as 'the oppressed''.[132] The image on the poster featured two well-groomed and proudly posed young white men, with Toronto's iconic CN Tower in the background.

During the 2015 federal election campaign in Canada, the Conservative party pledged to establish a telephone tip line for people to report 'barbaric cultural practices' to the police.[133] The campaign promise was a follow-up to Bill S-7, 'The Zero Tolerance for Barbaric Cultural Practices Act' (Royal Assent 18th June 2015), which was aimed at polygamous marriages and 'honor killings' (despite the fact that those things were already illegal).[134] The bill, the tip line, and related identity-politics wedges, correlated with an increase in violent hate crimes in Canada, especially involving Muslim women being verbally and physically abused in public places by total strangers.[135] The same party also introduced Bill C-24, the 'Strengthening Canadian Citizenship Act' (Royal Assent 19th June 2014), which enables the government to strip the citizenship from any person who is convicted of treason or a terror offense, if that person could become a citizen of a different country.[136] Though the bill evidently divides Canadians into two classes, 'old stock Canadians' and everyone else, and though the bill is evidently contrary to section 15 of the Canadian Charter of Rights and Freedoms,[137] nonetheless Prime Minster Stephen Harper hinted at his willingness to expand it.[138] Because of these and other movements toward a tribal kind of patriotism, voters in that year's election installed an opposition party in power, including a record number of Muslim MPs. The new immigration minister moved to repeal the Act in February 2016.[139]

Incidents like these are examples of a historically dominant in-group, in these cases white men, pushing back against the efforts of historically disenfranchised out-groups to tell their stories and be heard. White people might lose some of their exclusive advantages as the circle expands, but the loss of an exclusive advantage is not the same as oppression; the anger is directed at a straw man. The reality is that white people, with their history, are settling into a new place in the world where they are one people among many. What I find interesting, and also chilling, about these examples, is the way the in-groups invoke once again the ancient great wall of civilization in order to cast themselves in the role of out-group, and so prevent that decline.

The circle expands. Then it contracts again. The wall goes up, then it comes down. Lines are drawn in the sand, then they are erased and redrawn. Even in ancient times you can see this happening. Emperor Justinian of Rome, back in the 6th century, attempted a military alliance with Ethiopia. For this he was 'reproached...as if he had attempted to introduce a people of savage negroes into the system of civilized society.'[140] In this instance at least, Justinian tried to widen the circle, and in response his nobles tried to strengthen the wall.

Which of these two forces is the essence of civilization? Is history destined to fix upon one of them? Or, shall the tension between them go on forever? Sigmund Freud, for example, seemed to think that both of these forces could be at work at the same time, and he called this phenomena 'the narcissism of minor differences': 'It is always possible to bind together a considerable number of people in love, so long as there are other people left over to receive the manifestations of their aggressiveness,' he wrote. Even a philosophy of universal neighborly love can involve not the extinguishing of violence, but its redirection to other targets: 'When once the Apostle Paul had posited universal love between men as the foundation of his Christian community, extreme intolerance on the part of Christendom towards those who remained outside it became the inevitable consequence.'[141]

New questions; and I don't yet know the answers. But I think

I may have made a small discovery: *there are at least two candidates for the essence of civilization:* expanding circles, and rising walls. Could both of them be part of the same essence? Perhaps civilization is a process of drawing, then erasing and re-drawing, a line in the sand, nearer or farther from the centre each time. This complicates my search for an answer to the first of my root questions. But it's too early to declare the question unanswerable. The Heavenly City has many doors. I may yet find another way in.

§ 11. Plans for the Rational City

Another way to 'retcon' the philosophical history of civilization is to study different philosophically-imagined ideal societies, looking for features of that society that can also be found on the academic checklists.

In the Western philosophical tradition, the earliest and most influential model of an ideal community comes from Plato. (Like it or not, if you want to sit at the grown-ups table you have to read your Plato.) In his view, an ideal society is an aristocratic state ruled by incorruptible intellectual experts: philosophers. Here's the famous passage in the text where the argument is introduced:

> Until philosophers rule as kings in cities or those who are now called kings and leading men genuinely and adequately philosophize, that is, until political power and philosophy entirely coincide, while the many natures who at present pursue either one exclusively are forcibly prevented from doing so, cities will have no rest from evils...nor, I think, will the human race. (*Republic* 473c-d)

The philosophers, Plato explains in the next few pages, 'are those who love the truth' (*ibid* 475e), as opposed to everyone else, who only care about their own experiences and opinions (c.f. *ibid* 476d).

Plato also discusses how the philosophers care about knowledge and truth to the exclusion of nearly everything else: the philosopher would 'abandon those pleasures that come through the body...such a person is moderate and not at all a money-lover'. (485d) Indeed Plato's philosophers don't want political power, either. But they take on the responsibility of power because they are persuaded that 'the greatest punishment, if one isn't willing to rule, is to be ruled by someone worse than one oneself'. (347c) So, Plato's answer to my first root question is something like this: a civilization is a society ruled by the right kind of people: that is, the wise, the just, the ethically incorruptible.

Those who are not philosophers in Plato's ideal society are assigned jobs in accord with their natures. There's also a military class called the auxiliaries, and a working class called the craftsmen. So Plato's ideal society is not only one ruled by philosophers, but it's also a society guarded by the soldiers and built by the craftsmen. Everyone does the job that their natures make them best suited to do. He called this ideal society a *kallipolis*, a 'beautiful city'.

Most of the time Plato argues only that his imagined republic is founded on reason and rationality, as if that's all he needs to say about it. But in a few, subtle, easy-to-miss passages, he claims that rationality itself is founded upon a divine order in the universe. 'The philosopher', says Plato, 'by consorting with what is ordered and divine and despite all the slanders around that say otherwise, himself becomes divine and ordered as a human being can.' (*Republic* 500d) Such a person is: '...willing to take part in the politics of the city we were founding and describing, the one that exists in theory, for I don't think it exists anywhere on earth. But perhaps, I said, there is a model of it in heaven, for anyone who wants to look at it and to make himself its citizen on the strength of what he sees.' (*Republic* 592b) It's a carrot-and-stick approach. There's the promise of a better quality of life for everyone, if we follow his ideas. Yet there's also a threat of punishment for those who don't. His criticism of the life of the unphilosophical man is quite scathing: he calls them 'drones' and 'lotus-eaters'; he describes their behavior as 'frenzied' and 'without order or necessity'; he compares them to bees who flit from one flower to another apparently at random, without order or plan in their lives. He threatens that the unphilosophical man will eventually become a slave, at first to his own passions, and eventually to whatever tyrannical political leader takes power with the promise to protect the city against threats to individual freedom.

This strongly reminds me of some of the features of civilization mentioned by the academics: especially class stratification, and specialized labor. This particular feature was also carried forth by Plato's student Aristotle, who wrote that a basic distinction between those who command and those who obey is the foundation of the state:

> Equally essential is the combination of the natural ruler and ruled, for the purpose of [mutual] preservation. For the element that can use its intelligence to look ahead is by nature ruler and by nature master, while that which has the bodily strength to do the actual work is by nature a slave, one of those who are ruled. (*Pol.* 1252a24)

Aristotle's next move is to declare that people who are not Greek 'have nothing which is by nature fitted to rule'; the implication is that non-Greeks are all of the bodily-strength type and none of the intelligence-to-look-ahead type. Therefore, so his argument goes, 'a non-Greek and slave are by nature identical'. (*Pol.* 1252a34) Aristotle might be using the word 'slave' to mean any working class person, not just 'slaves' in the sense of people who are owned as the private property of a master. But even if that is the case, you can see the presuppositions of human nature here. You can also see the language of the Ancient Great Wall, invoked to strengthen the claims about human nature.

Indian philosopher Ananda Coomaraswamy observed that this argument in early Greek thought is almost the same in ancient India. (We Western philosophers like to say the party began in Greece, but the truth is it began independently in several places around the world). The paragraph where he describes this correspondence is dense:

> In Plato's thought there is a cosmic city of the world, the city state, and an individual body politic, all of which are communities (Gr. *koininia*, Skr. *gana*)... Who fills, or populates, these cities? Whose are these cities, 'ours' or God's? What is the meaning of 'self-government'?... Philo says that 'As for lordship (*kyrios*), God is the only citizen', and this is almost identical with the words of the Upanisad, 'This Man (*Purusa*) is the citizen (*Purusaya*) in every city', and must not be thought of as in any way contradicted by Philo's other statement, that 'Adam' (not 'this man', but the true Man) is the 'only citizen of the world'.[142]

The *Purusa* that is mentioned here is the primordial cosmic human being, the personification of the human race. Here's how the Rig Veda describes him:

> Thousand-headed was the Purusa, thousand-eyed, thousand-footed. He embraced the earth on all sides...
>
> When they [the gods] divided the Purusa, into how many parts did they arrange him? What was his mouth? What his two arms? What are his thighs and feet called?
>
> The *brahmin* [religious caste] was his mouth, his two arms were made the *rajana* [warrior], his two thighs the *vaisya* [trader and agriculturalist], from his feet the *sudra* [servile class] was born.[143]

In the idea of the *Purusa*, as you can see, we find the same notion of a labor-differentiated, class-stratified society that we found in Plato's *kallipolis*. While the connection to human nature isn't obvious here, it is clarified and veritably canonized in another sacred Hindu text, the *Bhagavad Gita*, as follows:

> Even a man of knowledge acts in accord with his own nature. Beings follow their nature. What can repression accomplish?... Better is one's own law though imperfectly carried out than the law of another carried out perfectly. Better is death in the fulfillment of one's own law, for to follow another's law is perilous. (3:33-35)

One could read this line from the *Gita* in an individualist way: better to live in accord with one's own personal relationship to Atman (the Higher Self, the primordial cosmic unity), than to live in accord with someone else's prescription. But there's also a political way to read this. In context: the *Bhagavad Gita* is a story about a man named Arjun, a charioteer and a member of the military caste, who doesn't want to do his job anymore. The god Krishna appears before him and persuades him to get back to work again. The argument that one should follow one's own law is the argument that Arjun should do his caste-prescribed job, whether he likes it or not. If he doesn't like it, he should remember that it's the job which matters, not its consequences (2:47-8), and that the job should be done 'as a sacrifice' (3:9), that is, as an enactment of religious devotion. Indeed the god Krishna claims the four castes have a divine origin: 'The fourfold order was created by Me according to the divisions of quality and work.' (4:13) Each person's fulfillment of their job 'maintain[s] the world-order' (3:20,25). Even Krishna himself has work to do. And if this is still unconvincing, if people still want other kinds of work to do, Krishna reminds Arjun that he shouldn't *want* anything anyway: 'He who is satisfied with whatever comes by chance, who has passed beyond the dualities (of pleasure and pain), who is free from jealousy, who remains the same in success and failure – even when he acts, he is not bound [to the wheel of rebirth].' (4:22) Again there are two ways to read this. One is personal, in which the gentle abstention from irrational desires will spare one much suffering. But it can be read politically, too: each person has a certain nature, which makes them suited to do a certain kind of work, in accord with a certain place in the political hierarchy. The stability and justice of the community depends on each member doing her own job. Coomaraswamy quotes from the same passage in the Gita, and interprets it in this political way, as follows:

> ...unless this community can act unanimously, as one man, it will be working at all sorts of cross purposes. The concept is that of a corporation in which the several members of a community work together, each in its own way; and such a vocational society is an organism, not an aggregate of competing interests and consequently [an] unstable 'balance of power'. Thus the human City of God contains within itself the pattern of all other societies and of a true civilisation. The man will be a 'just' man when each of his members performs its own appropriate task and is subject to the ruling Reason that exercises forethought on behalf of the whole man; and in the same way the public city will be just when there is agreement as to which shall rule, and there is no confusion of functions but every occupation is a vocational responsibility.[144]

Coomaraswamy has invoked the name of the City of God – and to this divine image my meditations now turn. (As an aside, it is precisely when a text can be read in two or more ways, like my reading of the Gita, that it becomes interesting and tends to stand the test of time. But I digress.)

§ 12. Dreams of the Celestial City

Western civilization has rolled along its way under the momentum of Plato's philosophical forward-push for something like two-and-a-half thousand years. Along the way it got a boost from Augustine, whose theological account offered a similar picture of a rank-organized community. In his argument, true civilization is a 'City of God', that is, a condition of order and peace obtained among people who have accepted Christianity. Here are his words:

> The peace of a household is an ordered concord, with respect to command and obedience, of those who dwell together; the peace of a city is an ordered concord, with respect to command and obedience, of the citizens; and the peace of the Heavenly City is a perfectly ordered and perfectly harmonious fellowship in the enjoyment of God, and of one another in God.[145]

This ordered concord emerges from hierarchal power relations, especially including slavery. No one, he says, is naturally born a slave; but people can be condemned to slavery as a punishment for a crime:

> By nature, then, in the condition in which God first created man, no man is the slave either of another man or of sin. But it is also true that servitude itself is ordained as a punishment by that law which enjoins the preservation of the order of nature, and forbids its disruption. For if nothing had been done in violation of that law, there would have been no need for the discipline of servitude as punishment.[146]

Augustine does *not* say, as Plato and Krishna said, that some people are naturally born for one particular class and not another. In this sense his argument is a distinct break from the hierarchical rigidity of the Platonic *Kallipolis* or the Hindu caste system. Yet Augustine's position on the legal correctness of slavery has precedent in two bodies of law that emerged from the Roman Empire's conquest of Europe. One was the natural law, *lex naturalis*, which claimed to describe how people (and animals) tend to behave. The second was *ius gentium*, the 'law of nations', which claimed to express moral customs observably common to all societies the Romans encountered. The natural law says we are all born free and equal. Yet the law of nations says that all societies have mechanisms by which some people can deservedly lose their natural freedoms. Usually, slavery is instituted as a punishment for some crime; noteworthy among them, and emphasized by Augustine, is the crime of being on the losing side of a just war. The proper punishment for that crime was death, but one could be enslaved instead, and this alternative was somehow a kind of 'mercy'. Given the way that the 'justice' of a just war is often applied to the winner retroactively, it is entirely impossible to say whether someone so enslaved really deserved it. (Notice, also, the logical fallacy of *post hoc* in the last line of quoted text; but I leave it aside for now.)

Augustine's idea takes another precedent from the famous Biblical account of the Heavenly City and the Temple of Solomon. The description of this city is both poetic and also vague, giving the modern architect great freedom to interpret the meaning: for instance the city is 'the Holy City, the new Jerusalem, prepared as a bride beautifully dressed for her husband'. (Revelation 21:2) The people of the Christian community are themselves: 'The light of the world. A town built on a hill [that] cannot be hidden.' (Matt 5:14) The description of this city in the Book of Revelation is long and carefully detailed:

It shone with the glory of God, and its brilliance was like that of a very precious jewel, like a jasper, clear as crystal. It had a great, high wall with twelve gates, and with twelve angels at the gates. On the gates were written the names of the twelve tribes of Israel. There were three gates on the east, three on the north, three on the south and three on the west. The wall of the city had twelve foundations, and on them were the names of the twelve apostles of the Lamb. The angel who talked with me had a measuring rod of gold to measure the city, its gates and its walls. The city was laid out like a square, as long as it was wide. He measured the city with the rod and found it to be 12,000 stadia in length, and as wide and high as it is long. The angel measured the wall using human measurement, and it was 144 cubits thick. The wall was made of jasper, and the city of pure gold, as pure as glass. The foundations of the city walls were decorated with every kind of precious stone... The twelve gates were twelve pearls, each gate made of a single pearl. The great street of the city was of gold, as pure as transparent glass. I did not see a temple in the city, because the Lord God Almighty and the Lamb are its temple. The city does not need the sun or the moon to shine on it, for the glory of God gives it light, and the Lamb is its lamp. The nations will walk by its light, and the kings of the earth will bring their splendour into it. On no day will its gates ever be shut, for there will be no night there. The glory and honour of the nations will be brought into it. (Revelation 21:10-26)

Notice, first of all, how much attention the writer gives to the wall here. The text is very specific about its dimensions and the different species of precious stones in its foundation. From outside it would look like a giant golden cube, more than 2,200 kilometers to a side! I think this emphasis on the wall is no accident. For one thing, its message is that heaven is not just any kind of place: *it is a city*. A city, let us recall, is 'the big picture' of civilization. It's the physical foundation for a politically organized community; a point reflected in the Biblical account by the reference to the kings (i.e. not just anybody) who will bring their splendor to it. It may be no accident that the city wall is mostly made of metals and gemstones, instead of wood or clay. For one reason, the materials represent various virtues, and their inclusion in the city's description is a way of saying which virtues can be found in the city. For another, inorganic materials reinforce the idea that the city is a feature of the world of thought and of spirit, and of human artifice, not the world of nature, wildness, and the fluidic messiness of the body. It may also be no accident that the city is described as a cube, that is, one of the Platonic Solids: shapes of perfect mathematical symmetry and simplicity. The cube shape, which occurs nowhere in nature except in sodium chloride crystals (an inorganic mineral again – and even the most perfect of them have flaws) also reinforces that the Heavenly City is unmistakably removed from the realm of the organic and the nonhuman. The picture also makes a strong contrast with the Elysian Fields, the heaven of the Pagan Romans: a place where, as the hero Aeneus is told by one of its residents: 'Not a one here has a settled home; in shady groves we dwell, and have our haunts in hollow banks of rivers, and in meadows refreshed by streams.' (Virgil, *Aeneid*, 6.673) Elysium is a land of happiness, comfort, and beauty, to be sure, but it's decidedly not a city.

It's possible that the Biblical author emphasizes the wall here simply because real-world cities of his time had walls, and he was only describing an idealized and glamorized version of cities he already knew. Even so, the Holy City's wall remains a visionary instance the Ancient Great Wall, and at the same time a visionary instance of the house and the hearth that separates the human realm from the wild outside. There is no temple in the city because the whole city is a temple – this leads us to the way the very idea of a temple invokes an antithesis between the sacred and the profane in much the same way the idea of civilization invokes an antithesis of the civilized and the uncivilized. In this respect it is perhaps also no accident that the description of the Heavenly City begins *outside* the walls. It is as if to say we begin our journey to

God, whatever that might entail, from a position of profanity (a word which once meant nothing more than 'outside the temple' and only later came to mean vulgarity and 'to treat (what is sacred) with irreverence, contempt, or disregard'[147]) toward a condition of holiness. The twelve gates of the Holy City remain open, and so the City is always accessible; but nonetheless, the distinction between the in-group and the out-group remains solidly in place, presupposed and unquestioned.

Castes are not specified in Augustine's text, as they are in Plato and in the Bhagavad Gita. But human nature is still invoked to justify why some people are higher than others. Not any individual's own nature personally, but the 'nature' of human societies and social orders. Of those who find themselves in the higher position, Augustine says:

> ...those who are truly 'fathers of their families' are as much concerned for the welfare of all in their households, in respect of the worship and service of God, as if they were all their children. They desire and pray that they may all come to that heavenly home... Until that home is reached, however, fathers have a duty to exercise their mastery which is greater than that of slaves to endure their servitude.

Notice the stunning display of blinkered class myopia: Augustine appears to believe it pains rulers to rule, worse than it pains slaves to obey! Augustine then concludes on a note that echoes the Rational City of the philosophers: a correspondence between the father of a household and the leader of a city. 'A man's household, then, ought to be the beginning, or a little part, of the city; and every beginning has reference to some end proper to itself, and every part has reference to the integrity of the whole of which it is a part.' (*ibid*, ch. 16)

This dream of a heavenly city gives us another essence for civilization. It is a class-structured society, in which a mythology about human nature, the authority of the gods, and the authority of the gods' representatives on earth, enforces the class structure. And just for the sake of tying up this meditation with a neat little bow, here's Coomaraswamy agreeing that a true civilization is a society modeled after a divine plan:

> Is not Plato altogether right when he proposes to entrust the government of cities to 'the uncorrupted remnant of true philosophers'...and altogether right when he maintains that 'no city ever can be happy unless its outlines have been drawn by draughtsmen making use of the divine pattern' – that of the City of God that is in heaven and 'within you'?[148]

I think what makes the City of God such a powerful and compelling idea is that it's easy for nearly anyone, or for nearly any group of people, to imagine that they are the ones who know what the divine plan is, and that therefore they are the ones who should rule. It is a *validating* idea: it fulfills a basic fantasy about power, place, and meaning. Particularly, it confirms the upper-class fantasy that God himself, the ultimate law-giver, the highest and most unassailable of political authorities, personally certifies that the powerful shall remain powerful and that the poor shall stay poor. As such it is another instance of the Ancient Great Wall, which as we have seen separates the human from the inhuman: here it separates the elites from the commoners, the prosperous from the deprived.

How vastly different is this model of civilization from the model of the academics! Nearly all the academics, from Toynbee to Morris, regarded civilization as an essentially *progressive* society. Coomaraswamy, that other celebrant of the City of God, wrote that industrial civilization's progressiveness is precisely what's wrong with it:

> On the one hand the inspired tradition rejects ambition,

competition and quantitative standards; on the other, our modern 'civilisation' is based on the notions of social advancement, free enterprise (devil take the hindmost) and production in quantity... It is fundamentally, the incubus of world trade that makes of industrial 'civilisations' a 'curse to humanity', and from the industrial concept of progress 'in line with the manufacturing enterprise of civilisation' that modern wars have arisen and will arise...[149]

Modern industrial civilization is enterprising, dynamic, ever-changing, and ever growing – and proud of these qualities. The *Kallipolis* is none of those things: it is a steady-state society, impossible to change, because its order is constituted by 'divine reason'; the Heavenly City is similarly impossible to change because it is constituted by God. Accordingly, the desire to change one's place in society, to renounce one's caste obligations and do something different with one's life, is condemned by God. This changelessness touches each citizen in the centre of her personal identity. For in the *Kallipolis*, as in the City of God, as in the cosmic *Purusa*, you are what you do. But you don't get to choose what you do, as this has been chosen for you by your nature, as represented by the caste in which you were born. It follows that you don't get to choose who you are.

It may appear as if I'm arguing that unlike the Heavenly City, modern industrial civilization has no great walls. Actually, industrial civilization has walls of its own, and it's perfectly capable of invoking God to defend them. Industrial civilization also has critics within its own walls: Kenneth Clark, who loved religion for its art and not art for its religion, called industrialization a 'squalid disorder' and 'a new form of barbarism'.[150] But I get ahead of myself – I'm already addressing the second of my root questions before I have a complete answer to the first. We still do not yet have sight of our destination – a full understanding of the essence of civilization – but our journey is now properly underway.

§ 13. Tales of the State of Nature

Here's a third way to 'ret-con' the idea of civilization, and so answer the first of my root questions. We can conduct a thought-experiment in which we imagine what human life might be like *without* a state, and without all the things that states imply: that is, without laws, without centralized governance, without class stratification, without institutions, and the like. The idea is to speculate about what life would be like if human behavior was guided only by human nature, and nothing more. Then, the thought-experiment searches for the condition of that natural life that might make people want to form a law-governed civil society. The name philosophers use for this imagined pre-civilized world is 'the state of nature'.

The conclusions you will draw after exploring this world depend very strongly on your opinion of human nature. Are we human beings basically respectful and generous and kind? Or, are we basically selfish and competitive and aggressive? Might human nature be some third, as-yet-undiscovered thing? Might we have more than one nature? Or, might there be no such thing as human nature at all?

A thought experiment very much like this was in Vitruvius' account of the first house. His 'men of old', as we have seen, lived in fear of the natural world until, in the course of some unspecified accident, fear gave way to curiosity. The space was thereby cleared for other virtues, like courage and creativity, to follow. Then:

As men made progress by becoming daily more expert in building, and as their ingenuity was increased by their dexterity so that from habit they attained to considerable skill, their intelligence was enlarged by their industry until the more proficient adopted the trade of carpenters. From these early beginnings, and from the fact that nature had not only endowed the human race with senses like the rest of the animals, but had also equipped their minds with the powers of thought and understanding, thus putting all other animals under their sway, they next gradually advanced from the construction of buildings to the other arts and sciences, and so passed from a rude and barbarous mode of life to civilization and refinement.[151]

Vitruvius' assumptions about human nature are generally positive: he thinks we are a curious and industrious kind of creature. Aside from fear of the forces of nature, he identifies no particular problem with life in the state of nature, except that it's a life more fit for animals than for people. The transition to civil society is portrayed here as quite natural and almost unremarkable.

Similarly, the Roman poet Lucretius, writing around the same time, thought that the transition from nature to civil society was prompted by the dangers of the wild:

> For many centuries, men led their lives
> Like roving animals, no hardy soul
> Steered the curved plowshare, no one understood
> Planting or pruning...
> When the nighttime came,
> They'd lump their shaggy bodies on the ground,
> Much like wild boars, under a coverlet
> Of leaves or brush...
> What made them much more anxious
> Was that wild animals would often make
> Their sleep a fatal risk; if they caught sight
> Of a lion or wild boar, they'd leave their homes,
> Their rocky caves, and in the dead of night
> Concede their leafy beds to their savage guests...

Like Vitruvius, Lucretius imagines that the origin of civilization is in humanity's effort to protect itself from the dangers of the wild. He sees early humanity as a generally curious, hard-working, and co-operative race, who make the transition to civilization quite easily. But Lucretius' story goes a little beyond Vitruvius. He also speculates on the first marriages, and the first peace treaties, and on how these seeds of deliberate social convention-making grew into the fullness of organized urban life, complete with walls:

> Next, with the use of fire and huts
> Or furs for clothing, when a woman stayed
> Joined to one man in something like a marriage,
> With offspring recognized, that was the time
> When first the human race began to soften.
> Fire kept their bodies from enduring cold,
> Lust sapped their energies, and children broke
> Their parents' haughty spirit by their wheedling,
> And even neighbors started forming pacts
> Of nonaggression. *Do not hurt me, please,*
> *And I'll not hurt you,* were the terms they stammered...
> So day-by-day,
> They changed their former ways of living, taught
> By men of lively wit and kind intent.
> Kings started founding cities, building walls
> Around the heights for refuge and defense.[152]

In other versions of this thought experiment, conducted by different philosophers, the transition to civil society is not so easygoing. It's a specific response to a specific problem that arises from the 'nature' of life in the 'state of nature' (please pardon the equivocation).

Thomas Hobbes (1588-1679), an Englishman, writing philosophy during the English Civil War, decided to do what all good philosophers do during times of chaos: attempt to reason about the chaos. Though he was living in Paris at the time and was quite safe from the fighting back home, he became a serious student of the accounts of the war brought by refugees and exiles, most of them from the Royalist side; that is, the side that lost. From these experiences he would develop a series of profoundly revolutionary ideas about individual freedom, the natural equality of all people, but most of all the necessity of a strong centralized government.

In the first premise of his argument, Hobbes thought that human nature was generally selfish and competitive: 'So that in the first place, I put for a general inclination of all mankind, a perpetual and restless desire for power after power, that ceaseth only in death.' (*Leviathan,* ch. 11) The idea here is that whatever else people may want, above all else they want power, that is, the ability to *do* things. This desire for power is 'restless' and 'perpetual': people always want *more* than they presently possess. Actually Hobbes also listed a few other things people want, such as 'ease', 'sensual delight', and 'praise'. But, like power, these things are almost always in short supply. There's never enough for everyone to have as much as they want.

In the next premise of the argument, Hobbes asserts that no one, in the state of nature, has the right to destroy themselves; or in other words, everyone has the right to 'the preservation of his own nature', that is, the right to survive. From this, Hobbes says it follows that everyone has the right to self-defense:

> ...it is a precept, or general rule of reason, that every man, ought to endeavour peace, as far as he has hope of obtaining it; and when he cannot obtain it, that he may seek, and use, all helps, and advantages of war. The first branch of which rule, containeth the first, and fundamental law of nature: which is, to seek peace, and follow it. The second, the sum of the right of nature, which is, by all means we can, to defend ourselves. (*Leviathan* 14)

Putting these two premises together, Hobbes concludes that people in the state of nature inevitably come into violent competition with each other.[153] And because of this situation of permanent violence, people live in more-or-less constant fear. It could be argued that Hobbes agrees with Vitruvius, that human life in the state of nature is permanently gripped with fear. But where Vitruvius said people fear the natural world, Hobbes said people mostly fear other people.

And so, in fearing each other, people compete all the more strenuously, and end up in a more-or-less permanent state of war:

...if any two men desire the same thing, which nevertheless they cannot both enjoy, they become enemies; and in the way to their end (which is principally their own conservation, and sometimes their delectation only) endeavour to destroy, or subdue each other... Hereby it is manifest, that during the time men live without a common power to keep them all in awe, they are in that condition which is called war; and such a war, as is of every man, against every man... (*Leviathan* 13)

Perpetual warfare, according to Hobbes, is the specific social problem of life in the state of nature, to which the idea of civilization provides the solution. In Hobbes' argument, civilization is represented by the concept of a 'commonwealth' or a 'common power' (already hinted at in the quote above), which is able to end the perpetual war by making people afraid of the government instead of each other. This commonwealth emerges from a 'covenant', a 'mutual transferring of right...which men call CONTRACT' (*Leviathan*. 14), by which people mutually agree to give up their personal natural right to self-defense, handing it over instead to a central political authority that can act on everyone's behalf. Finally, to ensure there's no mistaking how powerful and terrifying that common power must be, Hobbes names it after the Biblical sea monster: the Leviathan.[154] Here's the passage in the text where he describes this process:

> This is more than consent, or concord; it is a real unity of them all, in one and the same person, made by covenant of every man with every man, in such manner, as if every man should say to every man, *I authorize and give up my right of governing myself, to this man, or to this assembly of men, on this condition, that thou give up thy right to him, and authorize all his actions in like manner.* This done, the multitude so united in one person, is called a COMMONWEALTH, in Latin CIVITAS. This is the generation of that great LEVIATHAN, or rather (to speak more reverently) of that *mortal god*, to which we owe under the immortal God, our peace and defence. For by this authority, given him by every particular man in the commonwealth, he hath the use of so much power and strength conferred on him, that by terror thereof, he is enabled to form the wills of them all, to peace at home, and mutual aid against their enemies abroad. (*Leviathan* 17)

Hobbes' idea is that the Leviathan solves the problems of fear and war, which obtain in the state of nature, by demanding an exchange of rights. People trade in their right to natural freedom and self-defense, and in exchange receive security and protection. Notice also Hobbes' use of the word 'civitas', the Latin root of the word civilization. It's appearance here is not an accident: Hobbes regards this exchange of rights, and the Leviathan-commonwealth it creates, as the very essence of civilization itself: 'In him [the Leviathan] consisteth *the essence of the commonwealth*; which (to define it,) is one person, of whose acts a great multitude, by mutual covenants one with another, have made themselves everyone the author, to the end he may use the strength and means of them all, as he shall think expedient, for their peace and common defence.' (*Leviathan* 17; emphasis added.)

Yet Hobbes' monster-state is only one possible conclusion to draw from the 'state of nature' thought experiment. Suppose we ran the experiment again, but with a different presupposition about human nature? We would arrive at a different conclusion about what life in the state of nature is like, and about what, if anything, prompts the transition to civilization. The philosopher John Locke (1632-1704), another Englishman, writing only a short while after Hobbes, believed that human nature is generally rational, and that people inherently know how to get along with each other. 'The state of nature has a law of nature to govern it, which obliges every one. And reason, which is that law, teaches all mankind, who will but consult it, that being all equal and independent, no one ought to harm another in his life, health, liberty, or possessions.' (*Second Treatise of Government*, ch. 2) Locke believes this natural law is planted in everyone's hearts by God; so there is no question in his mind of some knowing the law and others not. As for the right to punish those who break the natural law: Locke says it extends only so far 'as will suffice to make it an ill bargain to the offender, give him cause to repent, and terrify others from doing the like' (*ibid*). In other words, the purpose of punishment is deterrence, nothing more. So life in the state of nature, as he sees it, would certainly not be a Hobbsean state of war. But in Locke's state of nature, punishments might not be fair: 'Ill nature, passion and revenge will carry them too far in punishing others.' From that unfairness emerges the necessity of civil society: 'Therefore God has certainly appointed government to restrain the partiality and violence of men.' (*ibid.*, ch. 2)

Locke's starting place in this thought-experiment is quite different from that of Hobbes. But his conclusion is very similar. Both say the transition to civil society is a clear benefit to humanity; both argue for the necessity of a strong central government; and both say the authority of that government must be respected, whether people like it or not. It will fall to French philosopher Jean Jacques Rousseau (1712-1778) to bring to the table a more radical possibility: that the transition from the state of nature to civilization was actually a colossal disaster.

Jean Jacques Rousseau thought differently about civilization because he lived differently than most civilized men of his time. Born into a middle-class family in Geneva, at a time when the city was an independent state, he spent most of his youth alone. He was often sickly; he was not especially handsome; he had few friends. His mother died when he was nine days old: an occasion he called 'the first of my misfortunes'.[155] His father loved him, but he was raised mostly by his uncle, who frequently beat him for even the smallest misdemeanors. Throughout his life he enjoyed walking in the countryside and in the wild, most of the time by himself. He wrote in his journals that he didn't much like people, and that people didn't much like him: 'Seeking refuge in mother nature, I sought in her arms to escape the attacks of her children. I have become solitary, or, as they say, unsociable and misanthropic, because to me the most desolate solitude seems preferable to the society of wicked men...' (*Reveries of a Solitary Walker*, pg. 95) Similarly, he wrote in his *Confessions* that he needed 'torrents, rocks, firs, dark woods, mountains, steep roads to climb or descend, abysses beside me to make me afraid.' (*The Confessions*, pg. 167) Even so, he often secured various jobs that allowed him to see into the world of high society. He contributed to Diderot's *Encyclopaedia*, and he often picked up employment as a secretary or a tutor for various aristocrats, including the French ambassador to the Republic of Venice. He probably regarded himself as an outsider to civilization; never its full member, never its full beneficiary. In fact I think through most of his life he was rarely ever happy. Having not much of a 'stake' in civilization, so to speak, he perhaps felt more free to criticize it, and find it wanting.

Rousseau's career as a philosopher arguably began when, at age 37, he responded to an essay contest posted by the Academy of Dijon. Contestants were to answer the question: 'Has the progress of the sciences and arts done more to corrupt morals or improve them?'[156] (This phrase, 'progress in the sciences and arts', should immediately remind you of the academic checklist-makers.) Unlike most other respondents, Rousseau boldly answered that progress actually corrupts us. On learning (a year later!) that he won the contest, he published an expanded version of the argument under the title *Discourse on the Origin of Inequality*. In its opening pages he fires across-the-bow shots against Hobbes and Locke, saying that they assumed people in the state of nature had the same ideas about property, political authority, and justice, and the like, as they themselves had. 'In constantly talking of need, greed, oppression, desires, and pride, they [the philosophers] have imported into the state of nature ideas they had taken from society. They talk of savage man and they depict civilized man.'[157] In other words, Rousseau accuses his predecessors of succumbing to what we today would call observer bias.

As an aside, note that Rousseau's use of the word *l'homme civil* is the first appearance in print of anything resembling the word 'civilization' or 'the civilized man' in its modern meaning.[158] The word also appears in its 'big picture' meaning in Rousseau's preface to the same text, where he addresses himself to the political leadership of the Republic of Geneva: *les chefs d'une société civile*. (Not that he really admired Geneva; he was actually thumbing his nose at Paris.) Secondly, note that Rousseau used these words some ten years before they were used by Mirabeau the Elder, who normally gets the credit for using them first. Thirdly, note the appearance of the word *sauvage*, in the same sentence: the shadow of the Ancient Great Wall. But I digress.

What is Rousseau's vision of life in the state of nature? It's the life of 'the noble savage'; an archetype that he is credited with inventing, although he did not use the term. The Noble Savage is a romantic ideal; a person who is 'uncivilized' in the sense that he or she lives by passion and instinct alone, and without advanced technology or science or art, but who is wise, heroic, good-hearted, and at peace with most everyone around him. The strongest of this character's instincts is empathy and compassion: in Rousseau's words, 'an innate aversion to the sight of a fellow creature's suffering.' (*ibid*. pg. 45) The 'savage man', as Rousseau called him, may well be a more worthy human being than the civilized man, because the civilized man knows how to silence the voice of empathy within him: 'Someone may with impunity slit the throat of a fellow man under the philosopher's window, and the philosopher need only put his hands over his ears and argue a bit with himself to prevent nature, which is rebelling inside him, from making him identify himself with the man being murdered.' (*ibid* pg. 47) Now, the archetype of the noble savage is clearly a fantasy, as pretty much everyone today acknowledges. It's also a bit of an insult to real-world indigenous people. But the instinct toward empathy and compassion, of which the archetype of the noble savage is the visible symbol, is not a fantasy; we have seen that already in the meditation on the expanding circle.

Rousseau believed, contrary to Hobbes and to some extent Locke, that life in the state of nature would be mostly pleasant and peaceful. Nevertheless it's not a desirable condition: for in that state, 'There was no education or progress; the generations multiplied unproductively, and because each began anew from the same point, centuries passed by in all the crudeness of the earliest ages; the species was already old, and man remained ever a child.' (*ibid* pg. 51) Thus Voltaire's jab, that reading Rousseau made him want to walk on all fours, completely misses the mark: Rousseau wants us to stand upright and look to the distance. Here we see shades of an idea that would later resurface in Kenneth Clark: the idea that civilization is a future-oriented society; that some impulse toward 'progress', however defined, dwells at its heart. So, Rousseau looked for something that might have happened in the history of our species that could have initiated the transition to civilization. He found it in property boundaries.

> The true founder of civil society was the first man who, having enclosed a piece of land, thought of saying 'This is mine', and came across a people simple enough to believe him. How many crimes, wars, murders and how much misery and horror the human race might have been spared if someone had pulled up the stakes or filled in the ditch, and cried out to his fellows: 'Beware of listening to this charlatan. You are lost if you forget that the fruits of the earth belong to all and that the earth itself belongs to no one!'[159]

Stakes, ditches – *dividing lines on the surface of the earth* – this is the beginning of the same Ancient Great Wall which, as we have seen, surrounds the beating heart of civilization. Rousseau then charted the series of steps which, in his view, must have logically followed, to lead our distant ancestors toward civilization. After the division of property in land there came the 'sense of superiority over the other animals'. (pg. 56) Then there was the acquisition of 'the rough idea of mutual commitments and the benefits of keeping them'; then the development of language; the construction of huts and houses (remember your Vitruvius?); the cultivation of farmland; the 'first stirrings of the heart', which lead to family life and the division of labor between the sexes. The next step was the emergence of leisure time – '...and this was the first yoke they imposed on themselves and the first source of the evils they were preparing for their descendants.' (pg. 59) For in leisure time people could gather in groups, 'gaze on the others,' and 'want to be gazed upon himself'. (pg. 60) In other words: leisure time is the origin of the *competition for prestige*, and the attendant problems of envy and scorn and pride, and the kind of revenge-based violence that Hobbes and Locke said characterized the state of nature. At this stage, according to Rousseau, we were no longer in a pure state of nature. But we were not yet fully transitioned into a civil state either: 'This state was the true youth of the world.' But this transition stage is the source of our problems: 'All subsequent advances appear to be so many steps toward improvement of the individual but, in fact, toward the enfeeblement of the species.' (pg. 62)

The final and irreversible step to civilization, according to Rousseau, was the development of two technologies: agriculture and metallurgy: 'For the poet it is gold and silver, but for the philosopher it is iron and wheat that first civilized and ruined the human race.' (*ibid* pg. 62) The poet who Rousseau refers to here is probably Lucretius, who wrote that humanity's problems begin when greed overtakes honor:

> But later on, with wealth
> And the discovery of gold, the strong,
> The beautiful, all too easily forsook
> The path of honor, more than willingly
> Chasing along behind the rich man's train.
> (Lucretius, *ibid* pg. 78)

But metallurgy and agriculture may be the more dangerous things. Agriculture allows one person or small group of people to produce more food than they personally needed to survive. And metallurgy allows the creation of weapons. Together, they allow for an armed man to sit on the pile of extra food, declare it 'his', and give orders to those who might need that food, and threaten those who disobey with death. So for Rousseau (and in a different way for Lucretius), the problem is not the state of nature. *The problem is the transition to civilization.* More specifically, the problem is the establishment of private property rights, and the enforcement of property rights through fear of violence. 'Thus, the encroachments of the rich, the thievery of the poor, and the unbridled passions of everyone, stifling natural pity and the still-hushed voice of justice, made men greedy, ambitious, and wicked.' (pg. 67)

The solution to this problem, according to Rousseau, is a kind of re-tooling or re-designing of the order of civil society. He proposes a new Social Contract, in which we trade in our natural rights to the whole community, and in exchange we receive an equivalent value in civil rights. The idea is to make legal equality overcome physical or natural inequality. (Think of it this way: would you rather have your problem with your bigger, stronger neighbor resolved in a trial by law, or in a fistfight?) This exchange of rights is guided by a strong concept of that which is in the interest of the whole community; a concept Rousseau calls The General Will.[160] Moreover, in addition to correcting the problems arising from the transition to civil society, the social contract also empowers each person to become a fully flourishing and free human being: In Rousseau's words:

> ...although in civil society man surrenders some of the advantages that belong to the state of nature, he gains in return far greater ones; his faculties are so exercised and developed, his mind is so enlarged, his sentiments so ennobled, and his whole spirit so elevated that, if the abuse of his new condition did not in many cases lower him to something worse than what he left, he should constantly bless the happy hour that lifted him for ever from the state of nature and from a stupid, limited animal made a creature of intelligence and a man.[161]

So there we have it: the foundation of 'big picture' civilization lies in a social contract of some kind: its process is a transition from earlier, troubled modes of life, to better ones. It would appear as if the answer to my first root question is settled. But I am not yet satisfied. In my next meditation, I shall explain why.

§ 14. Civilization Without Cities

Now, the trouble with Vitruvius, Lucretius, Hobbes, Locke, and

Rousseau, is that they spun their tales of the state of nature in near-complete ignorance about the lives of actual Aboriginal people. The two Romans I've mentioned must have known about non-civilized peoples in Europe living outside the frontiers of the Roman Empire, but they wrote nothing about them. The three moderns here did mention Aboriginal people on Turtle Island, although only ever briefly. Hobbes wrote that 'the savage people in many places of America...have no government at all; and live at this day in that brutish manner, as I said before'.[162] Rousseau said that the transitional stage between the state of nature and civil society 'is precisely the stage reached by most of the savage peoples known to us'.[163] Locke was the most harshly judgmental: he spoke of the 'several nations of the Americans' who are 'rich in land, and poor in all the comforts of life' because: 'For want of improving [their land] by labour, have not one hundredth part of the conveniences we enjoy: and a king of a large and fruitful territory there, feeds, lodges, and is clad worse than a day-labourer in England.'[164] But beyond these token acknowledgements, none of these writers made any extra effort to study Aboriginal societies and lives. We might claim, rather charitably, that good information about them wasn't available in Europe at the time, so these writers had no choice but to speculate in the dark. Even if that were true, we today, who *do* have access to good quality information, cannot claim ignorance.

A complete account of all the world's indigenous people is far beyond the scope of this work. And I don't wish to give the impression that all indigenous people think alike. In Canada alone, there are about fifty indigenous languages, six major 'cultural areas' (fuzzily-defined geographical regions in which the indigenous cultures are roughly similar), and 615 communities involved in treaty relationships with Canada, which together make up more than fifty First Nations.[165] But I think I can safely claim this much about all of them, or nearly all of them: when you look at the different worlds they lived in, you quickly realize that Hobbes and company got 'the state of nature' very wrong.

With the benefit of more than a hundred years of anthropology to guide us, as well as the words of indigenous people themselves, we find that people living in pre-urban communities do not live in perpetual fear of each other, as Hobbes supposed. Rather, we find people live in perpetual *indebtedness* to each other. We also do not find, as Locke imagined, that the central problem in pre-urban life has to do with unjust punishments for breaking the law of nature. For in fact the central problem in the lives of pre-urban peoples is the competition for a special commodity that is always in high demand and always in low supply: *prestige*. To be fair, Hobbes did say that competition for glory was part of life in the state of nature. He concluded that the competition would lead to permanent warfare; but in fact the pursuit of glory tended to lead indigenous people to develop principles of generosity. Historian Daniel Paul, a Mi'kmaq writer whom we have already seen in this movement, observed that among his people, honor and glory were won primarily by benefitting others:

> ...the urge to compete was a trait instilled in children at an early age and reinforced throughout adulthood. The competition to be the best hunter, the best leader, the best fisherman and so on kept the larders full and assured that the most qualified graduated to leadership. For most of their lives women also competed intensively to produce the finest clothing, designs and other things needed and valued by the Nation. However the motivation for competing in Amerindian societies was quite different from the motivation in European societies. In most Amerindian cultures one competed to provide the best service and the most wealth to the community. In European societies the competition was to see how much wealth one could accumulate for oneself.[166]

Paul also notes that the competition for honor was so strong among the Mi'kmaq that those who felt shamed or defeated in this competition might become deeply depressed, to the point of attempting suicide. (*ibid* pg. 26-8)

As we look deeper, we find more items from the various checklists of civilization. Paul draws special attention to numerous features of Mi'kmaq society that demonstrate one of Newman's three essential traits of civilization: complexity of the value system. The Mi'kmaq had a territory ruled by a democratically elected Grand Council and divided into seven districts; a religion supported by long-standing traditions; similar long-standing customs for storytelling and art and boat-building technology; organized education for the young; organized care and adoption of orphans; provisions for physical and mental health care; leadership by consensus and persuasion instead of by threats and fear; and a strong emphasis on hospitality, generosity, tolerance for differing opinions, and personal honour.[167] They did, occasionally, fight wars or commit acts of cruelty, like any complex society almost anywhere in the world. But, as Paul emphasizes, they never did this to expand territory: wars were fought to gain glory or to avenge wrongs.

Another of Newman's traits of civilization is rationality. Yet with even a casual *prima facia* look at the evidence, we see plenty of aboriginal rationality, deployed in a variety of circumstances, and for a variety of purposes. We have already seen The Peacemaker place reasoning at the centre of the Iroquois Confederacy's constitution: a pre-urban political philosophy. As another example, here are the words of Mato-Kuwapi, of the Santee-Yanktonai Sioux, describing the Sun Dance ceremony and its origin in pre-urban theology:

> When a man does a piece of work which is admired by all we say that it is wonderful; but when we see the changes of day and night, the sun, moon, and stars in the sky, and the

changing seasons upon the earth, with their ripening fruits, anyone must realize that it is the work of some one more powerful than man. Greatest of all is the sun, without which we could not live...[168]

Reasoning this way also led indigenous people to reach moral conclusions. For example, a man named Young Chief, of the Cayuses nation, told the superintendent of Indian Affairs for Oregon, that he could not sell his people's land because: 'The Great Spirit, in placing men on the earth, desired them to take good care of the ground and to do each other no harm...' (McLuhan, *Touch the Earth*, pg. 8)

Writing literature is an often-emphasized feature of civilization: it appears on Gordon Child's list, among others. If we broaden the usual definition of literature to include not only writing, but also an organized tradition of verbal storytelling, we find that many 'state of nature' societies had a literature equally as subtle, rich, complex, beautiful, and (dare I say it?) long-winded as the literature of any more technologically advanced people. One of the oldest documented surviving bodies of literature in Canada is the organized oral tradition of the Haida people. It includes mythologies, histories, memoirs, and songs, much of which takes many hours to recite aloud. Its central story, Raven's Tale, takes two hours by itself. The oldest print edition bequeathed to us by history is a transcription of a performance by a poet named Skaay, recorded by anthropologist John Reed Swanton; for 'quality control' the publication was supervised by Skaay and other Haida myth-tellers. Swanton was so impressed with the work that he compared it to a Homeric epic.[169] That these texts were committed to memory by professional myth-tellers, rather than committed to paper, makes them no less interesting as literature. Remember, Homer's poems, and anonymous cycles such as *Beowulf*, *The Epic of Gilgamesh*, and most of the Bible, are also oral performances that someone decided to write down.

If all it takes to be a civilization is to be organized, literate, rational, and so on (as the checklist-makers supposed), then it's clear we must conclude many, if not most, indigenous societies were civilizations. Fernández-Armesto would likely agree: he pointed to examples of societies that: '...preferred to live in relatively small communities and dwellings built of modest materials; but this did not stop them from compiling fabulous wealth, creating wonderful art, keeping – in most cases – written records (or something very like them) and, in Java, building on a monumental scale.'[170] There are also cases of communities that deserve to be called civilizations even though their dwelling centers were arguably not true cities: centers like Uxmal, or Great Zimbabwe, for instance. What, then, shall we make of the items on the checklist that we do not see in aboriginal societies? In a statement that seems to belong to a previous century, University of Calgary professor Tom Flanagan wrote that 'natives were 'uncivilized' because they lacked intensive agriculture, permanent settlement, writing, advanced technology and organized states.'[171] In direct reply, Mi'kmaq historian Daniel Paul said: 'In one form or another First Nations had all of those things, which to me are not measurements of being 'civilized' anyway...'[172] Paul's logical strategy here is to suppose that if we looked hard enough, we'd eventually find that among all aboriginal societies taken together, every item on Flanagan's checklist is present. But he also denies that the checklist has anything to do with civilization – a very curious position. There were other positions he could have adopted: for instance, the position that agricultural-technological civilization is morally corrupt and that therefore the uncivilized are the virtuous. Such is the point of view of many other Aboriginal observers, and more than a few Europeans who criticized their own societies; Jean Jacques Rousseau being a famous example. Instead, Paul judo-flips the concept, by saying that Aboriginal societies are the true civilizations and that Europeans are the barbarians. Paul does not say 'Civilization is such-and-such', as Western-trained philosophers (like me) habitually do. Instead he describes a measure for judging the relative merits of one society over another, and he invokes the name of civilization to do it:

> When writing on the subject of civilization, one must understand that the ability to read or write a European language does not create a superior civilization. Nor does the ability to point exploding sticks that cause instantaneous death or injury, or to launch missiles that could blow the world apart, provide a moral basis to declare one's culture more civilized than another. The question to ask when judging the values and merits of a civilization must always be: 'How does the civilization respond to the human needs of its population?' By this standard, because they created social and political systems that ensured personal liberty, justice and social responsibility, most Amerindian civilizations must be given very high marks.[173]

Notice the oblique reference to communications and to war-making capacity: two of Moore's four criteria for measuring how developed a civilization may be. Notice also the general criticism of industrial civilization, in which it may appear as if Paul has common cause with Coomaraswamy, who criticized the West from a similar direction. 'The one [the *Kallipolis*, the city of God] considers man's needs, which are 'but little here below'; the other [modern industrial civilization] considers his wants, to which no limit can be set, and of which the number is artificially multiplied by advertisement.'[174] But the *Kallipolis* is still a walled city. Daniel Paul's Mi'kmaq Nation is not.

Allow me a short digression to consider two counter-arguments. Someone could argue that an indigenous society that presents hallmarks of civilization like this is not, *ex hypothesi*, in the state of nature. Therefore it has no relevance to the criticism of Hobbes and others in his tradition. To this it may be replied: the evidence of the civilization of indigenous societies strongly supports the conclusion that no such state of nature, as imagined by Hobbes and others after him, had ever actually existed anywhere on earth. The most we can say is that humanity once lived in a pre-*urban* condition. Another critic might observe that the state of nature argument is only a thought-experiment, whose logic depends on theoretical rather than empirical considerations. Therefore it need not reflect anyone's actual living conditions, historical or contemporary. To this it may be replied: even a thought experiment must account for relevant facts. To go without such information is to make the experiment especially vulnerable to observer-bias, and indeed to irrelevance.

It should be obvious, now, that one can have small-picture civilization, that is, the civilization of ethics and behavioral etiquette, without a city. Indeed it seems likely to me that humanity has *never* lived in a pure-type 'state of nature', but we have always lived in communities that possessed at least some of the qualities of civilization, big picture and small, to one degree or another. But this only leads me to wonder why scholars like Flanagan, Bagby, and others, regard city life and its related activities, the 'big picture', as so essential. Kenneth Clark, for instance, said that manners and etiquette are only a kind of by-product of civilization, and not civilization itself: 'Fine sensibilities and good conversation... can be among the agreeable *results* of civilization, but they are not what make a civilization, and a society can have these amenities and yet be dead and rigid.'[175]

Are all these writers only working from different and mutually unrelated definitions of civilization? Or is there something deeper at work? What, after all these meditations, have I learned?

§ 15. Gathering the Fragments

From the academics and the checklist-makers, we learned that civilization is the 'big picture' of a large, organized, complicated community living in a built-up environment, and it's the 'small picture' of behavioral ethics and the mastery of various arts and technical skills.

From our meditation on the first house, we learned that civilization is another kind of event: it is the establishment of an integral hearth fire where humanity creates for itself a centre of belonging, a dwelling place, a home. We separate the human realm from the rest of the earth, not necessarily with antagonism, but certainly with clear distinction.

From the Ancient Great Wall, we learned that civilization also divides the human realm into the separate tribes of 'us' and 'them', along multiple vectors and planes, but especially along vectors of class.

From the Great Peacemaker of the Iroquois, and his counterparts in other societies, we learned that civilization means thinking instead of killing.

From the Expanding Circle, we learned that the boundary between 'us' and 'them' is permeable and can move, so to include more and more people in its orbit of belonging.

From Plato, Augustine, Confucius, and the unknown authors of the Vedas, we learned that civilization is a rationally ordered city, where everyone does the job that their natures render them best suited to do.

From the theorists of the State of Nature, we learned that civilization is a social contract, in which everyone agrees to live by the same rules and put up with a few inconveniences, in exchange for a social order that makes almost everyone better off.

From hundreds of nations of Aboriginal people, we learned that civilization does not necessarily require a city.

We have seen civilization accounted on *two* major vectors: the 'big' picture and the 'small' picture. Both vectors involve a spectrum between extremities of moral judgment. At one end of the 'big picture' spectrum, civilization represents all that is great and glorious about humanity's achievements and potentials: building cities and monuments, creating art and literature, raising up heroes. At the other end, civilization represents a society's capacity for conquest, colonialism, and oppression. Along the 'small picture' spectrum, one hand represents that which distinguishes all humanity from other animals. The other hand represents that which distinguishes the upper class from the lower, and the rich from the poor.

What do all these fragments have in common? What, if anything, dwells at the intersection of both pictures? The first and most obvious thing is the notion of an *event*. We find this front-and-centre among the academics and the checklist-makers, who described civilization as the process by which a community grows and complicates itself. We find the notion of an event in the meditation on the first house: for the meditation was, after all, a story we told ourselves about a time in human history before anyone built houses, and a story about why we built them, and what became of us when we did. Other meditations told us similar stories about events that changed the way we lived: the raising of city walls, the journey to the Heavenly City, the division of the Cosmic *Purusa*, the transition from a state of nature to a state of civility.

Are all these different visions of civilization united merely by the fact of being stories? Or, is 'civilization' just an absurdly complicated concept that means different things to different people? Ending this thought-opera on that note would leave no (large) logical flaws in the account. But it would also be intellectually lazy: it would be like giving up too soon. Is there something all these stories have in common with each other?

If there is, it might be the answer to my first root question. Before I leave my meditation-place above this lake, I have to find it.

I stand up and look around. The answer is somewhere in front of me. For all these stories are written upon the landscape before me, and the city behind me, and upon my own mind and body.

§ 16. The Essence of Civilization

I now have a testable hypothesis to answer the first of my root questions. The story of civilization is written in the fourfold language of forces-at-work, materials-worked-upon, with-what-results, and toward-what-aim. It is a story about a process of transformation and creation, in which humanity itself is both a force-at-work, and at the same time a material-worked-upon. Yet this needs explaining.

First, *Forces-At-Work*. This includes all of a given society's means of production, transport, and communication. It thus includes many, perhaps all, of the items noted by the academic checklist-makers. There's economic forces such as labor power and availability of credit, engineering power from draft animals to machinery, and all the various physical means of production, distribution, trade, and disposal of waste. It also includes whatever natural energies it can bring into its control, or somehow hijack for its purposes: the growth of plants and animals, the harnessing of winds for sailing ships, and fuel sources from wood to the nucleus of uranium atoms.

Second, *Materials-Worked-Upon*. These include the resources of the earth, such as food, construction materials, potential energy reserves, as well as the earth's territory and ecological systems. It certainly includes the land-territory upon which we build our cities. Yet of all the materials that a civilizing process works upon, I think the most significant is humanity itself. For among the forces at work there are also intellectual and cultural forces that both teach and also enforce a conception of human nature – that is, a conception of what people are like, what we are capable of, and what can be expected of us, and whether people are predisposed to act one way or another. The civilizing forces, as I shall call them from here onward, include traditions in mythology, art and music, religion and ritual, politics, economics, architecture and land planning, philosophy and rhetoric, and the seriousness and momentum that history might bestow upon them. There's also institutional arrangements such as schools, corporations, churches, monetary currencies, communications media from cave paintings to email, hierarchies in religion and the army and in corporations, codified laws, police services, and courts. The forces of the 'small picture' include some of the same traditions of the big picture, as well as locally unique traditions of storytelling, sports and games, foodways, proverbs, jokes, peer pressure, dinner table etiquette, even insults and malicious gossip. There are also psychological forces working on humanity's picture of itself, such as the wish to be accepted by, or to emulate, the prominent charismatic people in one's world: from the high school prom queen to an internationally famous movie star. The aggregate of all these forces, and their simultaneous expression of and pressure upon human nature, is the core of the process of civilization.

A friendly critic might object that my use of the word 'human nature' doesn't fit the case here. The word normally refers to the fixed and unchanging features of something's or someone's way of being in the world, and that those features cannot be freely chosen. The OED defines the word as: 'The essential qualities of a thing; the inherent and inseparable combination of properties essentially pertaining to anything and giving it its fundamental character.'[176] (One must be careful invoking a dictionary definition to make a philosophical point, for the dictionary does not do philosophy.) I acknowledge that people are born with various pre-determined potentials and dispositions, arising (for example) from genetics; this seems obviously true. Yet each person's distinctive way of being in the world emerges from numerous influences, not just her pre-determined dispositions. Moreover, it grows and blossoms slowly over time, following individual choices, and the opportunities or challenges of one's environment: for instance, the encouragement from parents and teachers and religious leaders. Other potentials lie dormant, never to be developed, for lack of individual interest or environmental opportunity. If we are all 'half nature and half nurture', as the saying often goes, the civilizing forces are undoubtedly able to 'nurture' people in various ways. So, to refine my working hypothesis somewhat: civilization is the process by which human forces like politics, economics, culture, and so on, become increasingly decisive in shaping what it means to be human. Different societies will deploy those forces in different ways, and so produce a more-or-less different picture of what it is to be human. But the principle is the same: the people become who they are through the increasing influence of the civilizing forces. Our environments shape us, yet at the same time we shape our environments; in effect, and over the very long term, we thereby shape ourselves.

The same critic might also wonder how deeply into humanity's essence the civilizing forces may reach. Surely there is a limit? In reply, let us observe that the civilizing forces work upon the material of our bodies, no less than upon our behaviors. The emerging scientific field of epigenetics studies how a person's lifestyle and environment can leave markers on one's genome, and that these markers can be transmitted to one's children. To choose one example: a group of studies published in *Nature* discovered that low-level stressors endured for long periods of time, such as the stressors of poverty, can shrink the size of the brain,[177] and affect early brain development in ways that are 'clearly visible in the brain structure and seem to appear at birth, which suggests that prenatal exposure to these stressors can be involved'.[178] Poverty was also found to suppress the gene responsible for serotonin transporter proteins, a condition linked to depression; it also made the amygdala more active (*ibid*). Taking a look at how the civilizing forces work upon people over many generations, we see that their influence can change our genetic code more permanently. A scientific study published in 2014 looked at more than 1,400 ancient human skulls and found that the development of behavioral modernity (abstract thinking, future planning, communication with symbols, etc.) correlated with a reduction of testosterone. The evidence for this was a measurable change in human morphology: a shortening and a rounding of the human face, and a reduction in the size of the brow ridge. As the study itself says:

> The fossil evidence reflects a significant reduction in androgen-mediated craniofacial masculinity between the MSA/MP and LSA/UP, coincident with genetically and archeologically visible increases in human population size and density and with a markedly increased rate of cultural evolution... This suggests to us a change in average human temperament toward greater social tolerance and reduced aggression during the Late Pleistocene and continuing into the Holocene, in the context of greater population density and improved payoffs for cooperation.[179]

In simpler language: as groups grew larger, co-operation and social tolerance became increasingly important; these behavioral changes led to hormonal changes in their bodies. These hormonal changes, over many generations, changed and 'feminized' the shape of our faces. The civilizing forces, applied over many generations, influence the essence of humanity even at the level of our DNA.

Changing human morphology is a 'big picture' view; we can also see the civilizing forces at work on our bodies in the 'small picture'. We shape ourselves with simple procedures like exercise, healthy dieting, and caring for the sick; and with more invasive procedures like tattooing, vaccination, surgery, and genetic engineering. Indeed, scientists in the Human Genome

Project announced in 2003 that they had decoded all of the human genome, and that they then intended to chemically synthesize one.[180] We work upon human bodies when we conscript and train them for military service, or theatre performance, or slave labor. Or, if the price appears acceptable, people might volunteer themselves for body-destroying careers such as extreme athletic training, or industrial labor that exposes people to toxic substances and hazardous environments. We also work upon our bodies with psychological and cultural forces, when we ascribe different meanings to different kinds of bodies, and then ascribe different expectations for behavior from, and toward, the possessors of different bodies. We say that human bodies are male or female: some cultures accept additional genders, others do not. Similarly, we say that our bodies are black or brown or red or yellow or white, and we say something about what those colors might mean in any case. If we say those colors are meaningless: that, too, makes a statement (as does the way we live up to that statement, or fail to do so). We say that some bodies resemble the animals, for better or worse: this man is as strong as an ox; that woman is as sharp-featured as an eagle; this child is as curious as a cat. Notice also how animal words are often used as racist insults (and I won't repeat any of them here.) We might say that we are 'made in the image of God' – or that only some of us are so made.

Third, *With-What-Results*. Here in this third station, we speak of the many visible and lasting artifacts of a civilization, including its arts, literature, and architecture (everything Kenneth Clark took to be the civilization you can look at); its industrial and commercial output; the advancement of its technological power and widening of its energy capture; its new political complexities. These are all signs of life; marks left on the world showing that someone or some people once passed by this place, and perhaps made it their home for a while. Thus to speak of these artifacts is also to speak of a state of consciousness concerning them, a way of being in the world involving them, which are in turn enacted affirmations of some model of humanity. To build an aqueduct or a temple, to write a sonnet or a symphony, is at the same time to describe something about one's state of consciousness, one's way of being in the world, and thus what one's life is 'about', in whole or in part. In the station of results, we thus observe the creation of a legacy of ideas concerning what it means to be human, what the 'good life' is, what people should do with themselves and how they should relate to each other and the natural world. Invariably and perhaps unintentionally, alongside its artifacts, a civilization produces a history of what life is like for people who, willingly or not, live by the prescriptions of a certain world view. We see it in the awards given to certain poets, dramatists, musicians, soldiers, politicians, entrepreneurs, and so on; but not to others. We see it in the laws that we enforce, the ways we enforce them, and the degree to which we regard the laws of our predecessors as binding on us, in the present day, and upon the unborn generations to come.

This history is a result of the process of forces-at-work and materials-worked-upon. But this history also participates in that process. There's a spiral relation between the forces and the materials. For the changed material becomes a new force, which takes its place among the other forces-at-work in the next iteration of the spiral. This is most evident when the material-worked-upon is humanity itself. We are fashioned into one form or another, and at the same time dispatched onward in one direction or another, by forces of our own conjuring – religion, warfare, politics, the market, humanitarian aid, scientific enquiry, monumental engineering. We human beings both build our world and at the same time receive configuration from it. Having been so configured, we dispatch ourselves in various directions that might not have been possible but for the new configuration. From the form and meaning of our bodies, to the largest economic and political arrangements, we both actively shape ourselves and at the same time passively fill the shapes we are given. Then we cast new shapes for ourselves that the precedents of history opened for us. Whether that spiral is constructive or degenerative, and what that may mean in either case, depends on this next element of the process.

Fourth, and ultimately, the essence of civilization spirals on *Toward-What-Aim*. Here we must ask the question we have been avoiding for thousands of years: what is the *point* of civilization? What is the whole process of civilization ultimately *for*?

It cannot be only to protect us from the environment and all its natural hazards. That's certainly part of it, yet there's also many things we call 'civilization' that have nothing to do with that aim. Watching cat videos on your phone will not save you from disease.

It cannot be only to pursue 'progress' in science and technology. That, too, can be part of it, but we can be civilized without being technologically powerful. Often, the happiest lives are spent working in gardens with our hands, instead of in factories with our machines.

It cannot only be to grow our material wealth. For it is entirely possible to be as rich as a king and at the same time as insufferably uncivilized as a child throwing a temper tantrum. What's more: it's possible to create the kind of wealth that actually makes us poorer as a whole, when the means of production are actually means of destruction, and the 'goods' they produce are only cleverly disguised trash-compactors. How many forests must be felled, how many mountains shorn of their peaks, so that we can have more dreary shopping malls, more souvenir fridge magnets, more plastic-wrapped pre-peeled oranges?

The ultimate point of the process of civilization, if I may put this four-fold mess into one sentence, is the production of the civilized person. In this respect I name Albert Schweitzer as the philosopher who grasped the essence of civilization more completely than anyone else: we have seen his assertion that the 'ultimate object of civilization' is 'the spiritual and moral perfecting of individuals'. To put it another way: civilization is the ongoing, interactive, multi-modal, planet-wide, and millennia-long experiment by which we resolve what it means to be human, not by discovery, but by *invention*. Part of this experiment involves taking the wild and frightened animal spirit out of us, and putting in its place the soul of rationality and cultivation. But even that does not precisely fit the case. For I am not convinced we were wild animals in the first place, and there's no consensus on what it means to be rational or cultivated. But we can say this much: the civilized person is the figure whose personal qualities are his civilization's virtues. His style and temperament are his civilization's ideal; his goals are the most worthy of all his civilization's goals. He is both a product of the workings of the civilizing forces, and at the same time he is one of their directors, guiding them to make more people in his image.

But exactly what image? Is he the Sage Gentleman, described by Confucius? Is he the educated aristocrat of Plato's and Aristotle's philosophy? Is he the Buddhist arhat, the Christian saint, or a humanist intellectual? Does he have to be one of the elite? Is he Byron's Childe Harold, or Goethe's sorrowing Werther? Is he John Henry, or Alexey Stakhanov, or Joe the Plumber? Does the civilized man have to be a *man*? Perhaps our best model of a civilized person is Elizabeth Bennet, or Maeve of Cruachan, or Theresa of Avila. The aim of civilization is to produce the civilized person – but also to negotiate and experiment with different ideas about who that civilized person is, and what more and what else she can be. Any given society that would call itself civilized has at least one answer to the question of who is civilized and who is not; it must also have the means to influence the world so as to procure evidence in favor of its answer. For the answer to the question: 'Who is the civilized person?' flows from the process of civilization: a process always composed of ever-changing forces-at-work, with humanity itself among the materials-worked-upon. In this sense, civilization is humanity's most metaphysical activity: it is the activity of humanity realizing itself, that is, making itself 'real', by making itself more and more an exemplar of its model of the ideal human being, the fully civilized person.

This first movement is finished; I rise from my place above the lake and go home. Tomorrow I shall rise again, and travel across the ocean to a new meditation-place, and face a new question.

An Interlude

§ 17. Far From the City, and Far From Home

The academics reading these meditations might wonder why I am about to devote a large measure of the argument to personal impressions formed while on a working holiday in Central Europe, instead of delivering the argument directly, impersonally, and straight. The answer, in part, is that I'm a human being and not a computer. As much as I aim to articulate the logic of an argument with clarity, coherence, and evidence-based support, as is the duty of a professional philosopher, so that argument is also *happening to me* as I write it. The narrative by which that argument happened to me seems as much part of the package as the air I breathe is part of my body. As an aside, no one would accuse Rousseau's *Reveries of a Solitary Walker* of being unphilosophical; and while I do not possess the stature of a Rousseau, I'm allowed to 'confess', too.

I'm also following the advice of the famed anthropologist Claude Levi-Strauss, who 'had to leave France to study Man'. I've traveled far from home many times in my life – and not usually as a tourist, but often as a temporary resident, or as the grateful guest of local people, whose lives entwined with mine for a little while. Almost every time, the adventure was as much psychological as geographic. For by escaping the cozy familiarity of my Canadian home and landing myself in the exciting confusion of a foreign place, I discovered new *ideas* no less audible to me than the strange music of my new surroundings. In the Irish hills of Connemara and fields of Meath, in the Vogelsberg of Germany, in the Swiss canton of Sankt Gallen, I encountered thoughts that transformed my life. Travel broadens the mind by shaking it up.

Thus, in the summer of 2015 I accepted an invitation from a friend and her family to visit a tiny village in Bohemia. They needed someone to look after their house and their dogs while on a month-long holiday. I adore the landscape of Central Europe: its high hills, its wide rivers, its walkable forests, its green and golden fields, its bounty of flowers and wildlife. I awaken each morning to the call of the neighbor's rooster; I hear sheep and dogs no further away than the next house; and more kinds of birds than I know how to name. I think I can smell the cleanliness of the air here, compared to the city air of Ottawa-Gatineau. I can see the high slope of one of the hills from the window of the room where I've set up a writing-place; and it's easy to imagine the land is calling me, inviting me to climb and discover what spectacles can be seen from the summit. These hills are not mountains, but they are rocky and varied; I'm told that draft horses are still used for logging around here because it's too steep to use tractors.

The house is small, but the right size for the family; its black timbers and colorful flowers fit it in the landscape like a scene in a fairy tale. Its ground floor is dark and cramped, because it's more than 200 years old and has been slowly sinking into the earth; it feels rather like a cave. The upper floor is newly renovated, and brighter; but because we are in high summer it's as hot as a greenhouse. I'm also told it's the oldest house in the village – although like the famous Ship of Theseus, or your grandfather's old axe, the house both is and is not the same house as originally built. Bees have colonized some hidden corner of the rafters, just over the front door. I can't see the nest, but I can hear them. I'm going to call this place the Hedgewitch House. It will be my honor to look after it while the family is away.

On the first night that I had the house to myself, I felt my solitude deeply. I have lived alone for most of my adult life; these past few years I've lived in a part of Canada where I can't speak the majority language. But here in this farmhouse, on the fourth night of my escape from the city, I'm the only human being. I had met some of the neighbors, and they were all very welcoming and kind, but they are all still new to me. I can barely approximate what people are saying when they speak to each other. I have almost no idea what to do if the house is burgled. This is very likely the most isolated I have ever been. It is easy to imagine that there have been others more isolated than I am now: adventuring mariners who have sailed around the world by themselves; the lone Apollo astronauts who orbited the moon while their two companions walked on its surface. I've been introduced to a few neighbors and they know I'm here while the family is away; I've been told which of them to call on if there's an emergency. But I think that isolation is more acute in the presence, and not the absence, of others: their presence, their language that I can't speak, their customs and relations that I do not know how to join, are the immediate evidence of how far away from my world I have come.

This will be the perfect chance to contemplate civilization from a distance, and to contemplate its alternatives from nearby.

The first occasion to do this appeared in the early morning hours before sunrise on 8th July, when I had been alone in the house for only two days. I was awakened by the dogs: they don't really like that I sleep upstairs where they can't get to me, and I could hear them clambering on the doorknob, wanting to go outside. I went downstairs and fed them. A thunderstorm was brewing in the distance. Helli took my hand in her mouth and led me to her food dish. Something about her demeanor seemed different. With the storm coming, and with the hour of the night being what it was, my head filled with stories of gods and fairies who take on the appearance of a hungry late-night visitor, needing shelter. I refilled their water and their kibble, and resisted the urge to look into their room, in case the real dogs were sleeping there and the dogs I just fed were spirits in disguise. (Aren't logically-minded people like myself supposed to be immune to such thinking?)

I went back up to my room. The storm is closer: wind whips the trees around. Lightning jumps from cloud to cloud. The definition of the sublime as a class of the aesthetic, given by the 18th century Irish statesman and philosopher Edmund Burke, could be usefully invoked here. The sublime, as he defined it, is the beauty of an awesome and terrifying power, such as a thunderstorm or a flood or other destructive natural phenomenon, viewed from a position of perfect safety.[181]

I decided to open the window and talk to the storm. Maybe it is the same storm that found me when I was hill-walking in Germany with the woman I loved at the time. That storm, eleven years before, inspired a new direction in my thinking that stayed with me ever since. If it is the same storm, what should I say? It occurred to me that when one is at a loss for words, one should say 'thank you'. There is almost always something or someone nearby to whom one owes a sign of gratitude. So I say: 'Thank you, Storm, for inspiring my thinking.' I describe some of the things going on in my life that make me sad. But I make no requests. The philosopher is gently reminding me that this kind of anthropomorphic thought is probably illogical. The storm is most likely just a storm, and nothing more. And that may be not so bad after all. Still, talking to the storm feels strangely cathartic. Perhaps I am so in need of an understanding friend that I'll take a nonhuman force that won't respond to me over a fully human one who might demonstrate that she does not understand me. It's easier to imagine that the storm is listening to me, and that by saying nothing, it's absolving me.

I wonder if ancient people, living in something like Rousseau's 'state of nature', looked upon natural immensities the same way. Might this have been the 'accident' Vitruvius mentioned but didn't explain – an occasion when it was possible to absorb the sights and sounds of power, from a position where the power posed no danger, and where they could inspire thought, imagination, and ecstasy, instead of fear?

§ 18. Prague and Empire

A local friend of my host family picks me up in the morning to take me to Prague. She works as a real estate agent there, so it's no trouble to bring me along. She drops me at a small square in the old part of the city, on the west bank of the river. I've been looking forward to this for months. Prague was not destroyed in the bombing raids of World War Two. So, notwithstanding renovations that were made in the years after the fall of Communism, it's a preserve of what Europe looked like before the war, and all the way back to mediaeval times.

I've seen mediaeval precincts in European cities before, but not on this astonishing scale. It's not just that everything is continuous and intact. It's also that everything is cramped together, ornamented to the point of headache, flooded with people, and astonishingly *tall*. The sidewalks have geometric mosaics made of cobblestones. It's a sign of a whimsy and joie-de-vivre, but also a sign of wealth and power. (They're also good for flood-prevention: heavy rain water can seep into the ground instead of fill the streets, as it did when the communists paved everything with asphalt.) I find myself exploring side alleys so that I don't have to push through crowds. I reached the plaza in front of Prague Castle, but the castle facade is covered in scaffolding and safety sheeting, so there's not much to see. I head down the hill again, on a different route, in hope of finding the Charles Bridge; but I take some side paths, just to see what might be there to discover. There are stories and histories to everything here, and there's almost always an English-speaking tour guide telling it to a group of people. But on this first visit I prefer to make my own tour, and see the sights unmediated by the interpretation of the tour guides. I come across a Knights of Malta stronghold, a plaque in honor of Beethoven, the Irish Embassy, several interesting-looking toy shops and coffee houses. I'm a little disappointed to have found no bookstores yet.

At the foot of the Charles Bridge I see something that tells me part of the story of this city without needing any tour guide to explain it. The architecture here speaks of power and empire. There's a guard tower at the foot of the bridge. Larger-than-life statues of kings, warriors, bishops, and the like, flank the edge. I later learned the bridge is part of a sacred procession-way, originally laid out by astronomers. I meet at various stations the monuments in honor of the power-wielders of the society that erected them. The bridge is also thronged with tourists, as well as those who make their living from them: mostly artists and souvenir-sellers. There are some beggars here too, leaning on their elbows and knees, holding out caps or paper cups to silently ask for charity. Some of them are 'employed' by gangs who collect their money each day, and who mercilessly punish those who don't accept their 'protection'. At the east foot of the bridge there's another guard tower. Just beyond it is a cathedral facade, and a magnificent statue of Charles IV, King of Bohemia and later of the entire Holy Roman Empire. Now I think I understand something about this city. It is a display-stage for power, for the majesty of empire, for *magnificence*. It is a glorification of the partnership of those two mediaeval mainstays of authority, the churchman and the warlord. But even while it speaks of the greatness of empire, so it also speaks of the fantasy of empire. The statues, the spires of churches and guard towers, the ornament on every building facade, are the remnants of a social world that no longer exists, and which is so badly understood by most people that it's easy to impose one's own imagination upon it. You can pretend that the warlords were always victorious and just; that the bishops were always wise; that the working classes were industrious, clever, and happy. Even the little Museum of Mediaeval Torture is part of the fantasy. Atmospheric lighting and dressed mannequins show the tools once used to hurt people in a cartoonish light. This changes the exercise of power into a spectator show, where the guilt or innocence of the tortured doesn't matter, and the justice or injustice of the torturer isn't discussed. We read that it was all completely terrible, but it's all in the past now, and we've all moved on. In 500 years will this museum display a bucket and cloth for waterboarding? Will we see a mannequin clipped with rusty jumper cables to a leaking car battery? (I resist the urge to ask that of the museum guide. Philosophers can ask the tough questions without becoming assholes.)

The Museum of Alchemy has a sandwich board outside its door promising 'an authentic and unforgettable dark-ages experience'. The assertion of the reality is what caught my eye. It reminds me of a comment by Baudrillard about the reality of God. To paraphrase him to fit my context: if something is real there will be no need to assert that it is real, but if something is unreal there will be a desperate and urgent demand that it be asserted as real.[182]

We are sufficiently removed in time that we can look upon these monuments and see them as beautiful, and not to see them as they were originally intended: *the power-instruments of a security state*. The guard towers are checkpoints. The statues are propaganda bulletins. They are to be awed and feared in equal measure. But the 21st century tourist experiences them with neither: he looks on them with wonder, and with curiosity, and with imaginal selfishness: the latter is proved by the way he photographs everything, as if to check off every box on a tally list of 'must-see' sights. (I shot nearly 500 photos on this day; I'm just as guilty.) The tourist imagines the mediaeval society as he wishes it was, perhaps with a nod to how brutal it was, but also with an eye to how he might imagine himself living in it: a strong king, a wise bishop, a jovial peasant. I stop looking at the monuments on the bridge and watch the tourists for a while. The overwhelming majority of them follow a very strict routine. They approach a certain statue on the bridge, remark to friends about how amazing it is, photograph it, photograph themselves or each other near it, read an explanatory plaque or listen to a tour guide, nod sagely to each other about the something-or-other of it all, then move quickly to the next monument. The whole routine takes less than one minute. I decide to investigate one of these statues for a full five minutes, just to see what would happen. The hawkers look at me quizzically. Their expressions to each other suggest they think there's something odd about me.

Yet having said all that, an obvious counter-argument appears. It is perhaps right that we experience the monuments of a by-gone empire precisely as 'living museum' pieces and precisely not as the instruments of the power of a present-day government. The warrior-king no longer threatens anyone with imprisonment or torture or death for breaking criminal laws, nor does the sage-bishop threaten anyone with eternal suffering in the afterlife for breaking divine laws. Therefore we are able to see them in the aesthetic light. Burke's definition of the sublime appears in my mind again. As it is with storms, so it is the same with the remnants of an ancient empire, such as the guard towers and cathedrals and castles of the Holy Roman Empire, and the statues of the great and the good that line the procession of the Charles bridge in Prague. To be fair, these security-state installations also protected the people of Prague from bandits and similar threats from outside the town. The city fathers may also have expected an attack from the Turks, who in 1529 besieged Vienna, only 330 kilometers to the southeast. Still, the awesome power that they represented, the power of the high mediaeval security state, no longer threatens anyone. That power, then, can be enjoyed in the mode of the sublime, and not, thankfully, in the mode of fear and awe.

Yet since that power is, or rather once was, a human force and not a natural phenomenon, we might be led to wonder whether we still have it in us to produce an high mediaeval security state like the one whose remnants surround me here in Prague. And if the answer is that we do, then we should look upon the statue of the warrior-king, the sage-bishop, and the other exemplars of power, and instead of saying 'thank you', we should say something like this: 'Never again.' Never again shall we kneel to the priest who claims to speak for the divine panopticon, the unblinking eye of God who observes and judges your every move. Instead, we shall be watched by video cameras with face-recognition software, and by massive dragnet-searches of your every keystroke and mouse-click on any electronic device in your possession, no matter how tenuously connected to the internet it may be. And we shall be judged by corporations for our brand loyalty, and by the police for our political obedience.

§ 19. Three Temples, Three Shrines

Across the Charles Bridge. I'm looking for the city's famous astronomical clock. It's a wonder of science and design: showing not only the time of day, but also the zodiac position of the sun and moon and also the phase of the moon, it is a 600-year-old work of mathematical genius. It's the third oldest of its kind in the world, and of those three it's the only one that still works. I've been looking forward to this for months.

The streets are a bit of a labyrinth here. I round a corner and find it unexpectedly: it's in profile to me, but it's unmistakable. It's also completely surrounded by a crowd of several hundred people. There's no way to see it 'right': I'm either standing at the foot of the tower that houses it, in which case I'm too close to get the full picture, or else I'm too far away to appreciate the genius of its mechanism and detail, or else I'm swimming through the crowd where my view is obstructed by a dozen 'selfie sticks' and the backs of tall people's heads. I find myself thinking more about the pickpockets than the clock. Curiously, the people in the best position to see it look at it directly only half the time. The other half of the time they look at it on the screens of their camera-phones. Then they inspect the photos they took, discard some of them, and take more. Hawkers move through the crowd, selling postcards and fridge magnets. The overall impression is that the clock is a wonderful thing, but that it must compete against a simulacra of itself for the attention it deserves. Beadrillard's notion of the HyperReal is in full play here. As is what some economists call 'opportunity costs'. The competition with other spectators for a good viewing angle, and the effort to ignore the hawkers, is how I 'pay' for the right to enjoy a good view of this 'free' spectacle.

I walk a few hundred yards to the north of the old town square and reach the old Jewish quarter. There's a synagogue which, a nearby tour guide explains, is the oldest continuously-used synagogue in Europe. I also hear that the Golem, the famous mannequin-monster, still lies in the attic, and that its last rumored movements involved killing two Nazi soldiers who broke into the building, back in the late 1930s. Just down the street there's a minivan with a mural painted on the side, to advertise a nearby Jewish restaurant. The mural features carica-tures of Jewish people sitting around a table. The Golem is the waiter. Two men stand around the van, inviting passersby to the restaurant, or to a tour of the Jewish quarter. They're dressed like some of the caricatures on the minivan: round hats, round glasses, big black coats, ringlets on their temples, bushy beards. They speak excellent English; one of them has an American accent. 'Are you Jewish?' he asks me. 'No,' I reply. 'Want to be Jewish for a day?' he asks. I suddenly wonder if I would offend him by saying no again. So I say, 'Not today.' In retrospect, I should have said yes. It might have been fun; and the food would surely have been delicious.

It's bittersweet to see these two gentleman here. On the one hand it's gratifying to know that something resembling a Jewish community survived here, following the Holocaust. (The reason Prague was not bombed by the Nazis, I had been told, is because the government of Czechoslovakia rounded up the Jews and handed them over. That was the price they paid to spare their city.) I find myself admiring the tenacity and endurance of their community. On the other hand these two men are also, in a curious way, as unreal as the rest of the old city. They're like living, heart-beating, air-breathing, human props in an elaborate theatrical set: the city's residents are themselves another feature of the history of the city made available for the viewing enjoyment of tourists. I listen to what some of the tourists say to them: 'Are there really Jews still living here?' The answer: 'Yes, there are. Lots of us.' A woman to her husband says: 'Gosh there's something strange about them. Let's go back to the clock.'

My last destination on my self-guided tour of Prague is Wenceslas Square. I was warned in advance to avoid it; my first impression was that my friends were right to warn me about it. There are too many cars, and too many big international retail chain stores, to be interesting. The one redeeming feature here is that I finally encounter a bookstore. I entered the square at the north-west end. I can see at the other end a small crowd gathered under the horse (the statue of Saint Wenceslas), and I can hear a woman's voice shouting something into a PA system. 'Good,' I say to myself. 'The square is still a gathering place for the people, still the site of grassroots political action.' As I draw closer I see that the crowd is completely ignoring the speaker. And then I see that the speaker is a religious fanatic. She's flanked by signs with Bible quotations, and two men carrying flags that say 'JESUS', one in English and the other in Czech. For a moment, my gaze moves between the religious speakers, the horse, and the corporate store fronts on either side of the square, and I'm reminded of the story of Jesus angrily kicking the bankers and loan sharks out of the temple. But the speaker's religious fervor explains why the people are ignoring her. Overt religiosity is in sharp decline in most Western countries; numerous surveys and census results show that Czechia is one of the least religious countries in the world.[183] This, incidentally, reminds me of the Jewish synagogue-museum. Are all churches destined to eventually become museums? Is the woman with the PA system the last grasp of a community that is dying the death of a thousand paper-cuts? Will those flags eventually fly in museums instead of in public squares? Perhaps that is precisely what she and her small number of supporters fear.

I need to go back to the Hedgewitch House. Prague is beautiful, but it's wearing me out. In fact I spent my last half-hour standing on an overpass above a rail yard, watching the trains come and go.

Second Movement: What's Wrong With Civilization?

§ 20. Models of the Civilized Man

Now I must consider my next cluster of root questions. *What's wrong with civilization?* Do the faults of civilization emerge from accidents that can be repaired? Or do they emerge from the essence, and so cannot be escaped? Philosophy tends to be an 'establishment' activity. One usually needs to be literate, educated, and in possession of enough leisure time to do philosophical work; and throughout history these requirements tended to be available only to the rich. Yet 'establishment' philosophy has a curious counter-tradition, in which philosophers obtain the necessary leisure time by deliberately renouncing their place in the 'establishment' and adopting a life of minimalism and naturalism, if not actual poverty. Diogenes of Sinope is a classical example: it is said that he lived most of his life in a wine barrel, and for fun he liked going to the marketplace to reprimand people for their consumerist obsessions. Heraclitus of Ephesus was first in line for the kingship of his city, but he abdicated in favor of his younger brother, and refused to participate in civic affairs. Socrates gave up most of his possessions, including his shoes, and enjoyed wandering the market of old Athens, exclaiming: 'How many things I do not need!' Similarly, at his trial, he chastised his fellow citizens for caring too much about their money: 'Wealth does not bring about excellence [*arete*, virtue], but excellence brings about wealth and all other public and private blessings for men.' (*Apology* 30b)

Asian philosophers who renounce civilization to pursue knowledge and enlightenment are perhaps better known, both in their homelands and in the Western world too. Among them may I draw attention to Siddhartha Gautama. Born the son of a king, he renounced his life of luxury and followed instead the life of a wandering holy man. Eventually his wandering took him to a forest, where he achieved his most important philosophical discoveries, meditating alone for many days. For instance, he found that the root of human suffering is craving for things we cannot possess, such as material wealth, and a permanent self. The Chinese philosopher Lao Tzu should also be included here. Employed for many years as the imperial librarian in the Kingdom of Ch'u during the Warring States period, he had already achieved some small fame as a wise man when he quit his job and went to live alone in the countryside. He is often depicted riding on a water buffalo, facing backwards so that he could speak with two guardsmen who wouldn't let him leave the city until after he delivered his last teachings. His book, the *Tao Te Ching*, contains numerous severe criticisms of conspicuous displays of power and wealth. Here are three of my favorite examples.

> Do not exalt the worthy, so that the people shall not compete.
> Do not value rare treasures, so that the people shall not steal.
> Do not display objects of desire, so that the people's hearts shall not be disturbed. (§2)

> The courts are exceedingly splendid,
> While the fields exceedingly weedy,
> And the granaries are exceedingly empty.
> Elegant clothes are worn,
> Sharp weapons are carried,
> Foods and drinks are enjoyed beyond limit,
> And wealth and treasures are accumulated in excess.
> This is robbery and extravagance.
> This is indeed not Tao. (§53)

> The Way of Heaven reduces whatever is excessive and supplements whatever is insufficient.

The way of man is different.
It reduces the insufficient to offer to the excessive. (§77)[184]

If the concentration of wealth is a sign of civilization, as some of the scientific checklist-makers believed, then these philosophers with their anti-wealth (or at least anti-consumerist) messages could be called philosophers of anti-civilization. I recognize the irony here, since some of the anti-civilized philosophers I named here did much to advance the cause of civilization, and are today counted among its foundational 'great men'. Siddhartha Gautama, for example, founded what is now the 5th largest religion in the world, Buddhism, with nearly 500 million practitioners.[185] Yet the wisdom of these ancient sages leads me to a possible answer to my second root question. Maybe our civilization has the wrong model of the civilized person. Maybe our present model of the civilized person is too materialist, and insufficiently spiritual.

Over the length of its history, Western civilization has imagined many different models of the civilized person: the Christian Soldier, the Renaissance Man, the Rugged Individualist, the Oxford Don, the Company Man, the High Society Lady. (It's noteworthy that so few of the West's posterfaces for civilization are female.) We could add figures from subcultures here too, like the Bohemian Artist, satirical figures like Forest Gump or The Very Model of a Modern Major-General, or melancholic models like J. Alfred Prufrock. Today, Western society still upholds some of these models. Probably the most prominent among them is the *Homo economicus* – the 'economic man' of every neoliberal economist since the foundation of capitalism. *Homo economicus* is the man who wants nothing more in life than to find the most intelligent way to make money for himself. Here's how Adam Smith, the 'Father of Capitalism', introduced him back in 1776:

...man has almost constant occasion for the help of his brethren, and it is in vain for him to expect it from their benevolence only. He will be more likely to prevail if he can interest their self-love in his favour... It is not from the benevolence of the butcher, the brewer, or the baker, that we expect our dinner, but from their regard to their own interest. We address ourselves, not to their humanity but to their self-love...[186]

And here's how John Stuart Mill described him almost a hundred years later, in a discussion of the study of political economy:

...'Political Economy' is not the science of speculative politics, but a branch of that science. It does not treat of the whole of man's nature as modified by the social state, nor of the whole conduct of man in society. It is concerned with him solely as a being who desires to possess wealth, and who is capable of judging of the comparative efficacy of means for obtaining that end.[187]

Notice that Mill claimed to isolate one feature of 'man's nature'. He leaves it open to suppose that our natures have other features, though he suggests those other features are not original to us but instead 'modified by the social state' (a reference to the State of Nature experiment). I do not doubt that people can be, and often are, calculatingly self-interested. Indeed a similar idea, the virtue of 'proper pride', appears in the work of Aristotle, some 2,300 years ago; and I do not doubt that the right kind of pride can be a virtue. But these narrow claims about humanity, as useful as they may be for the study of economics, are bait-and-switch tricks. They began, as you see here, as uncontroversial statements about one feature of human nature among many. But as the idea took on greater prestige, it came to be treated as the only important feature of human nature, and effectively the same thing as reason and rationality itself.[188] For example: John Rawls, probably the most influential political philosopher of the 20th century, stipulated in his book *A Theory of Justice* that an individual in the 'original position' (a kind of analogue of the State of Nature) is not envious of anyone, but 'his dominant interests are in himself', and that: 'The persons in the original position try to acknowledge principles which advance their system of ends as far as possible. They do this by attempting to win for themselves the highest index of primary social goods.' This model of rationality, Rawls says, is 'the standard one, familiar in social theory'.[189] *Homo economicus* values competition and individual wealth-maximization as the highest of all virtues. It repositions citizens as consumers, whose most meaningful expression of freedom is in how they choose to spend their money: Friedrich Hayek, an early 20th century economist who best articulated this world view, defined freedom itself in *The Road to Serfdom* (1944) as the ability to 'produce, sell, and buy anything that may be produced and sold at all'. [190]

Homo economicus emerged from the workings of the civilizing forces; he has now positioned himself to direct those forces as he wishes, craft them in his own image, and so make himself more real. For in a capitalist economy, the civilizing forces can be owned as the private property of individuals, in whole or in part, either directly or indirectly through corporations and investments. Indeed it is not an exaggeration to say that whomever owns some part of the means of production, distribution, and communication, owns a part of civilization itself (in its big picture, if not in the small). There is now no sector of human life upon which *Homo economicus* does not attempt to impose his language and his values. Governments offer tax incentives for investments, for instance. Corporations allow entrepreneurs to 'crowd fund' their investment capital from hundreds or thousands of people, and corporations give shareholders partial shelter from personal liability for the corporation's debts. In education, colleges and universities are increasingly managed as businesses instead of as services or as works of nation-building: students thus become 'clients' and their teacher's knowledge becomes 'course content packs'. In art and culture: thoughts, feelings, experiences, and stories become 'media content' and 'intellectual property'. Public infrastructure projects are replaced with 'public-private partnerships', in which most risks are assumed by city councils and governments, and most profits are gathered by the partner-entrepreneurs. Working class people in precarious temporary jobs become 'independent contractors', unprotected by minimum wage requirements and overtime limitations. The colonization of language also moves in the other direction, when spending money is legally protected as a form of political speech: a situation endorsed by the United States Supreme Court in the *Citizens United v. Federal Election Commission* (2010) decision. The values of *Homo economicus* surround us and filter our fields of view so completely that we do not see them anymore: recall Norbert Elias' point that a value system becomes fully 'civilized' when it has ceased to be a topic of conversation.

It often takes an outsider's point of view to see one's own values and to see their real consequences for people's lives. Here is an example from a friend of mine who moved from Canada to Medellin, Colombia:

The major cities are booming with international investment, and safety standards have increased dramatically in recent years. However, these improvements are contrasted by enduring issues of corruption and poverty. The Colombian government has taken impressive steps to make the economy more competitive and to invest in education and health programs. These changes, though, are a work in progress and public institutions lag far behind private ones. They have been in peace talks with the FARC and their guerrilla forces, which still control large regions of the countryside; but these negotiations are constantly interrupted by one party or the other breaking their fragile, temporary agreements. (C. Sadowsky, tour operator)

For another example, a strategic health plan for the Cree of James Bay, an indigenous First Nation in Quebec, saw the values of white Canadian civilization as follows:

As with most other Aboriginal peoples in Canada and around the world, the Cree of James Bay have faced many changes that have caused disruption in all aspects of their life and culture as it was situated before European contact... The accumulated impact of these matters has created *dysfunctional survivalist behaviours* among the Cree and the manifestation of many socially destructive situations in the communities... There is difficulty in endorsing a different cultural paradigm such as the way of life based on *competition and productivity* of the non-native civilization.[191]

What might make *Homo economicus* and his values bad for civilization? One answer might be: the consequence of his dominance over the sphere of civilized values is that too many people are made to needlessly suffer. Guy Standing, professor of economics at the University of London, coined the word *precariat* for people whose jobs and housing situations are permanently precariously insecure.[192] As I see it, the precariat is a consequence of *Homo economicus* and his occupation of the castle in the middle of the Ancient Great Wall. With him in the centre, it is nearly impossible for anyone to think for themselves, feel their own feelings, or even to live, except accord with his self-interested values – and even if they do live by those values, they may be punished anyway. I do mean 'to live' quite literally here, since the economic nonconformists are punished with depravation of the means of life: that is, unemployment, poverty, homelessness, starvation, and death. As wages stagnate or fall, and as the costs of health care, child care, rent, and tuition continue to rise, precariats have effectively replaced the middle class in most of Canada and America, since the economic crash of 2008.[193] An informant described to me what it feels like to be a precariat: he wrote that for most of his adult life he worked in the service industry, where:

...my job barely – BARELY! – covered rent, food, and bills for me and my then-wife Cathi. I didn't make enough to even pay my student loans, much less buy a car, put savings aside, or afford any form of health care. When we got sick, we depended upon free clinics and handouts from our families. When a shelf full of shoes fell and hit me in the head, my boss hustled me off to a doctor who was a friend of his, took all the medical records, and then got the doc to claim I had never seen him. (Those motherfuckers even told me to take five days off, then docked my pay for those five days, claiming I had just not bothered to show up. The lawyer I tried to hire claimed he could do nothing without proof, and all the proof had 'disappeared.') Another boss whited out our time-cards, and a third refused to give me my last pay check after I had given my two-week notice. (Her exact words were, 'Why should I pay you? You quit, so you're worth nothing to me now.') There was no way to get ahead; even when I worked two jobs and came home dead tired, there was never enough money to get us out of the pit, or even to a ledge where we might start to get a grip. This is still the situation for tens of millions of Americans – not 'bums' who 'want free stuff,' but working poor who are KEPT poor by a system that blames a working person for their own poverty, and which funnels all gains upward to a shrinking handful of 'achievers' and 'job providers' who use their prosperity to make those working poor even poorer. No wonder so many people are furious or despairing. For over half of the nation – yes, even for those 'privileged white males' – this is the reality of 21st-century America. For over a decade or so of my adult life, it was mine. I was fortunate. Most folks are not. (P. Brucato, who now works as a writer and game designer.)

The bosses who treated my informant like that were acting ethically wrongly in numerous ways; but their actions were consistent with the values of Economic Man. Keeping working people's lives precarious helps their employers make more money.

Previously I argued that the point of civilization is the creation of civilized people. My informant's story here suggests that we must modify that proposition. For there are people who work long and hard to embody the model of the civilized person, but who are nonetheless pushed to the edge of the Ancient Great Wall, permanently at risk of being thrown out. Let us say, then, that the point of civilization is still to create civilized people; but depending on the model of the civilized person, it may not be necessary to fully civilize everyone. It will be enough to fully civilize only a few. *Homo economicus* is one such model: for some people to 'succeed' at embodying him, others must be made to fail.

Another similar (though not precisely identical) model of the civilized person endorsed by the West, for which the civilizing forces also punish non-conformity, is the able-bodied, wealthy, sexually straight, Caucasian, adult male. Let's call him The Patriarchal Man. If my thesis about civilization is correct, we should see the civilizing forces move to punish people who renounce or who refuse to defer to that model. In the example of transgender women, that's exactly what we see. At the time I write these words, various American states have recently passed laws to prevent transgender persons from using the bathroom that fits with their gender identity.[194] The stated reason for these laws is to prevent men from posing as women, entering women's bathrooms, and assaulting them. Again: if my thesis is correct, then another, perhaps deeper reason for these laws is to punish people for deliberately rejecting the mantle of the patriarchal man. For a person born a man, and thus born in a position to assume the benefits and privileges of the patriarchy, yet instead who undergoes the chemical and surgical and social process to become a woman, appears in the eyes of the patriarchal man as evidence that there might be something wrong with the image of the patriarchal man. Never mind that the trans-woman gives up all the benefits of manhood in exchange for nearly none of the benefits of womanhood: this 'evidence' must be suppressed. So the law is summoned to compel trans-people to use a different bathroom, and face extraordinary personal and public humili-ation for doing so,[195] or alternatively face fines of up to $10,000, felony charges, and possible jail time.[196] Those who feel personally disgusted by the transgressors might take it upon themselves to punish the transgressors outside the law, for instance by killing them. An advocacy group for trans-people in America published evidence that the murder rate for transgen-dered women reached an historic high in 2015; and double the rate of the previous year.[197]

This can happen against persons with any kind of identity that challenges a politically-established standard, in large ways or small. Here at the Hedgewitch House, for instance, I was shown a book on Czech agricultural engineering that was banned during the Communist period, because its existence was proof that Russia was not the source of *all* scientific and technical progress in the world. (The book isn't banned anymore.)

To choose a more visceral example: In July of 1910, profes-sional boxer Jack Johnson defeated the former world heavy-weight champion Jim Jeffries, in a title match in Reno, Nevada. The fight had been widely promoted as an occasion when the white man, represented by Jeffries, could 'vindicate Anglo-Saxon manhood and save civilization' by defeating the black man, represented by Johnson.[198] So when Johnson easily won the bout, race riots exploded across America, in which eighteen people died. A New York newspaper of the time said of one of the riots: 'Three thousand white men took possession of Eighth Avenue and held [it] against police as they attacked every Negro in sight.'[199] To choose a more recent example: identity-realization was exactly the reason given by Thomas Mair, for why he murdered a British member of parliament, in June of 2016. At his first appearance in court, when the magistrate asked for his name, he said: 'My name is death to traitors, freedom for Britain', and he repeatedly called himself a 'political activist'. Mair's victim, Jo Cox, was a popular Labour party MP, and a supporter of Britain's continued membership in the European Union during the referendum on whether to leave the union. Mair said he murdered Cox 'for Britain', and to 'keep Britain independent'.[200] Similarly, when Anders Breivik was asked why he murdered 77 people in July 2011, he said that he did it to save Europe from an imagined Muslim takeover, and to punish Norway's Labour Party (of whom 69 of his victims were members of the party's youth wing) for allegedly allowing that takeover to happen.[201]

I think it's probably undeniable that our problems emerge, at least in part, from our celebration of terrible models of the civilized person. But I am sure it is not the *only* problem; and so, inventing a new model of the civilized person cannot be the only solution. Any such model is bound to be a Pinocchio, a little mechanical plaything who, given a taste of human life, wants more; he wants to become 'a real boy'. That's humanity in a nutshell – humanity is a wish (upon a star?) for a confirmed realization. We attain that realization by emulating and embodying some model of the civilized person. Yet any such model is also a Frankenstein creation, an artificial person who punishes people for withholding or denying that confirmation. What is meant by 'a real boy' here, and exactly how the civilized person can confirm it, is always subject to ongoing revision, through the workings of the civilizing forces. But those who refuse to embody the civilized man, or at least those who refuse to defer to him, will lose realization – and to borrow a phrase from Marx, the nonconformist 'loses realization to the point of starving to death'.[202] She might also lose realization on account of being beaten, harassed, publicly humiliated, disproportionately punished, excluded from participation in society and culture, and finally murdered. The killers realize themselves as exemplars of the civilized person by conquering whoever threatens the integrity and the glamour of the civilized person. So it seems likely to me that some kind of oppressive and potentially violent identity-politics might follow from *any* new model of the civilized person, even from the very best of them. So: while I think we do need to invent better models of the civilized person, I also think we need a deeper answer to my second root question.

§ 21. A Thought Experiment

In the last meditation I was only ruling out different options for an answer to my second root question. This is helpful; I might some day land on an option that I can't rule out. But if I am going to find an answer before I grow old, I am going to need a better method. So I propose to follow in the footsteps of some of my philosophical predecessors, and tell my own tale of the state of nature. The object of the tale, as we saw in the previous movement, is to find out what, if anything, prompts the transition to civilization. The object is also to find out what's 'wrong' with civilization. That is to say, whether there's anything in the logical foundations of civilization that explains why it fails so many people. The standard versions of the experiment tell a story of a fundamental problem with human social life, for which some model of state-level government was the solution. So we too shall look for what social, psychological, or political problems might appear in our theoretical pre-civilized state, and we shall examine whether the transition to civilization solves them – or whether, following Rousseau, the problem is the transition itself.

The standard accounts, from Vitruvius to Rawls,[203] say that the people in the state of nature live by instinct alone, or else by autonomous reason, but in either case without organized laws and formalities.[204] In our account, let's make a similar assumption: our experiment begins with a hypothetical community living in a pre-civilized state, with no such overt laws and formalities. However, I wish to modify the starting position, to reflect certain realities that the standard accounts generally ignore.

First assumption: A Multifaceted Human Nature. We shall assume that people in this condition can display any and all of the behaviors that philosophers have placed at the core of human nature: pro-social qualities like empathy, compassion, co-operation; anti-social qualities like distrustfulness, aggression, selfishness; absurdist qualities like suicidal passion. Let's assume that when we begin, none of these natural dispositions dominates any other: if one kind of nature is particularly prominent in one or more individuals, there are enough other individuals with opposite natures to counterbalance. We shall also assume this variety of natures appears in both men and women. Recent archaeological discoveries strongly suggest that prehistoric people lived with complete gender equality;[205] we shall therefore assume the same equality in our hypothetical community, at least at its starting position. Hobbes and others assumed that moderate selfishness was a fixed feature of human nature. I shall assume that moderate selfishness is one of many natures people may possess, and no stronger than any other. At any rate, I do not count the wish to fulfill natural needs as 'selfish', at least not in the common pejorative sense of the word. The instinct to eat, drink, seek shelter from the elements, and so on, which was assumed as a natural given by Hobbes, Locke, and Rousseau, is only 'selfish' in a very narrow sense. It might be argued that my opening position about human nature is not without its own bias; to say we have all natures, or to say we have no nature at all, is still to make a claim about human nature. In reply, I should say that my opening position, that human nature is multifaceted, is the one that best fits the evidence.

Second Assumption: Original Flourishing. Let us also assume that in our starting position, it was already possible for individuals and groups to lead fulfilling and happy lives. Perhaps they had fewer and simpler wants than we do today, and so they didn't have to work as hard to meet their wants as we do. Perhaps they 'bonded' more deeply with each other, as they would have shared achievements and life-threatening dangers together. Some scholars, such as anthropologist Marshall Sahlins and polymath Jared Diamond, have suggested that prehistoric people had more leisure time than we do; according to their calculations one man's hunting and gathering could support four or five people. Also, local climate conditions often made hunting or gathering impossible for a few months each year.[206] As Sahlins noted:

> ...hunters quit camp because food resources have given out in the vicinity. But to see in this nomadism merely a flight from starvation only perceives the half of it; one ignores the possibility that the people's expectations of greener pastures elsewhere are usually not disappointed. Consequently, their wanderings, rather than anxious, take on all the qualities of a picnic outing on the Thames.[207]

But following my earlier statement that the people of our hypothetical community have every kind of human nature, we'll also assume that some people in our community find that situation unsatisfactory. Some might regularly complain about hunger. Some might find the leisure time made possible by bad weather is more like 'enforced idleness'.[208]

Third Assumption: Intergenerational Dynamism. Another feature of social life, typically ignored in the standard accounts, is the transitional makeup of human communities. The standard accounts from Locke to Rousseau treat their hypothetical societies as if they are composed of the same people, the whole time, from beginning to end. Yet this is clearly not true of any society anywhere on earth. Indeed this point wasn't fully acknowledged by any social theorist in the tradition until Edmund Burke, in the 18th century.[209] So, in our experimental community, some of the talented and knowledgeable members die every year, or emigrate away; and every year, the community is refreshed by newborn children, and by immigrants, and by those youths who transition into adulthood. Any living society, human or otherwise, is like a river: it's never quite the same from one generation to the next. Yet the paths by which people move through life may remain roughly similar over time, like the eddy currents and whirlpools in a river that remain mostly stable while new waters flow into and out of them. In the science of ecology, such things are called 'dissipative structures'; other examples include hurricanes, cyclones, and living organisms themselves. The institutions and formalities of a society, like its laws and customs and institutional arrangements, are broadly like dissipative structures. So are the accomplishments of culture, like the artists and writers and musical composers whose works we celebrate years or centuries after their death. These things are not really 'things'; they are more like pathways for the movements of human bodies, thoughts, and feelings; they exist only so long as each generation inherits them, preserves or alters or reinterprets them, and bequeaths them onward to the next generation. The physical infrastructure is similarly dissipative, for although brick and concrete appear permanent, they too require people to regularly maintain them. Roads, bridges, farms, houses, towers, and cities, no less than ideas, can be preserved, not preserved, modified, or destroyed and replaced, as each generation inherits them and then transfers them to the next. To use another well-watered metaphor, we could say the 'ship of state' is like the 'ship of Theseus', which both is and is not the same ship from departure to arrival; its general shape remains the same, yet some of its planks are removed and replaced every day. So our hypothetical community must also flow like a river, remaining both stable and at the same time dynamic.

At this starting place in the experiment, our community's relationship with the earth mostly involves the work necessary to satisfy basic survival needs. I assume, at this starting place, that most people's survival needs are simple: they have bodily needs such as food, water, shelter, and care during times of vulnerability; they have psychological needs for acceptance, respect, and love. Yet I also assume each generation experiments with different ways of doing this work, in an attempt to find out which way of relating to things satisfies our survival needs better than other ways.

The last thing to set in place before the experiment begins is our hypothetical community's name. The first peoples of earth probably named themselves something along the lines of 'us', or 'our folk', or 'the people'. For the sake of this experiment, and in homage to Vitruvius, I shall name our people for a thing they can do that most animals cannot, except over short distances: they can walk upright. Walking on two legs allows them to see farther, travel farther, work with their hands, use more tools, and face the stars. So let's name our hypothetical community 'The Wanderers'.

The pieces are set, and ready to move. Let's see where they go.

§ 22. Facing the People

The standard accounts of this experiment begin at the place where people meet each other for the first time, and establish their first social relations. As our Wanderers have every kind of basic nature, so they shall have every kind of relation to each other. They will struggle, negotiate, and work with each other; they will speak to each other, or help each other, or threaten and steal from each other; they will generally do everything people do with each other today.

Those whose natural tendencies lean them toward aggression, distrustfulness, or territoriality – those inclined to take what they want by force – soon meet with others similarly aggressive. The logic of the experiment is such that none of these people can dominate others for very long; I borrow that assumption from Hobbes. But we have stipulated that the people of our community have every kind of human instinct. So there will also be people who respond to their neighbors with kindness, generosity, and love. These will meet others who are similarly generous and loving. They'll pursue their survival needs through co-operation and they'll easily succeed. Here we acknowledge Rousseau's assumption that empathy and compassion secures the happiness of life in the state of nature.

What happens when the aggressive people and the co-operative people encounter each other? It seems logical to suppose that the aggressors will dominate the co-operators. But it wouldn't be long before a second party of aggressors steps in to take for themselves a share of the exploited services of the co-operative people. Thus our community encounters the Hobbsean stalemate. We have already seen how Hobbes believed 'the sum of the right of nature' is 'to defend ourselves' (*Leviathan* 14) because life in the state of nature is 'a war...of every man, against every man'. (*ibid* 13) But even in a purely Hobbsean state of nature this would not always be the case, because of the facts of human vulnerability. We are born as infants, unable to walk or even lift our own heads. Should we live to the end of our natural time we must bear the infirmities of old age. In between, we might enjoy healthy adulthood most of the time, but we might get injured, or acquire a disease. Some people might be held by diseases and disabilities for most or even all of their lives: think of people with arthritis, for instance. Some people's life-long burdens are not physiological: they have to do with social constructions like racism, sexism, homophobia, religious hate, and the like. And, of course, everyone will spend about one-third of their lives asleep. In that situation, the right to self defense clearly cannot be exercised by everyone. Indeed, Hobbes has almost nothing to say about people who are unable to defend themselves. The most he says is that 'secret machinations' or a 'confederacy' of weaker persons could overpower a stronger individual. But that's not good enough for me. For my beginning position, my 'sum of the right of nature', is that flourishing human lives are ethically desirable and good. That must include the lives of the vulnerable, because if it excludes the vulnerable, it excludes *everyone*. And it would unfairly exclude some people more than others: for some human lives are more endangered, more disempowered, more vulnerable than others.[210] So, let us suppose that alongside the Hobbsean right to defend ourselves, our Wanderers also claimed another 'right of nature': *the right to ask for help*. Similarly, the non-aggression pact that Lucretius spoke of, '*Don't hurt me, please, and I'll not hurt you*', was likely only one kind of social contract among many that our Wanderers struck with each other. Given the facts of human vulnerability, they must also have formed mutual assistance pacts: '*Help me, please, and I'll help you.*'

By the way: the right to self defense has high prestige in Western society, not only because of the influence of Hobbes, but also because of its implicit place in the Second Amendment in the United States constitution. Furthermore, the Hobbsean view of human society as a 'war of all against all' happens to be especially useful to gun manufacturers and the military-industrial complex in general – an enormously wealthy and politically well-connected group of industries. If we saw the world as mostly safe, and mostly populated by kind and sympathetic people, we would buy fewer weapons. So it's in their economic interest to influence us, through advertising and political lobbying, to see the world as a 'Wild West', 'Mad Max' kind of place, and to hold the right to self defense as more important than any other. But I digress.

Our experiment with the Wanderers continues. The co-operative people and the aggressive people among them now encounter those whose natures lean them toward quickness and subterfuge and deception. Let's call this third group the cunning people. In their superficial appearance they will look like the co-operators, the better to gain the trust of others. But they will always take what they need in secret, or else they'll eventually take more than they give in open trades. I suppose the cunning people will be successful for a while. But they won't be successful forever. For one thing, they'll eventually meet other people who know all the tricks and thus know how to protect themselves. Once they are found out, they might also simply leave, and find new 'marks' to exploit. But this only sets them up for a cyclical repetition of the same failure. Soon enough, they'll meet others at least as smart as themselves, and they'll have to move on again. For another, when the cunning people find themselves in need of the help of others, people will remember how they cheated and lied, and will be much less willing to give. They will find that generosity and compassion are a kind of insurance policy.

The only successful strategy, the only response where more people meet more of their survival needs more of the time, is for everyone to become co-operative people. For the aggressive people soon find their fear-saturated standoff with other aggressive people never ends until one or both belligerents lay down their arms and declare peace. They also find that the co-operative people give more freely and more generously to those who co-operate in return. Similarly, the cunning people soon find that the best way to appear co-operative is to actually be co-operative. They have to fill their hearts with real empathy, the better to project the appearance of possessing it; but the moment they do that, they cease to be cunning and they become co-operative. Evolutionary ecologists have studied strategies for group survival, and they have generally found that co-operation is very common in the animal world,[211] and even more common in human societies than among animals.[212] One such study involving game theory, Prisoners' dilemmas, and public goods, found that when groups are small and memories long, co-operation always emerges as the best survival strategy. When groups are small, there is less incentive for freeloading; and when memories are long, people are better able to reproduce successful strategies from the past, and better able to recognize the freeloaders and kick them out.[213] The idea that human life is a 'dog eat dog' world where 'winner takes all' doesn't have to be true – and indeed it isn't true, more often than most people know.

In an earlier meditation, we saw some archaeological and scientific evidence that suggested increasing co-operation and empathy initiated civilization itself. A similar idea appeared in the work of various 19th century suffragette writers. To choose one example: Charlotte Perkins Gilman, in her book *Women and Economics* (1898), wrote: 'The subjection of women has involved to an enormous degree the maternalizing of man. Under its bonds he has been forced into new functions, impossible to male energy alone. He has had to learn to love and care for someone besides himself. He has had to learn to work, to serve, to be human.'[214] This, Gilman says, is a civilizing force: for in her view: 'To serve each other more and more widely; to live only by such service...this is civilization, our human glory and race-distinction.'[215] If Gilman's view is correct, I think it likely that only a small few of the aggressive people among our Wanderers felt any stirring of empathy toward any captive women, for the reason that domestic violence against women appears in every society documented by anthropologists, though it is less persistent and less severe in preindustrial, isolated, or non-patri-archal societies. Yet the idea that civilization is born of women teaching basic empathy to men has supporters among more recent anthropologists too, although they tell the story slightly differently. The advent of cooking, for instance, made it possible for people to gain more nutritional value from their food for less energy-expenditure in chewing and digesting. But the increased preparation time made the food more vulnerable to theft. So the cooks, most of them women, selected men whom they thought would be good protectors against other men. To preserve the loyalty of their protectors these women offered food, especially cooked food, and monogamous sexual relations. Men may also have become more willing to protect the children from abduction or murder when they were sure the children were 'their own'.[216] Aristotle may have thus been accidentally correct when he wrote that the foundation of a *polis* is a family.

It's a neat and tidy idea; yet we should remember that each story about life in the state of nature is in some way a reflection of its author's presuppositions and cultural assumptions. This theory about women as civilizing influences speaks to contemporary feelings about feminism, multiculturalism, and inclusiveness. It speaks to the embarrassment many white European-descended people (like me) sometimes feel about the colonial empires in their culture's recent past. It's very possible, even likely, that the softening of the aggressive instincts is only one of several forces that worked upon the Wanderers. But it's a force I think is more decisive than is normally acknowledged. Indeed, the idea that civilization itself was born out of empathy and co-operation, more so than out of mutual non-aggression pacts and fear of nature, appears to me as *a sign of hope and optimism.* But keep that sign in your pocket for later. Let's return to our experiment now.

Once the Wanderers find that co-operation and empathy offer an optimal solution to its various survival-related problems, it seems logical to suppose that more and more people become co-operative, so as to better meet their survival needs more of the time. The next generation would also experiment with different ways of relating to each other, as their predecessors did. But those who discovered the benefits of empathy and co-operation would teach their discoveries to their children and grand-children. So each new generation, even as it must do its own experimenting, receives the advantage of a store of knowledge about what works and what doesn't, passed to them by their parents and grandparents. This store of knowledge gives each generation a chance to make fewer mistakes than the last. At some hard-to-define moment in its history, the Wanderers inherit more knowledge than they create or discover. Perhaps after many generations and many hundreds of years, life would soon be very good for nearly everyone. But we also acknowledge Rousseau's claim that in a community where everyone's natural needs are mostly fulfilled most of the time, there might be no special reason for the process of civilization to begin.

§ 23. Facing the Earth And Sky

Besides encountering each other, the Wanderers are also encoun-tering the world. They explore it, hunt and gather food from it, build shelters to protect themselves from it, and marvel at the wonder of it. If the community is large enough, let's say about the size that anthropologists call a 'band' (that's twenty to forty people), they'll likely have a few among them who are perceptive and patient enough to study their environment and get used to its rhythms. They'll learn the best time of year to gather each different kind of nut and berry and tuber; they'll learn the behav-ioral habits of various animals and so hunt them more efficiently; they'll learn 'optimal foraging strategies', they'll find points of 'diminished returns', and they'll invent methods for preserving some of their food supplies for lean seasons. Nothing in their local environment is ever quite the same from one day to the next or one year to the next. One year's dry season might be hotter than another; one year's rainy season might last longer than another. Yet the people will learn to predict this. For instance they'll know when to expect rain by studying the shape of clouds and the smell of the wind. Again, much of this knowledge is teachable; each generation learns some of it from their elders. A sense of belonging in time begins to grow on them.

Eventually, they will build houses. The oldest recognizable houses known to archaeologists were built about 400,000 years ago, at Terra Amata, near Nice, in southern France. Traces of around twenty simple huts were found there: oval in shape, between 8m and 15m long, and 4m to 6m wide. They were made of long saplings or branches pushed into the earth and supported by a buttress of stones. A hearth fire was placed in the centre, and protected from wind by a screen of pebbles. The remains of some of the huts were stacked on top of others, suggesting that they were often damaged and replaced. However, no rubbish was found in close proximity to the huts, suggesting that the people who built them cared for them.[217]

The construction of permanent dwelling places, more than the establishment of settled agriculture, looks to me like an excellent place to fix the beginning of civilization. It is a moment when the people inherit, as much as they create, not only much of their knowledge, but also much of their material culture. Having said that, I think there was probably no single magic moment in history when our ancestors suddenly invented civilization. Contrary to Vitruvius, for instance, there was probably no single overnight moment when our response to the earth changed from fear to wonder. Our distant ancestors probably feared the natural world no more than they feared each other (perhaps also no less). They knew its dangers, but they knew how to face those dangers; and as their knowledge of a given landscape grew, they found fewer of its features dangerous. They also had moments of peace and quiet often enough that they could look upon the world with awe. Like my own encounters with storms in middle Europe, there may have been times and places where our Wanderers could face a natural power from a position of near-complete safety. Recent social-scientific research has also shown a strong inverse correlation between a society's religiosity and the natural amenities of good weather and beautiful landscapes: when a people dwell in an especially scenic land, they tend to be less formally religious. The 'natural amenities' of the landscape, the 'mountains, hills, lakes, beaches, and pleasant weather', provide the sense of the numinous that might otherwise be provided by ritual.[218] I know this from my own experience of life. As a child I went to church with my family every Sunday, but I felt the presence of the sacred more tangibly when alone in the conservation park near the village, or in my grandparent's maple forest. So our hypothetical community will have a very wide variety of responses to the environment: wonder, possessiveness, opportunism, fear, and love. Maybe they would tell stories about those experiences, or maybe they'd compare their feelings about the land in one moment to other similar moments in their living memory. Maybe their stories grew more complex over time – and so did the performance of the stories, as they added costumes, masks, iconic words and phrases and gestures. Perhaps they made rules about what time of year the story had to be told – or *not* told! But the next day, they went back to the work of hunting and gathering, and protecting themselves from danger, and experimenting with new solutions to their problems, as usual.

The civilizing process begins without anyone's realizing it. It creeps up on people, it whispers in their ears, it gently tugs on their sleeves. Its first stirrings might be easily mistaken for a rabbit in the grass, a light spring breeze, a tree branch that catches your hair as you walk by. It's nothing; you wave it off without a second thought. And you go back to work. But a little while later, maybe months or maybe years later, it happens again. Eventually you notice it happening more and more often. And you notice that it's been with you for a long time. You can't easily recall any time you've been without it. Civilization arrives as something apparently already part of your life. It's a bit like pulling your thumb out of your back pocket, and only then discovering your thumb had been there since you were born. Here's how I think it happens.

Our community built fires to share warmth and food and companionship; and soon they built houses around their fires, to shelter each other from natural dangers. This, I think, is a basic civilizing force, as follows. Where the nomadic person dwells in and with the world, the settled person dwells in and with *and upon* the world. To put it another way: where a wandering hunter-gatherer looks upon the world, she knows herself as an expert in the use of her territory's resources; a settler looks upon the world and knows herself as both expert and, to some extent, master. Not that the settler is any less vulnerable to the unexpected vicissitudes of nature: storms, diseases, predators, and the like may still undermine her work. But the settler has more tools at her disposal to protect against these threats, and to rebound from them. The most important of those tools is the more solid roof over her house. For the settler with her simple shelter has bounded off a patch of the earth, however small, where the forces of nature have less strength. And into this shielded space enters a new, transformed consciousness: the awareness of herself as a being who can exercise power over the world – at least the minimal power to push the frontier of nature's dangers slightly further away.

A brief aside: when I say 'transformed consciousness' here, I do not mean something to do with trance states, such as those which can be induced by music or rituals or by drugs. Rather, I mean the integration of new propositions into one's worldview and one's way of being in the world. It is an entirely non-mystical process, prompted by unexpected revelations of reality: seeing things you've never seen before, doing things or seeing others do things you've never thought possible before. This process is potentially upsetting and revolutionary if it also involves dismissing propositions that you might have held in your world view for a long time.

Into this newfound consciousness steps two additional discoveries, which together form a dilemma that we should properly call *political*. The first of these new discoveries is that a person can exercise more power over nature when she co-operates with others. The first huts may have been simple enough for one person alone to build; but a team of people can build the huts faster, larger, stronger, more numerous. Teamwork and collaboration find their first natural rewards. At the same time, some of the newly-empowered settlers discover that if they can exercise power over the natural world, so can others. And if they can do so better in teams, so can other teams. A kind of social tension might enter the settlers' minds; or perhaps it would be better to say that the rut that ended the previous meditation takes on a new meaning. This new tension stands between the need to collaborate in order to meet survival needs easier, and the need to protect one's work from being undone by others. To put it another way: in building houses, some people learn to trust each other, but others learn to suspect each other. These two kinds of early positions do not easily reconcile with each other. For one of them presupposes that we human beings are naturally aggressive and territorial; the other presupposes that we are naturally co-operative and empathetic. I suppose both of these forces were present in our earliest house-building ancestors, although as we have seen, the standard accounts emphasize only one of them. I do not yet know what will become of the tension between them. But before I investigate it further: let's look at something else that house-building does to our minds.

Vitruvius wrote that the impetus to build the first house grew from social gatherings around fires, and from our 'not being obliged to walk with faces to the ground, but upright and gazing upon the splendour of the starry firmament'. Philosopher Karsten Harries, in his own meditation on Vitruvius and the first house, observed that:

...by linking the origin of the first house to the awe-inspiring sight of the inaccessible timeless order of the stars, Vitruvius gestures toward what distinguishes even the first house from any animal shelter: beyond addressing physical needs inseparable from our bodily existence, it also addresses spiritual needs. Not only the body but the soul too needs a house.[219]

So, a house meets obvious survival needs such as the need for shelter, but it also meets new, complicated, *spiritual* needs. What might those spiritual needs be? I would say that a spiritual need is the need for a partner in the search for the highest and deepest things. In what way can the house act as such a partner? And what does that have to do with civilization?

One answer is already implied. As a social gathering place, the house already participates in social relationships whose sacredness is obvious: relationships like the family, and the friendship circle. The hearth is also an integral part of the oldest and perhaps most important of religious rituals: the sharing of food and drink and stories.

Another way to reach the sacred is by having a precedent in sacred storytelling. The building of a house has many such precedents: Biblical Adam's act of granting names to all the animals in God's creation (Genesis 2:19), or the lonely tent in the desert where Moses retreated from the people to talk to God (Exodus 33:7). To cast a wider net, it can be compared to Nehemiah's reconstruction of the Temple and the city wall in Jerusalem and his subsequent re-establishment of the Law (Ezra 3, Nehemiah 2:17-6:15, 8:1-3). The marking-off of space also reaches the sacred through language. The origin of the English word 'temple' is in the Greek *temenos* and the Latin *templum*, both of them words for a space enclosed, cut off from the surrounding area, or specifically marked out for the reading of augurs (that is, prophetic signs).[220] As noted by theologian-philosopher Paul Ricoeur:

What is most remarkable about the phenomenology of the sacred is that it can be described as a manner of inhabiting space and time. Thus we speak of sacred space to indicate the fact that space is not homogeneous but delimited — *templum* — and oriented around the 'midpoint' of the sacred space. Innumerable figures, such as the circle, the square, the cross, the labyrinth, and the mandala, have the same spatialising power with respect to the sacred, thanks to the relations these figures establish between the center and its dimensions, horizons, intersections, and so on. All these phenomena and the related phenomena by which the passage from profane to sacred space is signified — thresholds, gates, bridges, pathways, ladders, ropes, and so on — attest to an inscription of the sacred on a level of experience beneath that of language.[221]

Architecture configures space; it also configures the mind. An ordinary house, of course, is not a temple, even if its inhabitants have put a shrine in some corner. But a house is still a centre, of a sort; it may be a centre of a lesser order of magnitude than a cathedral, but it is a centre for its inhabitants nonetheless.

We also find this sanctification of space in ancient pre-modern customs and rituals surrounding the digging of the first post-holes for a new house. In early Norse houses, for instance, small gold tokens were often placed in the post-holes, bearing images of a couple in loving sexual embrace. Researcher Stephen Pollington noted that the tokens represent the gods Freyr and Gerd, and that they are 'designed to promote fecundity, well-being, health and harmony in the household'.[222] The work of building a new house, so blessed with rituals like that, becomes a reproduction of the work of the gods, building the first house, starting the first family, establishing the first fire and the first community. The house also becomes an *established centre*, that is, a place to return to when the working day is done; and the world surrounding the house thus becomes *intelligibly ordered*. As noted in the previous meditation: a house marks off, or carves out, a certain parcel of the surface of the earth, and thus separates it from the rest of the world. The marked-off plot of land is no longer a mere stretch of earth, no different from any other stretch in its vicinity. Rather, once marked off it becomes a definite *place*, a *centre;* and as such it will bear a name like: 'our home', or 'our land', or 'the rock where we belong'. Where once there was a wandering band on the trackless earth, there was now *a people in their homeland* – and again, there was also the feeling that their land was always their home. Even a nomadic tribe will have a homeland of a sort; they tend to follow a general route that brings them back to the same places, in an annual or multi-annual cycle. But settled people think of their landscape differently than nomadic people. Settled people think of the world in terms of its relation to an established centre: notions of 'near', 'far', 'similar', and 'different' take on the significance of being near, far, similar, or different *from home*.

The house as a centre gives to its inhabitants the consciousness of belonging both to their local natural surroundings and also to the cosmos as a whole: as Harries says: 'Architecture answers to the human need to experience the social and natural world as a non-arbitrary meaningful order. A mythopoeic intent is part of all architecture worthy of its name.'[223] The world, so ordered, centers upon a place where people may feel at home, at peace, at ease. It is where we may feel spared from whatever natural dangers might dwell beyond its circle of succor: dangers like wild animals, wind and rain and snow. It may still be a centre of labor, for instance the work of cooking, cleaning, fire keeping, child raising, and the like, take place at home. Yet the home is where such labor could be enjoyed rather than merely undertaken; it is where we may sometimes rest and play. In sum, the house as a centre of a meaningfully ordered world gives people a place where they can *belong*, both to the land, and to the others in the community. Notice the language of possession goes in both directions: we claim a land as ours, but the land also claims us; the land belongs to us, but we belong to the land. Knowing where you belong, and knowing how you relate to the things that surround you, is a large part of knowing who you are; and that kind of self-awareness surely counts among 'the highest and deepest things'.

Notice also, above all, that this new knowledge *emerged from the activity of building the home*. Thus by deploying our forces-at-work to cut the logs, dig the foundation, thatch the roof, and so on, we also deploy our forces-at-work upon our own minds, changing the way we think about things, and changing the way we see things.[224] Today you might think of yourself in relation to more than one centre: not only your home, but also your city's downtown core, and your workplace, and perhaps a prominent landmark in the region. Recall Joseph Campbell's observation that a society's highest values tend to be reflected in its tallest buildings: the mediaeval cathedral, the early modern political palace, the late modern office tower.[225] Our Wanderers may have a sense of space that is mostly natural: they can go to one area where they know there's good berry picking; they can't go to another area where they know there's a lion's den. Today your sense of space might be almost entirely architectural. This is partly a matter of design elements and the values they symbolize: classical designs representing mathematical symmetry and harmony; religious designs pointing upward to heaven; postmodern designs representing value-multiplicity and experimentalism. It is also a matter of what spaces are open to you and what spaces are closed. You can enter public squares and parks and some private properties like shopping malls, but you may not enter other people's homes, nor security-cordoned spaces like factories, without permission and a good reason. There are also public spaces that cannot be entered except in very specific ways: you can drive along a multi-lane highway, but not walk across it (unless you're willing to risk legal sanction, or death). All these conceptions of how you relate to space, where and how you can move in space, and what reference points you use for navigation, configure your history and your sense of the possible. Those, in turn, configure your sense of self-awareness, and your way of being in the world. Yet we have built these spaces and landmarks ourselves; we might have inherited them from previous generations, but they did not descend from on high. We shape our world, and the world we have made also shapes us.

The Wanderers banded together at first only to meet their basic survival needs. They eventually discovered that the best way to meet those needs was to co-operate with and care about each other. As their ability to share each other's feelings grew, so they also eventually discovered feelings of familiarity and belonging to each other. Where once was an aggregate of individuals, loosely related by family bonds, and held together only by survival necessity, there was now a community. But there came with this transformation the feeling that they had always been a community, that there was never a time in which they weren't a community. In the creation of communities, the Wanderers discover that they have needs beyond mere survival – needs for belonging, and for self-definition. They discover these needs in themselves precisely the same moment they fulfill them, when they discover that they are members of a tribe, and when they discover that they have a home. These transformations of consciousness are, in effect, the first small and subtle occasions where our distant ancestors took hold of their own hearts and minds, and used them as material upon which to impress their labors. They're as fragile as whispers, and just as easily dispersed into the wind. But they are, in essence, the same as the founding of a great city, or the declaration of the sovereignty of a great nation. Civilization begins in the transformations of consciousness that arise from pronouncing, through deeds if not through words, the propositions of presence and identity: 'We are here!'

§ 24. Facing the Darkness

There is yet one more immensity I have not yet discussed, which the Wanderers would undoubtedly have noticed from the very beginning. They would notice that all things are in motion, and nothing is still; and in the course of it, all things must pass, and everyone dies.

We have already mentioned how the Wanderers would have encountered threats from the earth, like wild animals, diseases, and natural disasters. We could add the passive threat of rough terrain, as some people may meet injury or death from misadventure on hillsides or rocky coasts. I stipulated early in this thought experiment that the Wanderers have every kind of psychological nature, and that each new generation brings new ideas and experiences and thus the potential to shake up any political or psychological stalemates and balances. So even as empathy and co-operation grow, there are still aggression and competition. To the dangers of the earth, we may therefore add the dangers of other people. Jealousy, envy, rage, fear, greed, and madness, can easily lead people to steal from each other, attack each other, and kill each other. I found that building a home can take on the character of the sacred; here I add that so can violence. As noted by René Girard, scholar of religion:

> The sacred consists of all those forces whose dominance over man increases or seems to increase in proportion to man's effort to master them. Tempests, forest fires, and plagues, among other phenomena, may be classified as sacred. Far outranking these, however, though in a far less obvious manner, stands human violence – violence *seen as something exterior to man* and henceforth as part of all the other outside forces that threaten mankind. Violence is the heart and secret soul of the sacred.[226]

Why did Girard regard violence as 'something exterior to man'? In his argument he mentions the way human violence appears to share something with natural dangers like diseases: both can destroy human lives. But more than this, he says that violence has no cure, because 'inevitably the moment comes when violence can only be countered by more violence'. This leads to what Girard calls the paradoxical nature of violence: 'The fact that evil and the violent measures taken to combat evil are essentially the same. At times violence appears to man in its most terrifying aspect, wantonly sowing chaos and destruction; at other times it appears in the guise of peacemaker, graciously distributing the fruits of sacrifice.'[227]

Even if some generation emerged with only peacemakers among them, and no aggressive people of any kind, the people would still notice violence as an everyday part of their lives. In order for them to eat, animals must be killed and dismembered, plants uprooted and flayed apart, nuts and berries crushed, tubers dug up from the earth. Any or all of these foodstuffs might be roasted in a fire, and then torn apart by fingers, knives, and teeth. Even in our modern Western dining rooms, everyone seated around the dinner table is armed with blades and piercing weapons – that is, knives and forks. Girard's thesis seems confirmed: the thing we do every day to avoid the evil of death, eating, is shot through with violence at every stage.

We must also add to this meditation the plain fact that those who escape all those dangers and live to a fine old age shall nevertheless die. And they would learn that there is absolutely nothing whatsoever that anyone can do about it. No amount of luck, or planning, or strength, or health, or magic, can preserve anyone's life forever. Most people do not like to face this fact. We often turn every small reminder of this fact into something trivial and easily brushed off, like a joke. Yet the inevitability of death is, has always been, and for most people always remains, a source of terror and despair.

Contemporary psychological studies have shown that people tend to worry about the death of loved ones, and process of dying, more than they worry about their own deaths.[228] But it is possible that the fear of death is so personal and intimate that we are reluctant to admit it, even in anonymous psychology surveys. Other studies have shown that when confronted with reminders of their deaths, people feel the need to bring children into the world,[229] or to create a legacy of works that might bring fame.[230] These are both forms of surrogate immortality: and as responses to reminders of death they are indirect signs of how strongly the fear of death works upon our minds.

Reminders of death also tend to make people feel more religious.[231] We should not suppose that the Wanderers already have religion (as Locke did); for religion is one of those checklist-features of civilization that an experiment like this one should explain rather than assume. Yet it is entirely plausible that mortality salience, knowledge of the fact of death, can explain why religion appeared in the world in the first place. Here's how I think it probably happened to the Wanderers. They noticed that when things die, other lives flourish. Saplings grow in the stumps of fallen trees. Animal carcasses provide food for insects and predators and scavengers. They might compare these observations to the rising and setting of the sun, the phases of the moon, and the turning of the seasons. So they might reason that life and death are somehow intertwined, or that life and death are two faces of the same phenomena. They might wonder at what substance or what energy is transferred from the dead to the living. They might notice, for instance, that when an animal is alive it breathes; its breath is sometimes visible on cold days and it looks like mist or campfire smoke; its touch feels like the wind; and when the animal dies its breathing ceases. Thus they might reason that the substance or the energy of life has something to do with breath, and they might imagine that when an animal dies its breath departs the body and moves away to somewhere else.

It's interesting to note that the words for 'spirit' in European languages comes from the Latin root 'spiritus', *breath*.

Our Wanderers might make similar observations about water as a life substance or life energy. Plants and animals are always more abundant near springs, lake shores, and riversides. Landscapes burst up with vegetation after a rain, and they diminish after a drought. Living animals are full of blood and other fluids; living plants are full of sap and nectar and oil; dead plants and animals lose their fluids and dry out. To this day, we still refer to the oils that can be pressed or distilled out of various plants as an 'essence'. Any of these beliefs about breath or water could be confirmed by dreams, or visions induced by psychoactive plants and mushrooms, or even the voices inside people's heads.[232] In all these observings and imaginings, the Wanderers would invent the idea of the soul – though the invention would feel like a discovery – and they might imagine that this soul survives death and moves on to another life, in another world, or in another form.

I make no claim here about whether we human beings really do have a soul. Nor do I assert nor deny that we 'are' souls temporarily clothed in flesh, as the popular belief goes. I'm making a rather more prosaic point here: people may have invented the *idea* of the soul as an attempt to understand the nature of life and death. This invention is a civilizing force: for the contemplation of the soul configures she who contemplates it. We've already noted some of the ways thinking about death changes people's behavior; here we could add that the person who believes she has a soul may expect that the consequences of her words and choices will follow her to the next life, or to the next world. She might do that which she thinks will earn the favor of the spirits who have already passed before her, knowing that they might be watching, and that when her own death comes she might have to explain herself to them.

Recent archaeological discoveries seem to confirm this

hypothesis. In Paleolithic times, from two million years ago to 10,000 years ago, people tended to dispose of human remains as far from the community as possible. They may have wanted to prevent the spread of disease. They may have worried that the soul of the deceased might still be nearby, and might have malevolent intentions. But by the Neolithic age, from about 10,000 BCE to about 2,000 BCE, people began building elaborate tombs for their dead, and those tombs were built much closer to the community. People had changed how they thought about their dead. Perhaps they simply made different precautions to prevent the diseases that come from contact with corpses. Or, perhaps they were producing enough surplus wealth to allow the leaders to display their power by building monumental architecture, starting with burial mounds. It is also possible that the work of building the monuments prompted the change in human consciousness. I'm thinking of Irish monuments such as portal dolmen, passage mounds, and stone circles, because I happen to be familiar with them. The most famous of them, Poulnabrone, in County Clare, was built about 4000 BCE, and the bodies of about twenty adults and six children were interred there. When it was finished, it became a permanent feature of a landscape, alongside the natural stone that surrounded it. And this sense of *the potential permanence of some human works* may have prompted a change in the way people contemplated time and history, past, present, and future. But whatever the reason, Neolithic people began to think differently about their relationships with the dead. With this changed way of thinking, it became possible to imagine that one's dead ancestors had a new role in one's life. They might no longer be lost and possibly dangerous spirits who had to be bribed or tricked into leaving the community alone. Instead, the ancestors could now become helpers, allies, teachers, or intermediaries between the living and other spiritual beings. And this would make it very important to know who one's ancestors are, and also very important to know where they are buried, what one owed to them, and what one could reasonably ask from them.

In this story about the origin of religion, we find the first major clue toward an answer to my second root question. For by inventing the story of the soul, we responded to death by distracting ourselves. The soul is a thought that turns our attention away from death. It helps us to ignore death. When death can't be ignored, it inspires speculation and hope for a future after death. It makes death appear friendly, and no more troubling than a decent night's dreamless sleep. Soon enough we find the Wanderers responding not to death itself but to the stories they tell about death: stories of the soul and what might await the soul in the next world. And these stories are wonderful, in the sense of being *full of wonders* – they are as beautiful and terrifying and strange as any dream. Yet the story of the soul promises something it cannot fully deliver: it promises us the truth. Dreams and mystical visions aside, for dreams are always in motion and they resist independent confirmation: it is logically impossible to know what death is. Remember your Wittgenstein: 'Death is not an event in life: we do not live to experience death.' (Wittgenstein, *Tractatus Logico-Philosophicus* 6.4311) Precisely because death is impossible to know, we may tell any story we like about what it is. But death neither confirms nor denies whether such stories are true. I am not saying that the story of the soul is a lie; I am saying it is impossible to confirm or to disconfirm – but that is not the important point here. The point is that death, when faced directly and without distraction, is almost always bringer of terror and despair. The story of the soul protects us from that terror and despair by allowing us to pretend that death is not so terrifying. In so pretending, we civilize ourselves, in the sense that we take greater deliberate command over our ways of thinking and living. But at the same time, we also deceive ourselves, for we treat some of our own social and cultural and imaginative creations as if they are naturally revealed realities.

There is a name for this kind of self-deception: *illusion*. Now I have a working hypothesis for what's wrong with civilization. It is a manufacturer of illusions.

Supposing, as I have said, that the purpose of civilization is to create the civilized person: at a fundamental level, the most un-civilized and 'primitive' thing that someone can do is die. For this is a basic activity that we have in common with animals and other life forms that we have never eradicated from our existence, nor improved upon to a degree of sophistication unattainable by other species. From this point, it might follow that the most civilized thing you can do is live forever. To put it another way: if civilization is the metaphysical activity of making ourselves real, we can try to realize ourselves by ensuring we never become 'unreal' – that is, by ensuring we never die. Philosopher Stephen Cave regarded the terror of death and the quest for immortality as the central driving force in civilization. It appears in what he calls four immortality narratives: first, 'staying alive', i.e. through medicine, scientific intervention, or even magic; second, 'resur-rection', i.e. the belief that our bodies could rise again after death; third, 'soul', that is, the survival of a nonmaterial spiritual entity following the death of the body; and fourth, 'legacy', that is the surrogate immortality of one's works and reputation. (Some people hope to live forever by uploading their minds into computers. I see that as a kind of legacy, for the 'person' that lives on after the body dies is only a digitized copy of a brain. But that might be as good a legacy as building a tower or writing a book.) Concerning all these paths to immortality Stephen Cave says, 'Our efforts to clear these four paths and prepare for the ascent up the Mount of the Immortals have thrown up what we know as civilization – the institutions, rituals and beliefs that make human existence what it is.'[233] Cave might be correct that the wish to live forever is a civilizing force; but I have grave doubts about the achievability of that aim. By working hard to simply stay alive we have made astounding advances in medicine. We have eradicated diseases, learned to correct congenital defects, and we now live on average twice as long as most people lived only a hundred years ago.[234] But we have not eradicated death. The wish for immortality by resurrection or by soul gave us all those magnificent cathedrals and mausoleums and mythologies. But this kind of immortality is impossible to be certain of, for reasons already mentioned: the evidence for soul, especially, is too ambiguous. Legacy, it seems to me, is the most practical and visibly achievable kind of immortality, but it too is uncertain: it is subject to forces that the person who seeks it can't control, because of course when she dies she won't be around to control them. If Cave is correct that the will to live is actually the will to live *forever* and that civilization is only a product of that will, then what are we to make of the fact that immortality is almost certainly *impossible to achieve*? Might it follow that civilization is only as Shakespeare summed it: 'A tale told by an idiot, full of sound and fury, signifying nothing'? Might civilization be nothing more than a centuries-long, planet-wide, and all-out pursuit of a glamorous, but ultimately unreachable chimera, borne of our own imagination – an illusion?

But I run ahead of myself. The experiment is not yet complete: our Wanderers have not yet built their first city. Let us return to the story.

§ 25. Planting the Fields

As we have seen, many of the scientific checklist-makers said that settled agriculture is one of civilization's most important features. So let's look at that development now. Our Wanderers, let us suppose, guessed that they would starve less often if they deliberately cultivated the plants and husbanded the animals that they want to eat. So they uprooted the plants that they wanted and re-buried the roots closer to their homes, in patches where they cleared out all the plants they couldn't eat or didn't want. They built special houses to hold the animals they captured instead of killed; or perhaps they built walls or ditches around the habitats of animals they wanted to hunt with greater ease. It is perhaps no longer sensible to call them Wanderers. So let is now call them *Villagers*. And let's see what happens in their village.

- Evidence for the earliest human use of fire is more than a million years old. But for much of that time, our ancestors used fire only occasionally, when opportunities appeared. The earliest evidence of fire for cooking food occurs about 500,000 years ago; the earliest evidence of controlled fire as a regular part of people's lives occurs between 320,000 and 350,000 years ago.[235]
- The first dogs were bred from wolves between 27,000 and 40,000 years ago (and thus long before the development of agriculture), somewhere in the Eurasian Steppes,[236] and possibly in Western Europe in a separate event about 4,800 years ago.[237]
- The first cultivation of wheat began somewhere in the Fertile Crescent, or the wider Levant region, especially the Karacadag Mountains of south-east Turkey, on or about 8000 BCE.[238]
- Rice was first cultivated in the Pearl River and Yangtze River regions of southern China, between 8,000 and 13,500 years ago.[239]
- The first domestication of corn (maize) occurred in the Balsas river valley of south-western Mexico, about 8,700 years ago.[240]
- Sugar cane was first farmed in the area of New Guinea about 8000 BC. From there it spread first to India, Philippines, and possibly Indonesia.[241]
- The oldest evidence for the cultivation of squash comes from Oaxaca, Mexico, and dates to about 8,000 years ago.[242]
- The first cattle were bred from aurochs in at least two independent events: one in Turkey, the other in Pakistan,

both about 10,000 years ago.[243]

- Pigs were also domesticated in two separate places, both about 9,000 years ago. One was somewhere in the Near East, the other in China.[244]

- Horses were first captured and put to work somewhere in Kazakhstan, about the year 3500 BCE.[245] The first clear evidence of their use in chariots dates to about 2,000 BCE, in the Eurasian Steppes.[246]

I don't need to describe in this meditation how and why these plants and animals came into the orbit of human management. What I need to do here is evaluate the extent to which managing them is a civilizing force, that is, the extent to which agriculture is a force that not only changes the world, but also changes us.

A first point to observe, is that our Villagers discovered that by chopping up their food, or cooking it, or doing both, they required less energy to chew and consume it. Though this may seem an obvious and even sophomoric point, it is an example of food preparation as a civilizing force. For the reduced energy requirement for chewing corresponds to a reduced evolutionary pressure to sustain large teeth. Scientists have studied this, and found that processed and/or cooked food requires 15 per cent less force to chew; this corresponds to the size of our teeth, 15 per cent smaller than that of *H. erectus*, our nearest hominid ancestor.[247] We've already seen how the increasing importance of empathy led to a change in the general shape of our faces. I do not expect that all civilizing forces affect humanity's essence in its morphology, but I do think it interesting that at least some civilizing forces affect us that way.

A second point to note. Some of these plants and animals require more collaboration among their human managers, and others less so. Rice farming, for example, and especially wet-field rice farming, requires much more collaboration than wheat farming, because rice paddies require extensive irrigation systems that people have to co-operate to build, dredge, and drain. If one family wastes or squanders their water, other families are harmed; so everyone in a given community would have to co-ordinate their collective water use. Rice farming (without modern technology) is also very labor-intensive, so farmers would plant and harvest their fields at different times, and arrange labor-exchanges to help each other out. Wheat, by contrast, requires less community co-ordination, and (usually) does not require irrigation; wheat can be watered by the rain. Wheat also requires about half the labor-hours of wet-field rice farming.[248] So, a wheat-farming family could manage their own fields with less attention to what's happening in their neighbor's wheat fields. (The advantage of rice over wheat, in case you're curious, is that rice produces more food per acre.[249]) As the people worked the land in accord with the different needs of their crops, so their work also affected their own minds in corresponding ways. Wheat farmers may grow more individualist and analytic-thinking, after many generations; rice farmers may grow more communal and holistic-thinking. Some psychologists have speculated that this explains many of the psychological differences between East Asian and Western cultures, as well as the differences between northern and southern China.[250] Northern China mostly farmed wheat; southern China had rice.

The transformation of consciousness that began with the first shelters, the awareness of oneself as a being who can exert power over the world, grows with the planting of the first fields. For unlike the hunter-gatherer, the settled farmer does not simply go to the tree, the field, the hunting ground, and so on, when she knows the time is right. She also decides exactly where the tree and field and hunting ground shall be. This additional degree of agency, however small at first, works upon her mind, and changes her perception of herself at the same time as it changes the shape of fields, streams, and landscapes. I make no claim here about which came first, the agriculture practices or the transformation of consciousness. It seems likely to me that they came about at the same time, each reinforcing the other.

The Villagers also discover that most salient practical advantage of settled agriculture: more food! It is possible for one farmer, or one farming family, to produce much more food than they can find by hunting and gathering; indeed, they can produce more food than they need for themselves. Hunter-gatherers can also produce surpluses, but not as often, nor as predictably, nor as large. Cooked food also keeps longer before it spoils. And when there's a surplus of food, reproduction quickens. The people of our village grow more numerous. This allows them to farm more land, which in turn allows them to have yet more children. Food surpluses also allow for the creation of stockpiles. Most cereal crops like wheat and rice can be dried and kept without spoiling for long periods. Cooked meat can be preserved with salt and with cold-storage cellars, such as in the souterrains found at Neolithic sites like Maeshowe, northern Scotland. It seems to me that the visible presence of a stockpile of foodstuffs would reinforce the transformation of consciousness that correlates with the rise of agriculture. A granary and a souterrain is a visible sign of humanity's agency, and with it humanity's (partial) mastery over the natural world: it's a way of saying, 'We are here.' It is also a sign of life, and a promise of fewer hungry seasons in the future.

The food surplus would likely be particularly interesting to the aggressive and the cunning people of the village, especially if some of them are among those who, precisely because of that surplus, don't have to farm. Remember, although I previously argued that the co-operative people would eventually prevail, I also stipulated that the other kinds of people never entirely disappear. Someone, or some group, whether aggressive or cunning or a mix of both, will see the stockpile as a new platform from which to influence or intimidate their neighbors. For whoever controls access to the granary also decides who eats and who starves. Hunger, or the threat of it, places those who have food in a position to demand services from the hungry. This creates a new kind of civilizing force in the world: *political power.*

Why is this *political* power? Power, in general, I define as the ability to do whatever you want. Philosopher Hannah Arendt observed that power 'in the singular', which she called 'strength', is that which inherently belongs to something individually. But political power, according to Arendt, requires a group of supporters.

> Power corresponds to the human ability not just to act, but to act in concert. Power is never the property of an individual; it belongs to a group and remains in existence only so long as the group keeps together. When we say of somebody that he is 'in power' we actually refer to his being empowered by a certain number of people to act in their name. The moment the group, from which the power originated to begin with (*potestas in populo*, without a people or group there is no power), disappears, 'his power' also vanishes.[251]

So, as the Villagers continue to experiment with agriculture, some group of them put down their hoes and ploughs and picked up clubs and bows. They stand themselves between the granary and everyone else. I assume it would be a group who does this, for a single individual attempting to blockade the granary would be easily overpowered by a number of others. A group can bring strategic advantages greater than the sum of the strengths of each individual member. Discipline is vital here: a disciplined group can more easily resist the retaliation of a much larger and better armed, but less organized, group. A disciplined group will also, to some extent, police itself; its prominent personalities will reward loyalty and punish treason. Let's call the group blockading the granary 'the big men'. At first they might do no more than grant a larger share of the stockpile to people they like, and a smaller share to those they don't like.[252] If this succeeds, then they might demand that others show conspicuous respect, or that others adopt their opinions more readily, in exchange for the larger share. Later, they might demand that people obey more specific orders: 'Clear this field to make way for new crops!', or, 'Build for us a bigger house!' The hungrier people are, or the more they worry about going hungry in the near future, the more obedient they're likely to be. These big men will eventually become the community's 'lords': recall that the word itself comes from the Old English words, *hlaford*, and *hlaf weard*, meaning 'loaf keeper'; that is, the person who keeps the *loaves* of bread.[253]

The power of the big men flows from their cohesion as a group, as mentioned; but it also flows from the obedience of those whom they command. Our Villagers, remember, have every kind of disposition and basic nature, in accord with our stipulation at the beginning of the experiment. So there will be rebels among them. They'll get angry when the inner circle issues orders, and they might decide to disobey. Or, perhaps the some of the big men get a little carried away with their newfound power, and they issue irrational or impossible orders. Perhaps the circle will dole out food from the granary more sparingly, in order to keep people hungry and therefore pliant, thus creating the impression that there is less food to go around for everyone – and thus another illusion enters the Villager's consciousness: *the illusion of scarcity.*

Some Villagers in our experiment decide they don't much like the way the big men run things. Perhaps they also feel that the village had grown too crowded. They might contemplate picking up their sticks and leaving. The standard account of the birth of civilization supposes that once fixed-field agriculture was well established, leaving the village was no longer a possibility. Here's one example of this account, in the work of anthropologist Marvin Harris:

As the population increased, they experimented with irrigation and began to fission off and colonize the drier parts of the region. Sumer, situated in the rainless but swampy and flood-prone deltaic zones of the Tigris-Euphrates, was settled in this manner. Confined at first to the margins of a natural watercourse, the Sumerians soon became totally dependent on irrigation to water their fields of wheat and barley, unknowingly trapping themselves into the final condition for the transition to statedom. As their would-be kings pressed for more taxes and more public labor, Sumer's commoners found that they had lost the option to move out. How could they take the artificial waterways and their irrigated fields, gardens, and orchards, representing the investment of generations of labor, with them? To live away from the rivers, they would have to adopt a pastoral nomadic way of life for which they lacked the prerequisite skills and technology.[254]

But I think this standard account isn't quite right. For one thing, people are clever: they can re-learn what they've forgotten. And there are always people on the geographic fringes of the village and its surrounding farmlands who never forgot how to hunt and fish and forage. Moreover, there is a natural geographic limit to how far from the village the inner circle can project its power. This limit is partially defined by the place where farmable land ends, and swamp or mountain or tundra begins. It's also partially set by how far food can be transported before it goes bad, and how far draft animals can carry it before they themselves need to eat it. These criteria, in turn, are set by factors like the roughness of terrain, and the availability of grazing vegetation along the way. (That's for overland travel, of course; goods can be carried much further by river or by sea.) It's simply impossible, at least until early modern times, for a state ruling party to tax or confiscate foodstuffs for their stockpile any further away from their centre than that limiting distance. Disgruntled Villagers need only move themselves beyond that limit – they quite literally 'head for the hills' – where they might resume a wandering way of life, re-learning how to do it from those who never settled in villages, or where they might start a new village.

There's some interesting historical evidence to suggest that in southeast Asia, that's exactly what happened. Historian James C. Scott argued that the so-called 'uncivilized' people of upland southeast Asia are not the remnants of pre-civilized cultures who were 'left behind' by city-building and state-formation. They are, instead, the descendants of people who made a deliberate political decision to quit their villages when some party of big men assumed power. Here's how Scott describes his thesis:

> [The hill people's] subsistence routines, their social organization, their physical dispersal, and many elements of their culture, far from being the archaic traits of a people left behind, are purposefully crafted both to thwart incorporation into nearby states and to minimize the likelihood that statelike concentrations of power will arise among them. State evasion and state prevention permeate their practices and, often, their ideology as well. They are, in other words, a 'state effect'. They are 'barbarians by design.' They continue to conduct a brisk and mutually advantageous trade with lowland centres while steering clear of being politically captured.[255]

Departing Villagers present the big men with a conundrum. As Arendt observed, a political party's newfound power evaporates the moment its political subjects disappear. If the big men want to preserve their power, they must do something to prevent Villagers from leaving. One option is to send soldiers to stand guard over the Villagers, as well as to hunt down and re-capture any who manage to slip away. But this cannot be a long-term solution. There's not enough food to support one full-time soldier for every farmer. Also, there will always be some number of

Villagers who grow tired of living in fear, no matter how hungry they are. Another party of big men could rise in the village: and the more the first party threatens it, the more the second party fights back, or assists Villagers who want to leave.

Hard power, in the form of violence and the threat of violence, including the threat of starvation, would lead to the same intolerable stalemate between differing factions of aggressive people which we already saw when our Villagers were still Wanderers. That stalemate was resolved as the aggressive people were softened by their ongoing contact with co-operative and compassionate people. Some version of that solution may also emerge here, but I think it won't do by itself anymore: the big men's group cohesion, a necessary foundation of the preservation of their power, mitigates against it. Rather, the big men will have to invent a new form of power, one that works upon people's minds, one that works in concert with the hard power of violence not only to deter people from leaving the village, but also to prevent the appearance of a rival party.

The community already possesses that form of power: *storytelling*. This is the same instrument by which the community overcame its fear of death. The big men will tell stories that can persuade everyone of the rightness and the necessity of their power, and the rightness and necessity of the Villagers' obedience. This move, the deployment of storytelling as party propaganda, increases the importance of storytelling as a civilizing force. It also leads to the next illusion.

§ 26. Crowning the King

The big men must tell a story that aligns the members of their circle with the unconquerable immensities of life and earth and death. The perfect stories for this purpose are stories about the most real of all beings: the gods. For the gods, like death, are blank canvasses upon which any picture can be painted. Their existence can never be proven nor disproven, because the dreams and omens through which they communicate can always be interpreted in multiple ways. So any intention, any history, and any behavioral program, can be attributed to them. The big men will tell a story that persuades the people that the gods themselves confirmed the power of the big men. It might be a story about how the gods are responsible for controlling the fertility of the earth, or controlling the outcome of battles or diseases or other events. The gods need not be omnipotent: it's enough to say that they are impossible to outwit, defeat, or escape; it's especially important to say they can be dangerous when crossed. Then some kind of significant relationship will be asserted, connecting the gods to the community, but especially to the big men. For instance, it might be a story of how the biggest of the big men are the gods' descendants. This story has the effect of *realizing* the big men; that is, making them more 'real', and making their model of the ideal person more real, and thereby making opposition to the policies of the big men akin to opposition to reality itself. To put it another way: since defeating or escaping the gods is impossible, defeating or escaping the influence of their descendants, the big men, will likewise be impossible. The stories will be complicated, and may require professional myth-tellers to memorize and to perform, so as to maximize their glamour and their hypnotic power. They may indeed be based upon actual historical events: for instance, they may take events in the lives of the village's founders and portray them as taking place at the beginning of things, when the world was first made. The stories may also be genuinely beautiful. But most of all, because the purpose here is to preserve the power of the big men, the story will have to say that the special relationship between the gods and the big men extends to no other parties.

The oldest surviving recorded law-code on earth, the Code of Hammurabi, tells exactly that story in its preamble:

When Anu the Sublime, King of the Anunaki, and Bel, the lord of heaven and earth, who decreed the fate of the land, assigned to Marduk, the over-ruling son of Ea, God of right-eousness, dominion over earthly man, and made him great among the Igigi, they called Babylon by his illustrious name, made it great on earth, and founded an everlasting kingdom in it, whose foundations are laid so solidly as those of heaven and earth; then Anu and Bel called by name me, Hammurabi, the exalted prince, who feared God, to bring about the rule of righteousness in the land, to destroy the wicked and the evil-doers; so that the strong should not harm the weak; so that I should rule over the black-headed people like Shamash, and enlighten the land, to further the well-being of mankind.[256]

To choose an example from my own ancestors: Irish mythology describes how the tribe of the gods, the Tuatha de Danann, fought and won two battles with a race of monsters called the Fomhoir. But the gods were eventually displaced by a tribe of mortal heroes called the Milesians However, the gods were not entirely banished, and indeed the two communities continued to trade and intermingle. In Lady Gregory's literary compilation of the old stories, *Gods and Fighting Men* (1904), it's said that certain kinds of people are the descendants of those three races. You can tell them by the qualities of their character, as follows:

It is what the poets of Ireland used to be saying, that every brave man, good at fighting, and every man that could do great deeds and not be making much talk about them, was of the Sons of the Gael [i.e. the Milesians]; and that every skilled man that had music and that did enchantments secretly, was of the Tuatha de Danann. But they put a bad name on the Firbolgs [another race of monsters]…for lies and for big talk and injustice.[257]

In a similar way, an 11th century Irish text called the *Lebor Gabála Éireann* declared that: '...every princely family that is in Ireland, save the Eoganacht, is of the seed of Nuadu Airgetlám (a god of kingship).'[258] And about the Celts of the continent, Julius Caesar wrote in *De Bello Gallico* that: 'The Gauls claim all to be descended from Father Dis (a god of the underworld), declaring that this is the tradition preserved by the Druids.'[259] These lines always made me feel as if my ancestors are in some sense still alive in the world. And this made the world feel more magical, more enchanted. Yet they are also examples of the next major illusion to appear in our growing experimental civilization: the illusion of the superiority of one kind of people and the inferiority of another; that is to say, *the illusion of the higher and lower men*. Remember what we mean by illusion here: it's the presentation of a human social construction as if it is a naturally-revealed reality. There shall, of course, always be differences between people: some will be taller and others shorter, some physically stronger and others weaker, some more intelligent and others more simple. And some social constructions are not presented as anything other than a social construction, and so are not illusions: traffic lights, for example, or institution of marriage. But the illusion of the higher and lower men will seize upon the most arbitrary and random fact about someone, such as the mere accident of his inheritance of political power, and it will cast that feature in a more glamorous light.

A particular variation of the illusion of higher and lower men is *the illusion of the virtuous prince*. In this case, the glamour is cast not only upon a society's nobility, but particularly upon a society's leading individual, its commander-in-chief. This illusion serves the same purpose as its predecessor: to preserve the political and economic powers of whomever happens to already possess those powers. What makes this illusion insidiously interesting is that, unlike some of the illusions previously discussed, the person projecting this illusion need not actually believe it.

Indeed, he may know perfectly well that the truth is the exact opposite of what the illusion portrays. The illusion of the virtuous prince was perhaps best described by Italian political scientist and philosopher Niccolo Machiavelli, who argued that a ruler should promote propaganda about his own character, in order to preserve his position. In a discussion of whether a prince should keep his word, or possess other moral virtues, Machiavelli says:

> A prince, therefore, need not necessarily have all the good qualities I mentioned above, but he should certainly appear to have them... To those seeing and hearing him, he should appear a man of compassion, a man of good faith, a man of integrity, a kind and a religious man. And there is nothing so important as to seem to have this last quality. Men in general judge by their eyes rather than by their hands; because everyone is in a position to watch, few are in a position to come in close touch with you. Everyone sees what you appear to be, few experience what you really are.[260]

To emphasize the importance of keeping up the appearance – not necessarily the reality – of being a good man, Machiavelli says that if a prince 'has these [good] qualities and always behaves accordingly he will find them harmful; if he only appears to have them they will render him service.' (*ibid.* pg. 57) To the question of whether a prince should actually be virtuous, Machiavelli's answer is that the prince should mostly *appear* to be so; he should also know how to be un-virtuous when doing so would be useful to him. 'For the common people are always impressed by appearances and results,' and, 'there are only common people.' (*ibid* pg. 58) Machiavelli's Prince could not be further distant from the benevolent and wise Guardians of Plato's Kallipolis, or Confucius and his Sage Gentleman. For those figures must actually possess humanity, righteousness, wisdom, courage, temperance, and justice; Machiavelli's Prince need only look like he does.

Previously, I argued that the best way to appear to be a good person is to actually be a good person. The myth of the virtuous prince puts that proposition to the test. But I shall say more about that test later. For the present meditation, it's enough to say that these two myths, that of the higher and lower men, and that of the virtuous prince, do not prevent all Villagers from leaving. But they do keep enough of them politically 'captured', fearful of starvation and enthralled by glamour, so that the big men retain their dominance.

§ 27. Building the Wall

The experiment continues. New generations are born; elder generations pass away. The flight of the dissidents to the hills creates a new type of social encounter: not just personal otherness, but also *political* otherness. The Hill People, having escaped the village, become members of a different village, a different clan, a different tribe. They'll fly a different flag; they'll paint their faces or their tents and houses different colors and patterns; they'll tell different stories about their origins. Over the generations that follow, the Hill People will develop their own customs, habits, stories, foodways, and social structures, their own way of being in the world, all following from their own different experiments with life. Given enough time and geographic remove, they'll develop their own language and religion, distinct from that of the Villagers. Our hypothetical community is now not one community, but two, or ten, or fifty thousand; it's as many communities as there are places on earth for people to settle together, and time enough for them grow distinct from other people in their separate settlements. But, for the sake of keeping our experiment simple, let's divide the community into only two camps: the Villagers in the valley, and the Hill People.

Furthermore, the flight of the Hill People and the appearance of political otherness also creates a new way to respond to the immensity of death. Contemporary psychologists have found that strong reminders of mortality tend to make people more conservative and nationalist,[261] and more likely to express racial or religious prejudices.[262] More than 200 scientific studies over the past 25 years confirm this.[263] As a recent and highly visible example, consider the political career of outspoken conservative businessman Donald Trump. During the state primaries, when candidates work to receive the official nomination of a national party, Trump ran a campaign which even the normally sedate conservatism of *The Washington Post* called racist and bigoted.[264] He won the Republican primaries in states where the death rate among middle-aged white people had increased over the previous 15 years.[265] The currently in-fashion explanation for this correlation between mortality salience and racism is that reminders of death prompt people to seek some kind of immortality; and that a vicarious immortality can be found in the survival of one's religious, ethnic, or political community. It seems to me that if that explanation is true, the Hill People in my experiment need not offer the Villagers a military challenge. Simple knowledge of their existence is enough to prompt the envious and fearful feeling that 'we' will not survive because 'they' will some day out-breed us, economically out-produce us, or even come down from the hills and kill us. They don't have to threaten anything; they just have to exist.

This potent combination of political otherness and mortality salience is, I think, the logical foundation of the Ancient Great Wall. It is the right kind of consciousness to lead to the effort to visibly separate 'us' from 'them'. From that basic political distinction can emerge many others: the 'safe' from the 'dangerous', the 'familiar' from the 'different'. As the wall grows more complex, it separates the 'civilized' from the 'primitive', 'pagan', and 'barbarian'. The visible sign of separation could be a physical wall surrounding the village: and here it's worth noting that the oldest walled settlements known to archaeologists have battlements. Jericho's famous wall, for instance, had a circular watch-tower with arrow-slits. The houses at Catal Hüyük, one of the world's first cities, had no doors or windows at ground level; people climbed the walls with ladders and entered through the roof.[266] For whatever reason, they perceived a necessity for armed defense against political 'others', that was greater than their necessity for a door at ground level.

However, as already noted, the wall doesn't have to be made of clay and stone. It can also be made of symbols, rituals, and political enactments. It can involve uttering a religious or political oath of loyalty to a chief or to a god, in the presence of an assembly of people who have made the same oath. For example, precisely that kind of ceremony was required of Saint Paul, to prove his commitment to the Law of Moses. Alas for Paul, in his previous career he was an enforcer for the Roman Empire, and had encouraged people to reject the Law of Moses. Some people in the crowd remembered him from those days; his appearance at the ceremony thereby caused a riot. (Acts 21:17-36)

My thought-experiment is nearly finished.

§ 28. The Illusion that Exalts Us

Our experimental village grows ever larger. More land is cleared for farms. The farms produce more kinds of crops and animals. Permanent materials like stone and brick go into the houses. Specialized buildings appear, such as temples, workshops, warehouses, stables, and tombs – and they too are built with brick and stone. Agricultural surpluses also grow, to the point where the food supply is large enough and predictable enough that some people can take up occupations unrelated to farming. Thus specialist tradespersons appear in the village: clothiers, carpenters, stonemasons, and merchants. Then a managerial class appears, with lawyers, judges, priests. The village may also produce poets, musicians, historians, accountants, engineers, and any number of professionals whose jobs require intellectual competence. The village becomes a town, and the town becomes a small city. So let's call our Villagers *Citizens* now, and the big men *the aristocracy*.

With this transition from village to city comes tough new problems. How shall we feed and house all the people? How to dispose of the waste they all produce? How to ensure that promises are kept and trades are fair? How to handle conflicts of all kinds, from interpersonal quarrels between citizens to political squabbles with other cities? To solve all these problems the people continue to experiment on themselves, trying out new ways of living and decision-making. The aristocracy participates in the experiment; they will want a way to solve them that also doesn't threaten their power.

The aristocracy continues to tell stories about the gods, as always; but now they also need stories about the rightness, or even the divinity, of the social order, and of the aristocracy's place at the top. (I lay aside for now the question of whether class stratification emerged spontaneously, or whether it was deliberately crafted.) We have already seen one such story: the Cosmic *Purusa*, of Hindu mythology. It lays out an elegant, simple, and effective model for a basic civilization in which, to paraphrase the saying, there's a place for everyone and everyone is in his place. Plato also offered a similar story. It's called 'The Myth of the Metals'. Here's how he tells it:

> I'll first try to persuade the rulers and the soldiers and then the rest of the city that the upbringing and the education we gave them, and the experiences that went with them, were a sort of dream, that in fact they themselves, their weapons, and the other craftsmen's tools were at that time really being fashioned and nurtured inside the earth, and that when the work was completed, the earth, who is their mother, delivered all of them up to the world. Therefore, if anyone attacks the

land in which they live, they must plan on its behalf and defend it as their mother and nurse and think of the other citizens as their earthborn brothers.

'All of you in the city are brothers,' we'll say to them in telling our story, 'but the god who made you mixed some gold into those who are adequately equipped to rule, because they are most valuable. He put silver in those who are auxiliaries [soldiers] and iron and bronze in the farmers and other craftsmen.' (*Republic* 414d-415b)

The point of integrating this story into the Kallipolis' education is to secure the people's loyalty, and their satisfaction with their assigned social place. Notice how the story includes a place for a god: the earth, which the story says is everyone's mother. But more importantly: Plato introduces the story as 'one of those useful falsehoods'. (*ibid* 414c) Earlier in his argument Plato said that a lie, used correctly and by experts, could benefit people: 'We have to be concerned about truth as well...falsehood, though of no use to the gods, is useful to people as a form of drug [i.e. medicine], clearly we must allow only doctors to use it, not private citizens.' (*Republic* 389b) In contemporary philosophy and political science, this argument has come to be called *the noble lie*.

Nor is this the only example of the noble lie in the Platonic corpus. In another of his books, the *Phaedo*, which (for added theatricality) takes place on Socrates' death bed, Plato thought it useful to endorse what I've called the illusion of the permanent self. Near the end of the dialogue he tells a story about the four rivers that encircle the earth and which allow the souls of the dead to move between the land of the living and the underworld. Along the way, each soul, 'led by his guardian spirit', arrives at a place of judgment that corresponds to how they conducted their lives, and each are rewarded or punished accordingly. (*Phaedo* 112e-114c) But the story concludes with a surprise twist:

No sensible man would insist that these things are as I have described them, but I think it is fitting for a man to risk the belief – for the risk is a noble one – that this, or something like this, is true about our souls and their dwelling places, since the soul is evidently immortal, and a man should repeat this to himself as if it were an incantation... (*Phaedo* 114d)

Plato, and his teacher Socrates, probably did believe that we human beings possess an immortal soul: there's arguments for this in several of Plato's other books, notably the *Meno*. Yet at the same time, this text treats stories about the afterlife as another of Plato's 'useful falsehoods', which together with the Myth of the Metals preserves the order of the Kallipolis.

The idea of the noble lie, applied by 'doctors' as a kind of 'medicine' for the benefit of the state and its people, is powerfully seductive idea. Politicians throughout history have found that persuasion and deception can be equally, if not more, effective than force, for the preservation and extension of their power. I want to emphasize that the idea of the noble lie is not merely academic. It remains a serious practical option that politicians, industrialists, investors, and members of the ruling class in general, regularly employ to preserve the current state of things in economics, politics, and society. For example:

- By the early 1700s, the food supply in affluent countries already came from the entire globe, much as it does now, thus making it possible for more people than ever before to be entirely unaware of the circumstances of food production. A report by the East India Company in 1701 said, 'We taste the spices of Arabia, yet never feel the scorching sun which brings them forth.'[267] Nor, for that matter, did many affluent European consumers personally feel 'the conquest of continents, the enslavement of nations, nasty warfare among the Eurasian powers that controlled the business, and burgeoning opportunities for pirates' (*ibid*) which made it possible for them to drink tea sweetened with sugar.

- Despite this overwhelming scientific evidence that shows that climate change and global warming are real and are caused by human industry, there remains a widely popular denialist movement, generously financed by oil companies, conservative public research foundations, and various 'dark money' (i.e. untraceable) sources.[268]

- Volkswagen installed emissions-control software on its diesel-powered cars, which enabled the cars to detect when they were undergoing an emissions test. The cars could burn their fuel 'cleaner' during the tests, but burn fuel as usual while driving. This was cheaper than building an engine that burns cleaner all the time. Scientists calculated that between 2009 and 2015, the excess pollution caused by these cars would lead to 59 deaths in the USA.[269] Yet as a testament to the strength of Volkswagen's brand, the company became the world's largest automaker in early 2016. One of its managers told a journalist: 'Thankfully, the bulk of the customers don't give a flying [expletive deleted] about these scandals.'[270]

- In early 2016, a whistleblower leaked to the world's media more than 11 million secret documents from Mossack Fonseca, a Panamanian law firm. The documents revealed that many thousands of rich people around the world used the firm's services to launder 'dirty' money (i.e. the proceeds of crime), to sidestep UN sanctions, and to conceal billions of dollars from their nation's tax collectors. Among the named culprits were twelve current or former heads of nation-states and sixty people linked to them as family or friends.[271] An executive for Mossack Fonseca was quoted in the documents saying: 'Ninety-five per cent of our work coincidentally consists in selling vehicles to avoid taxes.'[272] The revelation led to various consequences, including criminal charges for various tax dodgers, and the resignation of the Prime Minister of Iceland.[273] The scandal has come to be called the Panama Papers affair.

- The Tea Party, a grassroots Conservative political movement in America, was revealed to be not 'grassroots' at all, but funded by Charles and David Koch, two of the wealthiest billionaires in the world. As a Republican party campaign consultant told a journalist, 'The Koch brothers gave the money that founded it. It's like they put the seeds in the ground. Then the rainstorm comes, and the frogs come out of the mud—and they're our candidates!'[274] Concerning one of the think-tanks he founded, Charles Koch said: 'In order to avoid undesirable criticism, how the organization is controlled and directed should not be widely advertised.'[275]

I now see more clarity in my answer to the second of my root questions. I wouldn't be the first to suppose that the problem with civilization is its illusions. Sigmund Freud, in *The Future of an Illusion* (1927) thought that all religion was a fantasy. Karl Marx saw much of what goes on in modern economics as basically unreal. For example, we often assign to consumer products objective properties they do not in fact possess, such as the property of rising or falling in value over time; this he called 'commodity fetishism'. Similarly, he examined the buying and selling of products and services that exist only as numbers on balance sheets and not as materials or labor inputs, such as derivatives and futures; these things he called 'fictitious capital'.

I began to wonder whether this idea was merely academic. So I sent another informal survey to my friends, in which I asked 'What are the illusions that people know to be illusions, but treat as realities anyway?' You can see how my definition of illusion is implied in the question. But I was also curious to see how my informants would interpret the question. Here are some of the answers I received.

- That our rolling around this mortal coil is not, in fact, a lesson on futility.
- That each of us is vitally important... Maybe I meant to say, that mankind is the centre of the universe in significance.
- 'Economics' is the most obvious one. At least one prominent author referred to it as the 'voodoo science'. 'Money' is probably another.
- That the Canadian 'vote' actually counts. 'Camera obscura' a la Marx and all that.
- Whatever the media presents as the 'social structure' or the 'ideal' of social structure.
- Democracy.
- The patriarchy.
- Also the gay agenda.
- That the president actually runs this country.
- That people come to be successful solely on the basis of merit.
- That those who govern us are honest to a fault.
- Organized religion.
- [The idea that] 'We are all one.'
- Pick anything that exists only via social agreement: government, economics, the self.
- The vast invisible network of learned behaviors/courtesies that hold our society together. Through the day hundreds of times we wait at the crosswalk, take our turn in the coffee shop, pay our bills and turn the stereo down at night.
- Control in games of pure chance.
- Control in the world around you, and in your 'fate' or 'destiny'.
- Contracts.

- Traffic lines painted on asphalt.
- Video games.
- Our fears. And I don't mean fears like sharks or snakes or axe murderers. I mean fears like rejection, failure, not being good enough, etc.
- People's perceptions of other people and situations.
- That everything will be OK.
- Horoscopes, the idea of soul mates, the notion that a computer algorithm can find you someone worth dating? Uh, I might be a little down on love right now.

Much like my previous informal survey of the absurdities of civilization, this is certainly not a scientific survey. It says as much about the people who responded, as it does about any general trends. Indeed, some of my informants gave answers probably intended for comic relief, such as, 'Wearing a lucky hat to the World Series,' or, 'What you read on Facebook.' Out of 52 informants, four said 'democracy', three said 'money', three mentioned something to do with behavioral civility, and five mentioned something personal and intimate such as 'hope' and 'love'. Of course it's also possible that my informants didn't consider such things illusions until I posed my question. Such is the intrinsic danger of philosophical surveys. But I think it's reasonable to claim that many people believe that much of their social, cultural, and political world is socially constructed; and that many people believe 'socially constructed' means 'unreal'.

The fact that many people believe something is not, of course, evidence that the belief is true; we must avoid the fallacy of *ad populam* here. But we may nonetheless ask: if things like democracy, money, behavioral civility, and the like, are widely believed to be somehow 'unreal', then why do those things persist? I named this meditation after the famous line in the poem by Aleksandr Pushkin: 'The illusion which exalts us is dearer to us than ten thousand truths.' (*The Hero* ll. 64-65) Do our illusions persist because they somehow exalt us? Or, if they do not exactly 'exalt' us, might they have some other agreeable utility?

§ 29. Two Views of the Noble Lie

In this meditation I'll take a short break from the experiment to meditate on two 20th century philosophers, one from the political left and the other from the political right, and see what they have to say about the usefulness and the consequences of the Noble Lie.

From the political left: consider Brazilian philosopher and education theorist Paolo Freire. His career brought him into regular involvement in the lives of some of the poorest people in the world. In 1946 he became director of the Department of Education in the Brazilian state of Pernambuco, where he pioneered adult literacy projects for the state's poorest communities. After a military coup in 1964 he was charged with treason, imprisoned for 70 days, and then exiled. During his exile he wrote several books; on the strength of one of them, *Pedagogy of the Oppressed* (1968), he was appointed professor at Harvard University, and later, special education advisor to the World Council of Churches, based in Geneva. *Pedagogy of the Oppressed* treats education as a process of humanizing people, and oppression as any act which 'prevents people from being more fully human'.[276] What, then, does Freire mean by being human? In most of the text this question is answered in the negative: being human means not being an object, not being an animal. 'To alienate human beings from their own decision-making,' Freire says, 'is to change them into objects.' (pg. 66) In a section of the text strongly influenced by existentialist philosophers like Sartre and Jaspers, he says human beings are creatures who can meaningfully reflect upon, and meaningfully change, their own natures, as well as the world around them. 'Of all the uncompleted beings, man is the only one to treat not only his actions but his very self as the object of his reflection; this capacity distinguishes him from the animals...' And people, 'unlike animals, not only live but exist'.[277]

The relevance to the concept of the noble lie is this: the noble lie is the most important instrument by which the oppressor, whether a state party or a landlord or a corporate interest, interferes with this process of humanization, by treating people as receptacles for ruling class value programs. Freire uses the term *myth* instead of 'noble lie', but the basic concept is the same. In perhaps the most important part of the text, Freire enumerates these myths, as follows:

It is necessary for the oppressors to approach the people in order, via subjugation, to keep them passive. This approximation, however, does not involve *being with* the people, or require true communication. It is accomplished by the oppressors depositing myths indispensable to the preservation of the status quo: for example, the myth that the oppressive order is a 'free society'; the myth that all persons are free to work where they wish, that if they don't like their boss they can leave him and look for another job; the myth that this order respects human rights and is therefore worthy of esteem; the myth that anyone who is industrious can become an entrepreneur—worse yet, the myth that the street vendor is as much an entrepreneur as the owner of a large factory; the myth of the universal right of education, when of all the Brazilian children who enter primary schools only a tiny fraction ever reach the university; the myth of the equality of all individuals, when the question: 'Do you know who you're talking to?' is still current among us; the myth of the heroism of the oppressor classes as defenders of 'Western Christian civilization' against 'materialist barbarism'; the myth of the charity and generosity of the elites, when what they really do as a class is to foster selective 'good deeds' (subsequently elaborated into the myth of 'disinterested aid,' which on the international level was severely criticized by Pope John XXIII); the myth that the dominant elites, 'recognizing their duties,' promote the advancement of the people, so that the people, in a gesture of gratitude, should accept the words of the elites and be conformed to them; the myth that rebellion is a sin against God; the myth of private property as fundamental to personal human development (so long as oppressors are the only true human beings); the myth of the industriousness of the oppressors and the laziness and dishonesty of the oppressed, as well as the myth of the natural inferiority of the latter and the superiority of the former.[278]

You may recognize, in the last lines of this quoted text, a version of what I've called the illusion of the higher and lower men. To those who might argue that some of these myths are not myths but realities, Freire would likely reply that the speaker is resisting the discovery that he is oppressed, or resisting the discovery that he is an oppressor. Freire described a few examples of that resistance in his own experience and that of his colleagues, as they experimented with new methods of pedagogy. 'Beyond a doubt,' Freire explained, the people in his examples, 'were retreating from a reality so offensive to them that even to acknowledge that reality was threatening. For an alienated person, conditioned by a culture of achievement and personal success, to recognize his situation as objectively unfavorable seems to hinder his own possibilities for success.'[279] What stands out to me is Freire's view that the spreading of myth dehumanizes not only the oppressed, *but also the people doing the oppressing*: for it makes them unable to see the world in any other way than as 'an object of domination'. It also makes them unable to value their own lives except in terms of their possessions and the ranges of their dominions; and that, following Freire's logic, turns them into objects as well.

For them [the oppressors], *to be* is *to have* and to be the class of the 'haves'... The oppressors do not perceive their monopoly on *having more* as a privilege which dehumanizes others and themselves. They cannot see that, in the egoistic pursuit of *having* as a possessing class, they suffocate in their own possessions and no longer *are*; they merely *have*.[280]

A summary comment: Freire would argue that the noble lie fails because it preserves the stability of society at the cost of dehumanizing everyone, oppressor and oppressed.

Such is one view of the noble lie from the political left. Let us now consider a view from the political right: that of the 20th century German-American philosopher Leo Strauss. I choose him as a representative of the conservative view because he is now widely believed to have influenced senior advisors to US President George W. Bush to adopt the noble lie as an official government policy. The connections between Strauss' thought and Bush's foreign policy were mainly built by Strauss' critics. For example, Stephen Holmes, a law professor at New York University, said: 'They [the Straussians] believe that your enemy is deceiving you, and you have to pretend to agree, but secretly you follow your own views... The whole story is complicated by Strauss's idea—actually Plato's—that philosophers need to tell noble lies not only to the people at large but also to powerful politicians.'[281] Another critic, columnist William Pfaff, wrote: 'Strauss believed that the essential truths about human society and history should be held by an elite, and withheld from others who lack the fortitude to deal with truth. Society, Strauss thought, needs consoling lies.'[282] What is the evidence that Strauss himself actually held this view? No direct evidence for this view appears in his best-known work, *Natural Right and History* (1950). There is, however, an near-hit, in a discussion of the differences between political theorists (like himself) and politicians. First, Strauss says a political theorist can in some sense do more than an activist (Strauss uses the word 'active man') because the theorist is concerned with 'excellence regardless of when and where it is found' whereas an activist is concerned with 'whatever is nearest and dearest to him, however deficient in excellence it may be.'[283] If an activist engages too deeply with theory, he risks 'revealing the limitations of any practical pursuit,' and this makes him 'liable to endanger full devotion to practice.' (*ibid*.) Next Strauss quotes Edmund Burke, the 18th century Irish statesman and inventor of modern conservatism, saying 'political problems do not primarily concern truth or falsehood. They relate to good or evil'; Strauss explains this quote by saying:

> It may easily happen that what is metaphysically true is politically false. 'Established opinions,' 'allowed opinions which contribute so much to the public tranquility' must not be shaken, although they are not 'infallible'... Whereas theory rejects error, prejudice, or superstition, the statesman puts these to use.[284]

The consequences of shaking the 'established opinions', which 'contribute to the public tranquility' may, in this view of things, be very dire:

> 'Speculative inquiries' necessarily bring to light the imperfect character of the established order. If these inquiries are introduced into political discussion, which, of necessity, lacks 'the coolness of philosophic inquiry', they are liable 'to raise discontent in the people' in regard to the established order, discontent which may make rational reform impossible. The most legitimate theoretical problems become, in the political arena, 'vexatious questions' and cause 'a spirit of litigation' and 'fanaticism'.[285]

Since the argument appears in a discussion of Burke, it's possible that Strauss is merely interpreting Burke rather than expressing his own ideas. Nevertheless, by citing Burke so favorably here (and in a previous chapter, citing Rousseau with barely-concealed scorn), Strauss evidently endorses the idea that politicians must appear to be men of iron-clad conviction, regardless of their actual views. He endorses the idea that if politicians have doubts about the truth or the rightness of their plans then they must keep those doubts strictly private, or they must leave them 'to the schools, for only there they may be discussed with safety'. (*ibid*; quoting Burke again.) This is not precisely the same as the view Strauss is often accused of holding; and it is not especially close to Plato's view, which Strauss is often accused of reviving. It is, however, curiously close to Machiavelli's view that the prince must project a certain image of himself as strong and virtuous, and that he knows how to lie when necessary. The noble lie that Strauss affirms, if he affirms one at all, is the myth of the virtuous prince.

Deception in politics is problematic enough; but there's more. The Straussian-Burkean-Machiavellian politician, who knows how to lie about his character and his commitments, will wonder if his competitors and opponents also know how to lie. The informed reader will recognize this as a 'prisoner's dilemma' type scenario. This is not a merely speculative proposition: the careers of some of Strauss' students provide the case study. The connection between Strauss' ideas and American public policy was documented by Abram Shulsky, who wrote his doctorate under Strauss in 1972, and later became director of the Pentagon Office of Special Plans during the presidency of George W. Bush.[286] In an essay called 'Leo Strauss and the World of Intelligence (By Which We Do Not Mean *Nous*)', Shulsky says nothing more sinister than that Strauss believed texts like Plato's were written esoterically, that is, with hidden meanings; that the actions of foreign governments could also conceal hidden meanings; that social-science-as-usual was unable to grasp that 'deception is the norm in political life'; and finally that 'the study of the classics of political philosophy with Leo Strauss was a surprisingly good preparation' for a career in foreign policy analysis.[287] Strauss believed that any good writer, when threatened with persecution, would necessarily write in such a way that only a thoughtful few would understand him properly.[288] He regarded Plato as just such an esoteric writer, and that Plato's concept of the useful lie was the clue to his actual thoughts; Plato might have written in this careful way because he had just seen his mentor and friend, Socrates, executed by the state for practicing philosophy. (By the way, I reject the claim that Strauss himself was writing esoterically, for instance by putting his own ideas into Burke's mouth: for to follow his own logic, only persecuted writers do that, and he was not at the time persecuted.) However, from the claim that persecuted writers write esoterically, I think it is a very long stretch to draw the conclusion that therefore Strauss advised politicians to lie to the public. The Straussians (possibly but not necessarily including Strauss himself) regarded truth in the realm of politics as a inhabiting a dark and shifty corner where, one must assume as an axiom of logic, it's always possible that things are not what they appear to be. Here's Shulsky again, in a book called *Silent Warfare* (2002), describing that darkened corner:

If an intelligence service ignores its adversaries, however, it runs the risk of being deceived and of misinterpreting the world it is trying to understand. In intelligence matters, analysts can rarely be completely confident of the solidity of the foundations on which they are building; they must remain open to the possibility that their evidence is misleading. Intelligence is thus caught in a dilemma that reflects its dual nature. Intelligence seeks to learn all it can about the world, and its goal may be characterized by the biblical verse that Allen Dulles, President Eisenhower's director of central intelligence, adopted as the CIA's motto: 'And ye shall know the truth and the truth shall make you free.' But intelligence can never forget that the attainment of the truth involves a struggle with a human enemy who is fighting back – or that truth is not the goal, but only a means toward victory.[289]

I suppose that if you were an intelligence analyst playing a game of chicken with nuclear weapons, then this epistemology of warfare (as implied by the book's title) might seem sensible. For if you predicted that your country would be destroyed on a certain day, and then the day arrived and nothing happened, you'd feel a bit stupid but you would be alive. If, on the other hand, you predicted the country would be safe, and then the country was attacked, you'd feel nothing at all – you would be dead. When the truth is not measured by facts or evidence, but instead by whether interpretations of facts and evidence move you 'toward victory', then it might appear strategically correct to interpret every movement of your enemy as a potential threat, and to encourage everyone around you to see things the same way. What we have here is a illusion not yet seen in these medita-tions, and a kind of mirror image of the myth of the virtuous prince: that is, *the illusion of the devious enemy*. Following my understanding of illusion, as a work of human artifice presented as a revealed reality: the myth of the devious enemy seizes upon ambiguous or unimportant evidence and paints upon it a picture of what one already fears. In reality, it may be that the enemy is disguising weakness instead of strength; or that the enemy is in fact not an enemy at all, but rather someone who merely wants to be left alone. The interpretation of the enemy as deviously deceptive and immanently threatening might have seemed 'noble' to the Straussians, or if not fully noble than at least strate-gically correct, because, according to the logic of the illusion, it is better to be wrong about one's enemy than to be killed by him.

But the logic of this illusion is a road to paranoia. I'm not just making this up: an analyst in the CIA described the Straussians in precisely those terms: 'They see themselves as outsiders... There's a high degree of paranoia. They've convinced themselves that they're on the side of angels, and everybody else in the government is a fool.'[290] The idea of the noble lie fails from this right wing point of view because it never produces the consequences that it aims for. For the supporters of the lie, it produces never-ending fear; and for everyone else, it produces political, diplomatic, and military consequences such as those we saw during the presidency of George W. Bush. I write these words some fifteen years later, while the whole world is still reeling from those consequences. I'm sure I don't need to enumerate them.

I began this meditation wondering if there are any illusions that exalt us. I now think the conclusion that best fits the evidence is that our illusions never exalt anyone – not even the people who promote them. Perhaps some illusions – the model wife or husband, the beauty queen, even *Homo economicus* – temporarily exalt the few. But I think that eventually they all do more harm than good.

So I have to ask again: why do they persist?

§ 30. Rationality and Despair

There is at least one tendency in human nature whose aim is to dispel illusions: *rationality*. We've already seen philosophers who regarded reason as the essence of civilization. For my thesis, reason is but one natural disposition among many, although still a special one, because of its initiating and sustaining role in many of the civilizing forces favored by the checklist-makers: long distance trade, complex social values, writing, and the like. So I want to meditate on the nature of reasoning now, and find out what, if anything, might make rationality more prominent in the lives of the citizens in our experimental city, and what else might follow from its prominence.

I define reason as organized curiosity. Its checklist of require-ments can be quite long: self-awareness, autonomy, simplicity, patience, open-mindedness, struggle, courage, skepticism, honesty, precision.[291] Systematic critical reason – organized curiosity – is the most visibly successful approach to knowledge ever invented by anyone, anywhere. Part of the reason for this (get it? The *reason* for this!) is because of the way that it identifies all that is foolish, faulty, ambiguous, contradictory, without evidence, or without coherence, in all that we think and believe. Then it helps us to gently lay those faulty ideas away, leaving us fresh and ready to seek better alternatives. It seems to follow that reason is a force that would work against the creation of illusions.

The people in our experiment have been reasoning one way or another all along; their way of discovering the best solution to their problems was a quasi-scientific method of trial-and-error. Each new generation learns from the discoveries of its prede-cessors, although they also invent their own new responses. They may also revisit older, known-to-be-unsuccessful responses, if for no other reason than to rediscover for themselves that they still don't work. Those who have the most curious minds, and few moments of peace and quiet, become the city's philosophers and other intelligentsia, part time if not full time. And if they are also charismatic and eloquent, they might join the ranks of Toynbee's 'pioneers' or Kroeger and Clark's 'men of genius'. The actual history of early Western philosophy loosely reflects that pattern. The first philosophers in the Western tradition, or at any rate the first for whom we have a reliable written record, addressed themselves to metaphysics problems, especially the problem of change and impermanence. They wondered what substance, what force, or what way of thinking, could render our changing world intelligible. They came up with a rather dazzling variety of answers.

- Thales (c.600 BCE), the earliest (recorded) philosopher in the Western tradition, said that everything is water, presumably because water (or fluids generally) can be found in almost everything.

- Anaximander (c.611-547 BCE) said that everything is made of an indefinable substance which he called *to apeiron*, 'the boundless', or 'the unlimited'.
- Anaximenes (c.550 BCE) said that everything is *aer*, 'mist'; an infinite substance that condenses in places to create solid matter, and thins out in other places to create air.
- Empedocles (c.490-435 BCE) gave us the now-famous theory of the four elements: earth, air, fire, and water.
- Leucippus (c.440) and Democritus (c.460) together produced the first theory of atoms: the idea that the world is made of tiny indivisible particles. Their different shapes and combinations produce the variety of materials and changes that we can see in the world.

Let's suppose our experimental city has its own Thales, its own Pythagoras, its own Socrates. Eventually they find, as did the philosophers of our world's real history, that no matter what way they approach and respond to the immensities, there is always another way. They find that however much they interpret or discuss or explain things, there is always more to say. In whatever way they fight against the immensities, or worship them, or bargain with them, or avoid them, or love them, or hate them, or in any manner face and receive them, *there are always alternatives*. The more cosmopolitan their city grows, the more likely it is that they'll reach this conclusion: exposure to differing world views makes certain questions possible that wouldn't likely have arisen otherwise. I acknowledge Kroeger and Clark's observation that advances in civilization tend to occur during periods of internationalism. For this reason, perhaps, Herodotus, the 'father of history', wrote about a kind of cultural relativism. 'Everyone without exception believes his own native customs, and the religion he was brought up in, to be the best', and so culture is 'king of all'.[292]

Among early Greek philosophers, Heraclitus of Ephesus (born circa 500 BCE) came closest to describing that last point. His theory is that everything in the world is always in motion, and so it is not possible to 'know' it in any complete sense. 'You will not find out the limits of the soul by going, even if you travel over every way, so deep is its report.' (Fragment 35)[293] And: 'What awaits men at death they do not expect or even imagine.' (Fragment 84) The most one can do is grasp some understanding of the process by which things move. Heraclitus does this by comparing the world to a fire: 'The ordering [of the world], the same for all, no god nor man has made, but it ever was and is and will be: fire ever-living, kindled in measures and in measures going out.' (Fragment 37) As we have already seen, he also compares the world to a river: 'One cannot step twice into the same river, nor can one grasp any mortal substance in a stable condition, but it scatters and again gathers; it forms and dissolves... it rests by changing.' (51-2) The transformations of nature are guided by an universal rationality, called the *logos*: 'It is wise, listening not to me but to the report [*logos*], to agree that all things are one.' (36) But we shall never know all that there is to know about this *logos*, because 'nature loves to hide'. (10) No matter how long or how deeply we look for the *logos* of things, we never find all that there is to find.

Parmenides of Elea (c.500 BCE) gives us the opposite view. His work didn't involve postulating a new substance for the universe: rather, he clarified the rules of logic by which that substance, if there is one, could be discussed. First he stipulated that there is no such thing as nothingness: things either exist or they don't, and there's no middle ground. 'That which is there to be spoken and thought of must be. For it is possible for it to be, but not possible for nothing to be.' Since this is so, according to him, it follows that nothing comes to be and nothing passes away. 'For in no way may this prevail, that things that are not, are. But you, bar your thought from this way of inquiry, and do not let habit born from much experience compel you along this way.'[294] As you can see, Parmenides explains the fire of Heraclitus saying it's all an illusion borne of our deceptive senses. But Parmenides was wrong. It's not that our senses can't be mistaken, for obviously they can. His mistake was in failing to grasp the full implication of his own premises. Parmenides contends that the substance of nature, whatever it is, must be '...all continuous, for *what is* draws near to *what is*. But unchanging in the limits of great bonds, it is without start or finish, since *coming to be* and *destruction* were banished far away and true conviction drove them off.'[295] Now, the substance of the universe might be without start or finish, but not so we mere mortals; we are born and we die, and the universe both predates and postdates every person's little time on earth. It follows that no one person can ever understand all of it, all at once, by herself. And we are back with Heraclitus again.

To return to point: The incompleteness of any given explanation of the world, the way those explanations always leave more to say, ensures that the work of reason can never be complete. Indeed, reason can consider the possibility that no way of responding to the immensities is any better than another, or even that none of our choices have any meaning at all. This discovery can lead to a kind of looming despair. And insofar as rationality is a central force in the process of civilization, then we could wonder if the whole process of civilization must eventually end in despair.

You're laughing at me right now, aren't you?

Before you quote Camus at me – 'The struggle itself towards the heights is enough to fill a man's heart' – or that quotation's current-day, pop-culture equivalent: 'It's not the destination that counts, it's the journey' – think again. If your first response to this conclusion is to immediately recite a ready-to-hand, deep sounding, and emotionally gratifying pop-culture quotation, which appears to solve the problem in only one pithy sentence, it's almost certain that what you're really doing is protecting your illusions.

One of rationality's jobs, as mentioned, is to mark off the beliefs that are illusions and so dispel them. Yet the really insidious part here is that reason does not have to *prove* that certain beliefs are illusions. All it has to do is sow the seeds of reasonable doubt. Let's look at the example of religion. Maybe there is a God, or two, at work in the world – I won't say there is or there isn't, because I don't know that. But the mere *suggestion* or *possibility* that God is an illusion can prompt in the devout person a deflection technique, such as satire and dismissal, or personal offense, or reactionary defiance – all to avoid the *invalidation of his world view,* and especially to avoid the *despair* that can arise if those unwelcome statements turned out to be indubitably true.

Sigmund Freud made a similar point. 'What is characteristic of illusions,' he wrote in *The Future of an Illusion*, 'is that they are derived from human wishes.'[296] In particular, they are derived from the wish to 'remedy' the 'perplexity and helplessness of the human race.' (*ibid,* pg. 18) Freud regarded all religion as an illusion based on precisely that wish. But religions persist, partly because evidence in their favor is always ambiguous, and not amenable to reason: 'Just as they cannot be proved, so they cannot be refuted.' (ibid pg. 31) Mostly, however, religions persist because they allegedly protect us from chaos:

> If men are taught that there is no almighty and all-just God, no divine world-order and no future, they will feel exempt from all obligation to obey the precepts of civilization. Everyone will, without inhibition or fear, follow his asocial, egoistic instincts and seek to exercise his power; Chaos, which we have banished through many thousands of years of the work of civilization, will come again. (ibid pg. 34)

Against this position, Romain Rolland, the Nobel Prize winner for literature and one of Freud's best friends, countered that religion is not based on fear, nor even upon doctrine, but rather on a feeling: 'a sensation of 'eternity', a feeling as of something limitless, unbounded – as it were, 'oceanic'. This feeling...brings with it no assurance of personal immortality, but it is the source of the religious energy which is seized upon by the various Churches and religious systems.' Rolland added that it is possible to 'rightly call oneself religious on the ground of this oceanic feeling alone, even if one rejects every belief and every illusion.'[297] I myself have encountered this oceanic feeling, although very rarely, and not for many years now. I think it's fair to say that it is not the oceanic feeling that is the illusion, but the doctrines and ritual practices and obligations that religious systems pile on top of it. And those are illusions which, should they ever be dispelled, can lead to despair.

But religion is a 'soft target'. It's all too easy to say there's no evidence for it; all too easy to dismiss the oceanic feeling Rolland spoke of, which even Freud admitted some people do experience. A much harder target is economics, because economics clothes and houses and feeds us, and we're less willing to criticize the hand that feeds. So that is where I shall turn next.

§ 31. The Illusion of No Alternative

I have characterized reason as a force that dispels illusions and seeks realities. Yet there is at least one illusion that is peculiar to reason: *the illusion of no alternative*. This final illusion, it seems to me, emerges not so much from reason itself, but from the way that other civilizing forces colonize or hijack the power of reason for their own purposes. For rationality, having the power to dispel illusions, must appear as a threat to the illusions of the other civilizing forces. Rationality, then, must come under their spell, so as to prevent the dispelling. The other civilizing forces offer to the rational seeker a place where her intellectual seeking may find discovery, a place where she may feel as if she has grasped an absolute and final truth, and a place where the seeker may avoid despair. The function of the proclamation of No Alternative, then, is to suppress rationality's power to keep the seeker seeking. To which it may be asked: 'What should we do if the application of No Alternative leads to evident suffering and injustice?' The answer, of course, is to continue applying the No Alternative with greater discipline – such is the internal logic of the illusion. Indeed, the proclamation of No Alternative may come together with a statement about how some amount of suffering and misery is *necessary* and *good*. Evidence that the No Alternative produces perfectly avoidable depravations and oppressions will thereby be re-interpreted as evidence that the No Alternative must be applied all the more rigorously.

Examples of the assertion of No Alternative are easy to find. It's in politics, for instance in Margaret Thatcher's statement that '...there is no such thing as society. There are individual men and women, and there are families.'[298] The illusion can also appear in the form of a confounding of human social affectations with natural physical laws, so as to improve their apparent reality and impressiveness. For instance: David Ricardo, a banker and probably the most important classical economist of the 19th century, declared that the failure of Britain's 'poor laws' was as inescapable as gravity: 'The principle of gravitation is not more certain than the tendency of such laws to change wealth and vigour into misery and weakness.'[299] Similarly, Ferdinand Lasalle wrote of 'the iron and cruel law' by which workers' wages tend to fall to the point minimally necessary to sustain the worker's life.[300] This confounding of physical science with politics and economics is only the modernist version of the ancient myth of the virtuous prince, who connected his family dynasty with the gods, and so made himself more real, and made his rule appear unassailable.

The proclamation of No Alternative is frequently accompanied by an argument about the necessity of suffering and sacrifice. Here's one of the very earliest examples of this kind of thinking in classical economics: it appears in *Social Statics* by Herbert Spencer (first published 1851), in a rant against Britain's poor laws:

> To become fit for the social state, man had not only to lose his savageness but he had to acquire the capacities needful for civilized life. Power of application must be developed; such modification of the intellect as shall qualify it for its new tasks must take place; and, above all, *there must be gained the ability to sacrifice a small immediate gratification for a future great one.* The state of transition will of course be an unhappy state. Misery inevitably results from incongruity between constitution and conditions. Humanity is being pressed against the inexorable necessities of its new position – is being molded into harmony with them, and has to bear the resulting happiness as best it can. The process must be undergone and *the sufferings must be endured...* Intensified they may be, and are; and in preventing their intensification the philanthropic will find ample scope for exertion. But *there is bound up with the change a normal amount of suffering,* which cannot be lessened without altering the *very laws of life.* Every attempt at mitigation of this eventuates in exacerbation of it. All that a poor-law or any kindred institution can do, is to partially suspend the transition – to take off for a time, from certain members of society; the painful pressure which is effecting their transformation. At best this is merely to postpone *what must ultimately be borne.*[301]

The transition that Spencer is discussing here, for which he says suffering must be endured, is the transition to civilization itself. In the paragraphs that immediately preceded the above-quoted text, Spencer builds an insidious argument-by-analogy, in which he says that since the improvement of animal species comes about through the destruction of the species' weaker members, so it should be the same for human beings:

> Pervading all nature we may see at work a stern discipline, which is a little cruel that it may be very kind...it is much better that the ruminant animal, when deprived by age of the vigour which made its existence a pleasure, should be killed by some beast of prey, than that it should linger out a life made painful by infirmities, and eventually die of starvation. By the destruction of all such, not only is existence ended before it becomes burdensome, but room is made for a younger generation capable of the fullest enjoyment... The development of the higher creation is a progress toward a form of being capable of a happiness undiminished by these drawbacks. It is in the human race that the consummation is to be accomplished. Civilization is the last stage of its accomplishment. And the ideal man is the man in whom all the conditions of that accomplishment are fulfilled. Meanwhile the well-being of existing humanity, and the unfolding of it into this ultimate perfection, are both secured by that same beneficent, through severe discipline, to which the animate creation at large is subject: a discipline which is pitiless in the working out of good...[302]

Adam Smith, the 'father of capitalism', built a similar analogy almost half a century earlier; and he too connected it with the civilizing forces.[303] But where Smith ignores the ethical implications of his quasi-scientific observation, Spencer says that non-interference in the workings of 'nature' is a non-negotiable moral imperative upon which progress towards civilization depends – even when 'nature' leads to the destruction-by-neglect of the children of the poor. Indeed Spencer described 'state-almsgiving' as 'being kind by proxy',[304] and likely to stifle people's natural benevolence, the faculty upon which he says civilization depends, by making people think the poor laws did the work of sympathy on their behalf:

> For what faculty is it whose work a poor-law so officiously undertakes? Sympathy... The faculty of whose growth civilization is a history – on whose increased strength the future amelioration of man's state mainly depend – and by whose ultimate supremacy, human morality, freedom, and happiness will be secured. Of this faculty poor-laws partially supply the place. By doing which they diminish the demands made upon it, limit its exercise, check its development, and therefore retard the process of adaptation.[305]

As you can see, the logic of No Alternative, with its connected demand for a discipline of suffering, invoked the august name of Civilization among its very first appearances in modern economics. Spencer's motto of 'There Is No Alternative' to economic conservatism is repeated to this day.[306] It was a favorite saying of Margaret Thatcher, as is well known. More recently, German finance minister Wolfgang Schaeuble told Greek president Alexis Tsipras (while Tsipras was still opposition leader) 'there is no alternative to the path already taken, the implementation of an economic adjustment programme' if Greece wants to stay in the Eurozone.[307] In an essay boldly entitled *No Alternative to Austerity*, a columnist in London's *Financial Times* wrote that Francois Hollande, President of France, was 'virtually ignoring the structural reforms that are the only route to sustainable growth.'[308] Notice, by the way, the weasel-words 'reforms' and 'adjustment'. Here they do not stand for just any old kind of economic change. They stand specifically for *fiscal austerity*, that is, the cutting of national budgets and the privatization of state assets, in the hope that national debts would be repaid, and businesses would be stimulated to spend on job-creation the money they would have spent on taxes. But the mirage of a coming prosperity, to which there is no other path but through fiscal austerity, has already been vanished. In May of 2016 The International Monetary Fund published an essay that admitted austerity programs do more harm than good. They make inequality worse, and they stifle economic growth.[309] Economist Friedrich Hayek did the most to articulate the moral danger of allowing 'unitary ends' to direct 'the whole of society and all its resources'; any such effort, he says, is likely to be 'totalitarian in the true sense of this new word'.[310] On this particular point Hayek and I completely agree. What Hayek did not see, perhaps because he was so single-mindedly focused on the totalitarianism of Nazism and of Soviet communism, is that his preferred alternative world view, Neoliberalism, whose values are embodied by the model of *Homo economicus*, would eventually become equally totalitarian, according to his own criterion.

A second look at the Straussians may be helpful here. Researcher John G. Mason wrote of them that:

> For the Straussians modernity since Machiavelli has been a straight path to nihilism where all understanding of political virtue has been lost along with respect for a social hierarchy rooted in aristocratic values. To rediscover Virtue's true meaning, they argue we must return to the classical schoolroom and the pagan philosophers where moral teaching began – but this is a path is only open to a select few. For the rest of us, a return to organized religion, what Strauss called a 'pious fraud,' along with uplifting patriotic fables, are our only hope of avoiding the fall into total anomie.[311]

Strauss himself wrote nothing about foreign policy as such, and nothing about military intelligence analytics. There were, however, some few occasions when he wrote or lectured about normative political positions. One such occasion was in 1941, shortly after he had left Nazi Germany; he gave a lecture in which he attempted to explain the dangers of Nazism to an American audience. It's an interesting speech, not only as it is presents the views of an eyewitness to the rise of the NSDAP, but also as it invokes the concept of civilization as a cornerstone of the argument. I have already (but briefly) meditated upon his definition of civilization: it is 'the process of making man a citizen, and not a slave'; here is how he elaborates upon this point: 'By civilisation, we understand the conscious culture of humanity, i.e. of that which makes a human being a human being, i.e. the conscious culture of reason,' especially the two 'pillars' of scientific and moral reason.[312] The antithesis of this process, according to Strauss, is nihilism, which he defines as 'the rejection of the principles of civilization as such', and as: 'The desire to destroy the present world and its potentialities, a desire not accompanied by any clear conception of what one wants to put in its place.' (*ibid*. pg. 364, 359) Strauss said the Nazis were not purely nihilistic in that sense, but they were very close to it: they rejected the principles of rational civilization, but they *did* know what they wanted to put in its place: militarism and military virtues.

The admiration of the warrior as a type, the unconditional preference given to the warrior as warrior, is however not only *genuine* in German nihilism: it is even its distinctive feature... War is a destructive business. And if war is considered more noble than peace, if war, and not peace, is considered *the* aim, the aim is for all practical purposes nothing other than destruction. There is reason for believing that the business of destroying, and killing, and torturing, is a source of almost disinterested pleasure to the Nazis as such, that they derive a genuine pleasure from the aspect of the strong and ruthless who subjugate, exploit, and torture the weak and helpless.[313]

At least in 1941, then, Strauss believed that the greatest danger to rationality and civilization is nihilism, especially the 'German' militaristic nihilism, which glamorized warfare and destruction for its own sake. Nine years later, with the publication of his book *Natural Right and History* (1951), he still thought that nihilism was dangerous: but he identified a new source of it: liberalism. Modern liberal and enlightenment values, according to Strauss, allowed people to reject the idea that there is such a thing as an intrinsic morality, which he calls 'natural right'. In the absence of intrinsic morality, we embrace instead a kind of cultural relativism, which Strauss believes is the same thing as nihilism:

> The contemporary rejection of natural right leads to nihilism – nay, it is identical with nihilism. In spite of this, generous liberals view the abandonment of natural right not only with placidity but with relief. They appear to believe that our inability to acquire any genuine knowledge of what is intrinsically good or right compels us to be tolerant of every opinion about good or right or to recognize all preferences or all 'civilizations' as equally respectable. Only unlimited tolerance is in accordance with reason. But this leads to the admission of a rational or natural right of every preference that is tolerant of other preferences, or negatively expressed, of a rational or natural right to reject or condemn all intolerant or all 'absolutist' positions.[314]

Notice his invocation of civilization again. And notice this time civilization is not the cultivator of reason, but now it's that which is threatened by reason:

> In order to live, we have to silence the easily silenced voice of reason, which tells us that our [moral] principles are in themselves as good or as bad as any other principles. The more we cultivate reason, the more we cultivate nihilism: the

less we are able to be loyal members of society. The inescapable practical consequence of nihilism is fanatical obscurantism.[315]

Against the danger of fanatical obscurantism, the Illusion of No Alternative presents itself as the necessary policy. But I suspect Strauss did not foresee the depths of anti-intellectualism that politicians and political campaigners would endorse in the service of avoiding nihilism and securing loyalty. He likely did not foresee how 'truthiness' and 'post-truths' would take the place of facts and evidence in public debates,[316] or how government scientists would be intrusively supervised by media-relations 'minders' when they spoke to the public, to prevent government policies from coming under reasonable doubt.[317] I dare say the proclamation of No Alternative is almost always either a failure of imagination, an advertising or lobbying slogan, or a lie. And I further dare say that the more deeply this illusion is entrenched in people's minds, the more likely it becomes that people will protect it with violence. Evidence of this is already appearing, for instance, at the time of writing, at rallies for candidates in the 2016 American presidential election, instigated by supporters of both major parties.[318]

The thought-experiment is now complete. From it emerged a theory about what's wrong with civilization. The civilizing forces, as they shape our basic natures, also craft illusions to insulate us from nihilism and despair: but at the cost of the preservation of human suffering. Here in these meditations I have described several such illusions: the permanent self, the higher and lower men, the virtuous prince, the devious enemy. There may, of course, be more than these. For example, from the facts of human vulnerability we could discuss *the illusion of the self-made man*. Or, from the dynamism and the immensity of the earth and all its ecological processes, we could discuss *the illusion of humanity's dominance over the earth*. But I'd like to note one more thing that all these illusions have in common: they always eventually break. Reality always eventually reasserts itself. Civilizations tend to fall when their illusions can no longer hold back the facts of reality. Societies can rebuild following invasions, plagues, earthquakes and other natural disasters, even climate change; it is enormously more difficult to survive the loss of mythology. For when the illusions break down, our physical infrastructure and our social and economic practices tend to break down with them. Trade routes disappear. Currencies become worthless; prices suffer runaway inflation. Contracts and other forms of promise-keeping become unreliable. Punishments for the smallest crimes grow to excessive proportions, while those who commit the best and worst crimes remain free. Grasses and trees reclaim urban landscapes. Roads and bridges and cities decay. Monuments fall to ruin. The people themselves move on. They might eventually invent new illusions; but that is effectively the same as becoming a new society.

Following the shattering of the illusions, the revealed realities, by themselves, offer very little with which to fill the emptiness left behind by the shattering. For there is never only one way to interpret them and respond to them. There are always alternatives. Some alternatives may be better than others, of course; but there might be none among them that are absolutely certain. In the absence of the certainty provided by the now-shattered illusions, all that remains is the never-ending seeking. Rationality is the skill by which we undertake the seeking; it is also the skill by which we discover that the seeking shall never end. The endlessness of the seeking can make it appear as if there are no absolute certainties, no final truths; and that can lead some to despair. And all of this is part of the essence of civilization. And so I say again: the logical end of the process of civilization is a dance on the edge of despair.

It remains to answer one final part of my second root question: whether the problem of civilization is a matter of accident or a matter of essence. The conclusion I think follows best from the argument is this. Despair is not an existential condition of human life, like loneliness, or death. But it is a feature of reason and rationality. For despair has this terrible habit of emerging from any philosophical (or, for that matter, civilizing) investigation into 'the highest and deepest things'. Seeing as it is not an existential condition, there may be ways to escape it; or if not to escape it, then to learn to live with it, and to thrive and prosper in life notwithstanding it. But the argument has not yet come that far. At this place in my meditations, my answer to the second root question remains incomplete. But incomplete as it is, it points the way to the third root question.

Another Interlude

§ 32. Pastoralia

It's another full day alone in the Hedgewitch House, in Bohemia.

The dogs help keep the weight of solitude off me. Whenever I'm writing, they come and see what I'm doing. One of them, Helli, likes to take my hand in her mouth and lead me outside. She is very wise, in this way. Each time I come downstairs in the morning, Helli takes me to her basket of collars and leashes, leaving no doubt what she wanted me to do. When I sit in my writing-place instead, she hops on my lap with her front paws and licks my face. She whimpers when I tell her I have writing work to do; it's hard to say no to her. The other dog, Kringle, is much less exuberant, being much older, but he too loves company; about once or twice a day he'll get up from his bed and come to my side, seeking some affection. The dogs are much more used to human company than I am, it seems, and they can't go without it very long. Llyan, the family cat, is a similarly personable animal: he jumps on my lap whenever he's in the house (even if I'm on the toilet), and nuzzles every part of my neck and face, purring loudly. It's possible that he does this because he wants me to feed him, or open the door. Most of the time he's outside doing whatever it is that cats do when there's no humans about. But his affection is welcome, nonetheless. The company of these animals isn't a substitute for the kind of human touch that I was craving yesterday. Yet they do make the house less lonely. (Anyway, I've published sixteen books in the past twelve years. Melancholia has never slowed me down.)

The dogs and I like to go to a nearby lookout tower that I've half-jokingly referred to as the philosopher's research station. It's a walk through several fields to get there, taking perhaps twenty minutes; Helli bounds ahead, and pokes her nose into everything, then bounds ahead again; Kringle plods steadily behind me, on the leash. Helli comes to my side when I call her, most of the time. A few days back, when Melinda was showing me the way to the tower, Helli found and chased a hare. I saw it bound across my path, running for its life: Melinda had to call her back and leash her to stop her from doing it again. Today I had her off-leash in the same field, but my mind's eye was looking out for the hare. Even so, I thought of what other life might dwell in the fields: in the past week I've seen mice and voles, and bees on the flowers, and more kinds of birds than I know how to name. I haven't seen the owls yet, but I've heard them, and found their pellets on the ground. I'm told there are wild pigs in the forests, and that they could be a small danger if I'm caught unawares, but Helli would likely chase any off. There's a different kind of wealth here, than the wealth of the ancient city I visited yesterday. It's a wealth of life, and of forms of life; a wealth of natural sights and sounds; a wealth of fresh air, and rain, and earthly beauty. I love that we can freely walk through these fields; I love that these fields do not have clearly trodden paths; I love the clean smell of the air; I love the reward of the wide view when I reach the destination. Helli is certainly right to insist that I should go outside and play with her more often. Though I shall get less of my book written that way.

If the imaginal space of Prague involves the fantasy of empire, the imaginal space of the Bohemian countryside is the fantasy of a rustic dignity and 'frugal comfort' (recalling Éamon de Valera). It's the fantasy of a bountiful and generous earth, of permanent good weather, simple pleasures, and easy work. I hike up this hillside with these two dogs at my side and imagine that I'm following some Irish or maybe Germanic ancestor of mine, strolling up a hill just like this one, in a landscape like this one, perhaps with two dogs of his own. He goes about his day without hurry, and in full possession of himself and all the land that he can see from where he walks. I imagine that walking in this way, up this hill, with these dogs, and with this vista of green hills and golden fields all around, is a re-enactment – a re-embodiment – of my ancestral way of being in the world. I cross the road and enter the next field, and I remember that this thought is a fantasy. Farm life and countryside life are hard. It's early mornings, late nights, fine tuning, and heavy lifting; it's specialized technical knowledge and skills that I, a career academic, do not possess. It's putting one's life and livelihood in the hands of unpredictable events like the weather. It's animals who make demands on their keepers as surely as those animals provide love, or work, or (for that matter) wool for the shearing, milk for drinking, flesh for eating. I do not have even the most basic prerequisite for membership in the local community: the ability to speak the local language. I grew up in a village and still imagine myself as a small town boy, but I've lived in cities for most of my adult life, and I am quickly becoming conscious of what an urban creature I have since become. Colleges and universities are not set in farm fields (notwithstanding that I am a Guelph grad); they are features of that urban civilization, which I have come here to contemplate from afar. The thought of returning to that world does not give me much happiness, just now. But, if I am honest, if I did not return to the city I would miss the bookstores, and the pubs.

I reach the philosopher's research station. Kringle, being elderly, has to be tied up at the base of the tower: he's not strong enough to climb the stairs. Helli, being much younger, joyfully bounds up the stairs with me. Its platform reaches far above the canopy of the surrounding spruces. The sight of the world from here is beyond glorious. It makes me wish I could fly. Without intending it deliberately, I'm smiling. For a moment I wonder if it might be perfectly morally correct to say of one who remains unmoved by such a sight that his spirit is bereft.

Another reminder of my urban acculturation occurred to me a few evenings later, as I was cooking my dinner. In an urban environment, it's nearly impossible to know true silence. Here in the village, there are still ambient sounds in the air, but there's far fewer of them, and they're of a different quality. As I gather the pans and wooden spoons and other necessities for my meal, every little clack and bump I make sounds sharper, crisper, louder. The fine details are not being drowned out by the urban hum of cars and air conditioners and other machines that I've tuned myself to ignore. I stop what I'm doing for a moment and simply listen. I hear the sound of the sheep in the neighbor's yard, some overhead birds, a creaking of the timbers in the wall, and the grumbling in my own belly. Between these sounds, there's nothing. Nothing! So that's what Nothing sounds like. Interesting.

Or: that's what Nothing sounds like during the day. At night, the little creaks in the walls, and the slight movements in the bushes outside, and the Nothing, makes me think of rodents, predators, and burglars. When the host family was still here, all those little nothings didn't disturb me, since I trusted that the family would know the difference between an ignorable noise and a potential threat. Now that I'm alone, I can rely on the dogs for that; but as I'm the only human in the house, I'm the one who would have to do something about it.

After eight days of solitude, my consciousness has changed. My awareness of the passage of time, my awareness of ambient sound, my eating habits, even my sexual fantasies, have all changed. I become task-oriented instead of time-oriented; I'm concerned with getting a job done, instead of getting my labor hours filled. At home in Canada, on days I'm not teaching at the college, my routine involves waking late in the morning, working for a few hours, napping in the late afternoon, eating something, then remaining up and working until well past midnight. Here in the Hedgewitch House, there's no television, no games console, no high-speed internet (there's a basic service here; good for email, but not much more). So there's no reason to stay up so late. I wake and sleep with the sun. I have my tablet computer and some notebooks for writing, and the house has lots of books, so I'm not at a loss for something to do. But the need to stay up late isn't so strong anymore. I no longer feel as if I might be 'missing' something. And as for getting up in the morning, the dogs make sure of it, either by whimpering and barking, or by defecating in the front hall. If I ever felt that I might have 'missed' something, it was on a day when I got no writing done, or when there were too many people at the lookout tower for my comfort and so I didn't climb it, or when it was too rainy to go outside at all.

Another curious change to my consciousness: I found myself taking about an hour each day to do nothing. Nothing, that is, but watch the bees gathering the pollen from the little white clovers that grow in the grass, and watch Helli play-fighting with Llyan the cat, and watch birds in the trees fly round each other, and count which flowerbeds could use a little more water. In so much of my life, even back to my primary school days, I have sought solitude, craved quiet, felt invaded by the 'polite meaningless words' of others. (I have felt this even while wishing to be touched and kissed by a lover – I am a ridiculous contradiction, a tangle of foolish pride.)

When I first noticed how my mind had shifted into this new way of conceiving time – something I had rarely enjoyed in my adulthood – I felt extraordinarily surprised. My first deliberate thought regarding it was a memory of the story of Winnie-the-Pooh at Galleons Lap, when Christopher Robin tells his childhood friend there will soon come a time when he will no longer be allowed to do Nothing. Adults aren't allowed to do Nothing: adults must at all times be busily doing Something Productive and Useful, especially if the Something involves money. We judge and condemn people for idleness for instance with proverbs like: 'The devil finds work for idle hands'. Only children are allowed to do nothing. Only children – but not *all* children. I've met many people over the years whose childhood circumstances denied them the chance to do nothing. Could time to do nothing – thinking time, leisure time, rest time – be a human necessity? Solitude and idyll, I have found, are necessary 'research resources' for intellectual discovery. Might one of the problems of civilization be its habit of denying us the time to do nothing? Tuck that thought away for later.

This particular evening, as I do nothing, but contemplate the smell of the air and the trembling of the leaves in the slight evening breeze, I think about the science of ecology, and what it might offer my meditations on civilization. This was one of the dreamy little thoughts that prompted my research project in the first place. Now there's at least two ways to think about what I'm seeing. One is as an unfolding of harmony, balance, organic co-operation, and a kind of love. That is how I have tended to see it all through the journey. The other way, of course, is as an unfolding of drama, competition, territorial conquest, and as an arena for combatants to do violence to each other, with food and sexual partners and physical habitats as the prize for the winner. We've certainly looked at human civilization in both of these two ways, as well.

Suppose, for a moment, that this second way of looking at an ecosystem, that is to say as a battlefield, reveals the essence of it. We would logically expect, therefore, that the top predators would dominate and destroy their competitors, and then attack each other. We would also expect that in so doing they would destroy the basis of their own subsistence, and so they would starve and fade away. Their territory would be left as a monotonous mono-culture, and in every other respect an unlivable barren-land. Similar worries have been raised for human civilization: that we, too, might destroy the material foundation of our own survival, through our wars and competitions, and our endless demand for energy and wealth. Yet when we look upon the biosphere of the earth, we see that it has not destroyed itself. We see that for all its violence, it is still nonetheless *here*. The top predators have not destroyed everything – or if they did once, somewhere in the natural history of the region, nonetheless life in the region returned. More than that, we see that the earth is full of extraordinary diversity – though there are, obviously, some areas so damaged by human development and waste that they will not repair themselves in the humanly foreseeable future. In this village and surrounding fields, I have so far counted seven species of tree, fifteen birds, eight insects, five wildflowers, and six land animals – not counting the animals, flowers, food-crops, and fruit trees deliberately husbanded by local people. I suppose if I was a proper ecologist, I would count many more. (I later learned that most of the forests, hedges, wind breaks, and other 'wild' landscape features are also deliberately tended, and even guarded, by their owners. In this respect the landscape is comparable to the park back home in Gatineau.) The evidence of not only the survival, but also the diversification and flourishing of life on earth, tells us that the proposition that ecosystems are battlefields is false; or, alternatively, it tells us that violent competition is only one of several forces-at-work in the ecosystem. I prefer the latter conclusion; it seems to me better supported by the evidence. It also prompts interesting new questions. What other forces besides violence are at work? If the analogy between human society and ecology is strong, then what can we learn from ecology that we could apply to the great problems of humanity?

§ 33. New Horizons

The 14th of July is an overcast day in Bohemia, with low-hanging clouds, fast moving, bringing thoughts of rain. This morning I'm particularly looking forward to news about the New Horizons spacecraft, which today will pass by Pluto. The limited internet access here will suffice; I didn't see the live stream but I did see a wonderfully crisp and clear hi-res photo of Pluto itself, and this I find very exciting.

It amuses me to sit here on this wooden bench, surrounded

the sounds of baying sheep and barking dogs, singing birds and crickets, and the rolling clouds above, and to look up and to imagine I can see all the way to Pluto, and beside it, the spacecraft that embodies the very best of modern American engineering genius. Very little, almost nothing perhaps, delivers a sense of wonder and of optimism for the future as space exploration.

Unable to watch the live stream of the countdown to New Horizon's closest-pass to Pluto, I take to reading feature articles in various online newspapers about the mission. Almost all the arguments I read that day are animated by a kind of survivalist thinking. We should explore space and colonize other planets, so the argument goes, because that would be the best way to avoid an event that might cause the extinction of all human life on earth. Should earth fail, for instance due to runaway climate change, or an impact by an asteroid large enough to destroy the ecosystem, then human life would continue on Mars, or some other extraterrestrial colony. At the time of the Pluto fly-by, NASA is tracking 1,591 'potentially hazardous objects', meaning an asteroid with 'potential to make threatening close approaches to the Earth.'[319] In a discussion about a large asteroid that came perilously close to earth in early 2014, physics professor Brian Cox said: 'There is an asteroid with our name on it and it will hit us.' Similarly, physicist Stephen Hawking said that space exploration is 'life insurance' for the human race: 'It could prevent the disappearance of humanity by colonizing other planets.'[320] Finally (for now): Elon Musk, founder of the private and for-profit space exploration company SpaceX, has said many times he wants humanity to become an 'interplanetary species'. Here are his words:

It's the first time in four and a half billion years that we are at a level of technology where we have the ability to reach Mars... The sun is gradually expanding. In 500,000 million years—a billion at the outside—the oceans will boil and there will be no meaningful life on Earth. Maybe some very high temperature bacteria, but nothing that can build rockets.[321]

This argument for space exploration worries me for several reasons. One worry is practical: it has to do with the disproportionate alarm directed at a very remote threat. The expansion of the sun will not be a problem for us for many millions of years. NASA itself agrees the threat is negligible. 'No one should be overly concerned about an Earth impact of an asteroid or comet,' says one of its press releases. The threat from near-earth objects becomes significant only 'over long periods of time'.[322]

My other worry is philosophical: it has to do with the nature of the logic of survivalism. There's a striking similarity between the views of the 'dropouts' (I do not intend this term disparagingly); that is, people who leave civilization to build sustainable eco-communities, and the future-minded space colonizers. Both groups imagine that they possess the essence of humanity: one group regards that essence as having to do with simple, back-to-the-land or back-to-God living; the other regards it as the persistence of the human population. Both groups also imagine they are on a mission to save that essence of humanity, either from its corruption, or from its destruction. My worry stems from my wish that the purpose, the goal, the objective, of human life, and indeed human civilization, should be something more ambitious than mere survival. Survivalism, as a purpose for human life, and indeed as a mission-statement for what is sure to be the hardest engineering problem ever attempted in human history to date, is a mere tautology. You may as well say that the purpose of life is not to die. Or, that the purpose of travel is not to sit still. It's like a New Age spiritual quotation: apparently full of stars, but mostly as empty as the vacuum of space. Survivalism seems to denote a conspicuous lack of imagination. And how odd, isn't it, to find this spiritual emptiness dwelling so near the heart of what is likely to be one of humanity's most ambitious, most imaginative endeavors. With mere survival as our sole objective, we could colonize Mars with complete success, yet have no art, no music, no poetry, no justice, no freedom, no happiness, no pleasure, no love, no peace, no reason, no meaning. There would certainly be no wild life-forms beyond the ones we bring with us because we think they will be useful. And, for that matter, there will be no safety from the fall of civilization for *all* of humanity – for the chance to colonize Mars shall belong only to the elite. The rest of us shall remain behind, to wallow in our resource-exhausted and polluted earth, perchance to die.

I love space exploration; I am looking forward to a future where everyone who wants to, and not just the elite, can 'boldly go where no one has gone before'. But I feel a need to bring my thoughts back down to earth. So I close the computer and take the dogs out for a walk. We went to a new 'horizon' of our own: a path I had not followed yet, to a lookout point over the reservoir – a section of the Vltava river widened and deepened by a dam. I had only Melinda's emailed directions to follow, which I didn't write down, so as to be guided only by what I could remembers of them, and thus remain open to surprise and discovery. The path took me by a grain field, then into a hollow hedgerow, then a pine forest. All the while I was both worried about whether we would be caught by rain, but also hopeful for the spectacle at my destination, like a hero on a quest, antici-pating treasure. Eventually I found the lookout point: a rickety wooden bench facing a window in the trees that gave an excellent frame for the sight of the water below. It's not a wide view, like the lookout tower or the hunting stand; it's a secret view, as from a place where I could see all things without being seen. Here, as it turned out, I formed the question in my mind that would become the third of my root questions for this entire study. Are there any solutions to the problems of civilization that are not tautologies? Recalling my meditations upon Prague, I later rephrased my question: is there a way to defeat despair and assert optimism for the future, *which is not an illusion?*

A good answer to a question like that would be – wait for it – a new horizon!

§ 34. This is What Love Looks Like

So far in these meditations I've said almost nothing about the people I met here. And this seems to me a terrible omission. For they, too, inspired my thoughts about ecology and civilization, and often to my surprise.

Only three nights after I arrived, some of the neighbors lit the fire pit in the village centre. The fire reminded me of the 'integral fire' of Vitruvius and Frank Lloyd Wright; later I learned this fire is almost always the centre of the most important celebrations in the village. Some of the people cooked pork over it. Others, sitting on the picnic tables nearby, played guitar. I was invited, and I brought some beer to share. Only one of the people made an effort to speak to me: the rest mostly left me alone, although another shared some of the pork, and a few slices of melon. It was a Czech national holiday, celebrating the lives of two old saints who brought Christianity to the region. The townsfolk celebrated not having to be at work that day. Such was my first taste of the Czech sense of humor. I felt like I was witnessing a folklore event that might have been enacted in small settlements like this all over Middle Europe, for thousands of years. My hostess, who speaks both English and Czech, informed me that some of the songs were about ribald topics like drunkenness or masturbation. But I can tell they are lively and fun songs, the sort that might form the shared repertoire of a circle of friends who may have known each other for years, perhaps for most of their lives. The folk event reinforces their friendship, gives them an event to look forward to while working, and a means of forgetting their work when the work day is done. The songs might be unrepeatable in front of children, the people themselves half drunk, and the whole event half comedy, yet a tenacious thought keeps rising in my mind: this is what love looks like.

The following day, while walking the dogs, I was told that a local maypole in the village centre is part of a Beltaine tradition in which each village in the municipality has to watch that the folk of another village won't come and knock it down – while at the same time they might try to break another village's pole. There's also a tradition in which, around the same time of year, the mayor of the region visits every house, dressed like a king with crown and scepter, to share a drink with every family. The householder supplies the drink to him and to every visitor – non-drinkers are offered tea or hot chocolate. I'm sure the 'king' gets properly legless by the end, but I'm told, 'He has never failed to make it back home on his own two feet!' Many houses around here also have a fruit tree or two in the yard, with which they produce their own fruit brandy: the house where I'm staying has a small orchard of apple and cherry trees. The result is that on special occasions like the mayor's Beltaine tour of the region, or the holiday sing-along that I witnessed that night, there's no shortage of booze. This informally organized sharing of the material supplies of 'the good life' – this, too, is what love looks like.

Yet several days into my solitary stewardship of Hedgewitch House, the loneliness began to hit me. I spent five hours on the internet looking for someone to talk to. At the same time there was a chance for me to talk to some local people: another party was prepared in the village square, just outside the property gate. It looked like about fifty people were there. Some of the children race their bikes around the village. Helli chases them (on our side of the fence, of course) when they get close to the house. She loves it, but I suspect some of the children are a little frightened. It's almost midnight and it looks like there's still thirty people around the fire, drinking and laughing and carrying on. I can see the love, as last time. But tonight I also feel that there isn't a place for me among them. It's a language barrier, but it's also a solitude barrier. Something in me looks upon them, and tells me there's no reason why any of them would want to know me.

The solitude-barrier befalls me at least once a day, for the first few days of my time here. The dogs are determined to make me feel better. Helli whimpers when she wants me to go outside with her and I stay in my chair instead. Kringle mopes over to me with this sad and pained expression, and suddenly I want to make him happy because he looks lonelier than I am. He lets me pet him for a while; sometimes he leans on my leg; sometimes he noses my hand when I stop too soon, to tell me he wants more. Then he wanders back to his bed.

My solitude is agreeably interrupted every two or three days by Tomáš and Ivana. They both work in the city, but in the summer they live in a cottage about two kilometers from the village. This cottage, which they call the Hacienda, was built during the war by two German soldiers who deserted. It sits at the top of a steep slope over the reservoir, and offers a wonderful view. It also has no electricity, which at first surprises me. When I ask if electricity will eventually be connected here, they say no. Without electricity, there's nothing in the house worth stealing. Ivana is generous without hesitation, and full of smiles; it was she who took me to Prague a few days before, and who drives me to a grocery store once a week. She told me she doesn't like working as a real estate agent because it forces her to think of people around her, even friends, as potential clients. Tomáš was, at least at first, hard for me to read. For instance, when I once thanked him for a beer he gave me, and he looked away and waved his hand and said, 'Nothing.' This, I suppose, might be the local way of acknowledging thanks, as when we Canadians nod and say, 'You're welcome.' On two occasions he showed me an engraving of what the river looked like before the dam was built. It submerged a village, and divers sometimes swim among the ruins. Sometimes the steeple of the church is visible above the water.

About a week after my host family disappeared for their holiday, Tomáš and Ivana invited me to an evening dinner at their cottage. I brought the dogs with me, and arrived early. When I arrived Tomáš was wearing a shirt only half buttoned up, and his underwear, as if that was the most normal and natural thing in the world. It may have helped that we drank more than few cups of wine and beer, and some shots of Tullamore Dew, before Ivana and some other neighbors returned. Incidentally, I learned he is a medical doctor. And a chain smoker. An unexpected combination. He asked me what I would tell my friends and students back home about Czech people: 'You can see we don't just eat mushrooms and swing from tree to tree.' He was a fun loving, wise cracking, delight of a man.

At the dinner party I met Tereza and Honza, a young couple who will be married next month. They were welcoming and generous with food and drink, as always. Tereza works in museum restorations and Honza went to a prestigious Czech engineering school. They are building a log house that will be as energy efficient and off-the-grid as they can make it. For the moment, therefore, they live in a trailer near the skeleton of the house. Eventually they plan to fit the entire village with solar panels. They mostly spoke Czech, so I spent most of the evening sitting in a corner with Kringle, trying to be polite. But near the end of the night Ivana produced a guitar, and I played a few of my own songs, and felt more like I was contributing something.

Walking home from the Hacienda that night was a surprisingly spiritual experience. It's about two kilometers, and it was dark, windy, overcast (so no moon), and so for a few moments my world held only me, and two dogs, and the deep black world around us, and the orangey-grey clouds above. We were walking first through an impossibly black forest, then a wheat field, then the hedgerow-flanked road to the village, through a darkness and a windy wildness that seemed fresh from a mythic age. My borrowed flashlight showed me a dim pool of white in a sea of black and orangey-grey. I could have emerged at any time in history. I could have met anyone on the road and easily believed she was a mythical creature in disguise. Yet I felt at peace with this. For I could have believed that I myself could become a mythical creature, too. Such perfect moments demand to be remembered, treasured, experienced with the fullness of one's sensory being, and perhaps deliberately sought out – for tonight was one of the great reminders that human life is can be fragile, yet also precious and romantic in its fragility.

The Reidinger family returned. After so many days of near-total solitude, the noise of the radio and the children and the visitors, and the sudden crowdedness of the house itself, all made me realize how acclimatized to solitude I had become while they were away. I continued to walk the dogs in the fields and hills as I had done while alone, because it often seemed the dogs were anxious to go, and I wanted to get out from under everyone's feet. We went to that rickety little bench that overlooks the reservoir, which I have called my thinking place, even though I don't get much thinking done there: mostly I just sit and rest, try to keep the dogs close, and enjoy the view. On the way back, I spotted a deer in the wheat field. I'm proud of this because I almost never spot the deer back home, and because I saw this one before the dogs did. I got three photos of it, and then raised my hands in prayer to thank it. Alas, that is when it bounded away. Though this moment lasted perhaps only two minutes, it felt like a spiritual moment: I felt that I had been given a great gift. In my spiritual life, I do not have psychic or trance-vision or super-natural experiences, as other pagans say they do. I have moments like this encounter with the deer, where something of the inhuman world reveals itself to me, and offers silent conversation about the smallness and yet the uniqueness of my life when measured against the immensity.

One afternoon, near the end of my stay, a neighbor named Vasek shot a wild boar, and I was invited to watch him skin it. He and his partner love eating meat, but they don't trust the meat from grocery stores: they eat only the animals they hunt or raise themselves. I arrived to see him finish dismembering a boar that hung on a tripod by a hook in its jaw. When he finished he hung another to the tripod, and peeled off the pelt from the head downward. All the while he made casual conversation with his partner, with Petr, and with me; they shared a beer with me, and answered my ignorant questions with patience. My impression was much like that which I felt attending the gatherings in the village square: this is something people have done in this part of the world for hundreds of years. But I also began to think of the notes I had made about survivalism, and the Time To Do Nothing. For here I was witnessing something people have done to survive for thousands of years, and yet most modern urban dwellers like myself never see. In some cases, people are prevented by law from finding out where their food comes from. Several American states, for instance, have made it illegal to covertly film or photograph livestock farms. Some also require people to declare any association they may have with animal rights groups before applying for farm jobs.[323] (This, by the way, adds another case to my collection of civilization's absurdities: the crime is not animal cruelty, but the attempt to document the cruelty. Thankfully, no laws prevent me from documenting hunters or the processing of hunted animals.) Obviously, I have always known that the meat in my dinner is animal flesh; but there's been only two or three occasions in my life when I got to see this reality enacted before my eyes. As civilization works to take our Nothing-time away from us, might it also work to conceal from us where our food really comes from? A report from 2012 found that more than one-third of people in Britain aged 16 to 23 years did not know that bacon comes from pigs; four-tenths of the same group did not know that milk comes from cows; about one in ten of them thought that eggs come from grain crops like wheat.[324] What else might civilization work to conceal?

American author Joyce Carol Oats observed:

> Civilization is a multiplicity of strategies, dazzling as precious
> gems inlaid in a golden crown, to obscure from human beings
> the sound of, the terrible meaning of, their jaws grinding. The
> meaning of man's place in the food cycle is that, by way of our
> imaginations, we had imagined might not apply to us.[325]

Yet nothing appeared especially cruel or uncivilized about the
occasion I was invited to witness. I could see the bullet hole in the
pelts of both animals: small, and just behind the ear. The
creatures were probably killed instantly and painlessly. The
hunter's knife work as he skinned each carcass was clean,
efficient, and professional: a handicraft of evident practice and
skill. There was no blood and no mess, but he wore no shirt,
perhaps to spare his clothing any possible accidents. In that way
he seemed a giant Slavic god of a man: easily a head and shoulder
taller than me, with bright blond hair, a muscular build, and a
habit of hunting only during nights with no moon. His eyes are
sharp enough to need nothing more than starlight. Only the plain
greenish trousers tied with a string, and the Crocs on his feet,
showed that he was a 21st century man. What is more: the
creature was hunted not because of an anonymous market
demand, but instead because of a natural and nearby need: the
meat would soon be served at the feast following Tereza and
Honza's wedding. There is simply no comparing the industrial
factory farm with the event I was witnessing that day. It made me
wonder if some part of the solution to civilization's absurdities
may involve lifting its veils of illusion away.

On the second-to-last day, some of the family and I went to
visit Tereza and Honza, for a barbecue over the fire. Tomáš and
Ivana were there as well. Some of the pork we ate that night had
been hunted locally just a week before. I played guitar again, and
the didgeridoo. I got lots of gentle ribbing over my puzzlement

about how to use the trailer's dry toilet. 'So how was your Canadian visitor?' 'He came, he played guitar, he shit in my house...' Even in that, I saw once again the enactment of the oldest human drama by which we human beings share friendship and love: music and jokes and stories performed; food cooked on a fire in the centre of the circle, and shared out to all; a dog running about; a child asleep on a chair nearby; the round dark hills looming in the middle distances; curtains of clouds coming and going, and the stars above them.

As Petr drove me to the airport on the morning of my last day, the smell of the camp fire was still on my clothes. It was good.

Third Movement: What Shall We Do About It?

§ 35. Dance Macabre

Imagine a decadent ballroom, with crystal chandeliers, lace and velvet curtains, and classical paintings in shining gold frames. Imagine a chamber orchestra on the stage, performing for a hundred dancers, all in elegant silk suits and dresses, and classic Venetian carnival masks. Some faces show calm serenity, some ecstatic seriousness, some have a romantic tear painted on a cheek, and some wear a sly grin. Everyone greets each other with a bow, everyone dances with precision and grace, everyone touches and gazes on each other with ritualistic respect. But at midnight, a bell tolls. The music stops. The masks come off. We see that the musicians were all skeletons, and the dancers were all werewolves. They immediately tear at each other's throats with their teeth.

The conclusion about human nature we are to draw from the ballroom scene is that civilization is an illusion. All our behavioral civility, so the belief goes, is a paper-thin mask covering an animalistic nature that could resurge again at any moment. Although this view is evidently misanthropic, it remains surprisingly popular. Sigmund Freud endorsed something like it: 'Every civilization must be built up on coercion and renunciation of instinct,'[326] he wrote in *The Future of an Illusion*. Similar statements appear, for instance, in the writings of journalists who report on riots and protests. To choose one example: following the Stanley Cup riots in Vancouver, BC, in the spring of 2011, a columnist in a Vancouver newspaper wrote:

> The Stanley Cup riot reminds us that civilization is fragile, collectively and individually... The truth is that many of us will change our behaviour when circumstances change.

> Civilization is a form of social contract. And, in some situations, human nature deems the contract void. Large crowds are one such situation...[327]

The idea also tends to appear following outbreaks of political, or state-sponsored, violence. The American-Jewish historian Henry Feingold spoke of the 'illusion of civilization' following the Holocaust, for example. 'We believed...that Germany was civilized. Yet look what happened. Civilization is an illusion.'[328] The statement also appears in pop culture. In the film *The Invasion* (2007), a Russian ambassador says: 'Civilization is an illusion; a game of pretend. What is real is the fact that we are still animals driven by primal instincts... In the right situation, we are all capable of the most terrible crimes.' In *Scrooge* (1951), the first film adaptation of Charles Dickens' *A Christmas Carol*, one of Scrooge and Marley's business partners says to another, 'We're all cutthroats under this fancy linen.'

Going back in time a little bit, we find Herbert Spencer arguing for a state that is both laissez-faire and at the same time aristocratic. *The Man Versus the State* (1892) he said: 'The welfare of a society and the justice of its arrangements are at bottom dependent on the characters of its members,' and that only 'peaceful industry under the restraints imposed by an orderly social life' can improve people's characters; a point that would seem to confirm my general theory about civilization. But the effort would be futile because: 'The defective natures of citizens will show themselves in the bad acting of whatever social structure they are arranged into. There is no political alchemy by which you can get golden conduct out of leaden instincts.'[329] Going back in time even further, we find the Greek historian Thucydides, writing in the 5th century BCE, who also regarded civilization as a mere cover story. In describing a series of revolutions across the ancient Greek world prior to the Peloponnesian War, he wrote:

In times of peace and prosperity, cities and individuals alike follow higher standards, because they are not forced into a situation where they have to do what they do not want to do. But war is a stern teacher; in depriving them of the powers of easily satisfying their daily wants, it brings most people's minds down to the level of their actual circumstances... With the ordinary conventions of civilized life thrown into confusion, human nature, always ready to offend even where laws exist, showed itself proudly in its true colours, as something incapable of controlling passion, insubordinate to the idea of justice...[330]

I have no doubt that civilization is often fragile. Yet I recoil from the view that civilization is a mere mask for an animalistic reality. For one thing, the assumption that we human beings are wild animals at heart, is as much a *moral* proposition as an allegedly factual one: it configures us even as it pretends to explain us. It's also inextricably wrapped up in cultural values and observer bias. Self-centered and even narcissistic people are more likely to appear successful in business, politics, and the media, and so they are more visible. And in Christian theology, the 'Doctrine of Original Sin' tells us that humanity's predilection for terribleness was certified by God.

There is plenty of excellent evidence that human beings are capable of being utterly bestial to each other; but there is also plenty of excellent evidence to the contrary. Psychologists have found that we human beings co-operate with each other much more often, and more readily, than do our nearest relatives in the animal kingdom. Human infants and toddlers share tools and toys and food with only a little encouragement, whereas chimpanzees share food only after significant harassment; infant chimpanzees have to beg their mothers for a share of things.[331] A British nationwide survey by Common Cause Foundation discovered that 74 per cent of respondents believe that compassionate values are more important than selfish values. Yet 77 per cent of respondents also thought that other people hold selfish values in higher regard.[332] Most people, it would seem, underestimate other people's capacity for kindness. Contrary to the misanthropic view, which holds that we all revert to selfishness during disasters, some of the most visible signs of humanity's ability to co-operate appear precisely during and immediately following disasters. After the massive wildfire that destroyed most of Fort McMurray, Alberta, for example, the donations of food and clothes and other goods from across Canada far exceeded the evacuees' needs.[333] Similarly, after a mass shooting at a night club in Orlando, Florida, in June 2016, local blood banks were overwhelmed with hundreds of volunteer donors; staff had to ask them to come back on other days.[334] During the four days when all of Ontario and much of the north-eastern United States was without electricity in August 2003, informants from Toronto described to me how people checked in on their elderly neighbors daily, to see they had not died of heat exhaustion without their air conditioning; some people met their neighbors for the very first time that way. Foodstuffs that would go bad without refrigeration, especially ice cream, were shared widely and immediately. Restaurants served people for free, on promise of payments when the power was restored, since bank machines weren't working. Even without looking at compassion prompted by disasters, we can still see trends leading toward increasing co-operation and non-aggression: for example, at the time I write these words, there are fewer countries at war now than ever before in recorded history, and fewer people than ever before are dying in battle.[335]

Where, then, do the world's terrible people come from? Most of them come from social environments that trained them to be that way. As observed by anthropologist Scott Atran, who spent years studying the psychology of religious terrorists, militant fanatics tend to be very ordinary people. 'What gives them all fanatical focus is not some inherent personality defect, but the person-changing dynamic of the group.'[336] Philosopher Jonathan Glover extensively studied the psychology of ethics: he found that we have three 'moral resources', sympathy, respect, and identity, which generally help people resist doing terrible things. Those resources can be overwhelmed by extreme circumstances such as war. The third one, moral identity, can also be hijacked by political or social conditioning. As Glover says: 'There may be no resistance [to committing atrocities] when a person's self-conception has been built around obedience. In the same way, if someone's self-conception has been built round a tribal identity or round some system of belief, resistance to tribal or ideological atrocities may have been subverted from within.'[337] It may be that some of the world's terrible people were 'naturally born' that way. But the complete picture of the reality is likely to be that naturally terrible people are fewer than believed, and that their appearance is entirely explainable.

A critic might argue that evidence for a more compassionate human nature is full of observer bias. To which the answer is: Yes. It *is* full of observer bias: so is *every* claim about human nature. The study of human nature is the great black hole of philosophy: for every claim about what human nature is, there's an equal and opposite empirical observation. Sympathy, respect, and moral identity 'are the core of the humanity which contrasts with inhumanity,' wrote Glover. 'They are widely distributed, but to identify them with humanity is only partly an empirical claim. It remains also partly an aspiration.'[338] And as an aspiration, the claim that humanity can better itself has the advantage of not mistaking the logic of civilization, as the misanthropic view mistakes it. If civilization is a manufacturer of illusion, the reality beneath it is not a particular form of human nature, animalistic or otherwise. For civilization is not a disciplinarian; it is an artisan. Suppose we returned to the ballroom, just a moment before the bell tolls, and lifted some of the human masks. If we find the face of a wild animal there, it is because the animal is yet another mask. And all of these masks were fashioned by the people who wear them; each person fashions her own, and at the same time we all fashion each other's. For civilization and all its member forces is not a monolithic Leviathan from outer space that hangs over the world. Civilization is *us*. It is everything we do in trans- action with each other, with the earth, with our own solitude, and with the past and the future. It's every little move we make that furthers some image of what humanity is, and what humanity can be, and what it should be, and which builds up habits in one person and sets precedents for others. It's in the consent and participation we give to the works of nation-building: clearing land for roads and bridges and farms and cities; fighting wars; electing our leaders; prosecuting crimes in courts; playing sports and games; celebrating art, literature, music, drama; paying taxes; debating and arguing the public questions of the day. It's also in the ordinary and everyday things we do to show we care about each other: the simple 'please and thank you' and the, 'How are you today?' Each of us contributes to their own preferred image of humanity a little bit, every time we do something that confirms that we are who we imagine ourselves to be, or who we imagine we should be. So if we are violent, or compassionate, or hateful, or loving, it is because we have directed the civilizing forces to make us that way.

Beneath *all* the masks, beneath the all illusions of civilization, is not an animal, nor a zombie, but a *child* – who, when the mask is taken away, wonders who she is, and what the hell is going on. The third of my three root questions appears before me: can that child grow into a mature and happy adulthood without a mask? Or, to dispense with the metaphor and be more precise: can human beings and human society find hope and optimism for the future without the need for illusions?

I've returned to the lake near my house, to think about these questions. This time I'm seated by the lake's edge, the better to touch the water, and to see the stars on its surface. Twilight is creeping across the sky. The other tourists are heading home. All the ideas floating about this forest will soon be mine to gather.

§ 36. Progressive Negations

Knowing that the purely misanthropic view of civilization is almost certainly a mistake, I already have a touch more hope for humanity than I did before. To find if there are other sources of hope, I should clear the illusions away.

One type of logical proposition that might be useful for this purpose is a type called a *negation*: a statement which asserts that something is not the case. The procedure I have in mind is comparable to the scientific method of falsification. Scientists aim to falsify a theory, in order to clear the way for another theory that better explains observable phenomena and that predicts experimental results more accurately. Similarly, in police procedure, it is often far easier to prove what did not happen at a crime scene, or to prove that someone is not guilty of a crime, than it is to prove what did happen, or who is guilty. My method could thus be compared Husserl's phenomenological *epoché*, or to Descartes' methodological doubt.

The aim of using negations, like the ones I shall soon propose, is to put our use of the civilizing forces to the test of reality. It is, in effect, to declare a sacred 'no' to the social-political mythologies whose function is to narrow people's contact with reality, yet whose foundation in reality is weak. The logical procedure is as follows: for any given social-political principle that you suspect might be an illusion, state the corresponding negation of that principle, and then imagine what life might be like if the negation turns out to be true. Ask yourself diagnostic questions like these:

- Do any new and better ways of facing reality appear?
- Does any source of 'necessary' suffering now appear

unnecessary and avoidable?

- Most of all: is it possible for more people to live worthwhile and flourishing human lives – even if those lives might be very different from the ones we are living now?

If the answer to these questions turns out to be 'yes', we may be more confident that the social-political principle under examination is an illusion. This does not, by itself, mean that practices associated with it should be entirely abandoned. But it does mean that we can experiment more freely with new practices, and new ways of being in the world.

I'm ordering these negations from the easiest to the hardest: that is, from the ones I think most people would find acceptable and easy, to those I think more people are attached to, and thus less willing to release.

First: *Nothing is permanent. Nothing is eternal. Nothing is forever.* And isn't this one obvious. Many things last a long time – some things, like our planet earth, last billions of years. But even so, all things must pass; everything is in motion and nothing is still. You yourself are changing, as you read these words. You're growing older. Some day you will die. Let us not be distracted by thoughts of afterlives and immortal souls – such things may or may not exist anyway. You might, instead, hang your sense of permanence on social roles that remain reasonably consistent over time. To use my own life as an example: I'm a writer, a college professor, a homeowner, an eldest son, an uncle, a brother, a Canadian, an Anglophone, a friend. But even these may change over time. I can start playing new roles, and stop playing old ones. The other people with whom I play these roles change. And the expectations people have for occupants of these roles change all the time; which is a way of saying the roles themselves change. Looking at your present situation, in this very moment, the most unambiguously true statement we can make about what's actually happening to you and the world around you is that it is passing away.

Second: *You do not know everything.* I include this instance of Socratic wisdom as an antidote to the Illusion of No Alternative. For the person who claims to know that there is no alternative to some present or foreseen situation, is a person who claims to know everything there is to know about that situation. But surely it is obvious that the world is so vast, so complex, so varied in shape and form, and so open to re-invention, that no matter how much you know, there is always more to know. It follows that no one can know everything there is to know about any given situation. (Incidentally, this was a point raised by Adam Smith himself; it served as a premise in an argument for why government should not regulate the economy.) From this position, it follows that the world will always reveal itself in new ways; the world is always open to discovery; and (following the warrior-philosopher Worf, son of Mogh), 'There are *always* options.'[339] What is more: people will always be so different, so unique in their perspectives and experiences, that no matter how much you know about some situation, it's always possible that others know something about it that you don't. Against the illusion of No Alternative, I propose that it's okay to not know everything, and it's okay to acknowledge that you do not know everything. Take it from the philosopher Socrates, of whom the Oracle of Delphi said no one is wiser; yet he himself claimed to know only that he knew nothing. And regarding people: being different, it is always possible that they will surprise you. It is when your loved ones do something unexpectedly wonderful that we suddenly love them all the more.

Third: *You do not deserve to suffer.* Earlier in these meditations I speculated that some small measure of despair is a potential part of an honest contemplation of reality. So let me be clear about exactly what kind of suffering I'm speaking of in this proposition: the suffering of those whom the civilizing forces push outside the Ancient Great Wall; the suffering that appears when we pretend that certain illusions are forces of nature without alternatives. If you are someone who does not embody or does not defer to your society's model of the ideal Civilized Person, for instance because you are disabled, or poor, or an ethnic minority, or a religious minority, or gay, and so on, still you do not deserve to be punished for that. We do not have to say that all people are the same, nor do we have to make them all the same, in order to treat people with basic respect. A statement of universal moral worthiness like this one is part of the message of nearly every important religious and humanist peace-maker, including Jesus, Mohammed, the Buddha, Khalil Gibran, Martin Luther King, Mohandas Gandhi, Nelson Mandela – the list can go on. Yet this message still needs to be proclaimed, for as long as the Illusion of the Higher and Lower Men remains strong among us. Only someone who is still captured by that illusion would claim, for example, that the fourteen engineering students at L'Ecole Polytechnique in Montreal, who were murdered on 6th December 1989, deserved it because they were women; the killer said as much in his suicide note.[340] It's the same for the more than fifty people who were murdered by a gunman in June 2016 in a night club in Orlando, Florida,[341] or the thirty-two people killed by an arsonists in New Orleans in 1973;[342] none of them deserved to die because they were gay.

Fourth: *There is nothing wrong with human nature*. As a follow-up to the previous proposition: there is no pre-determined fault in human nature that civilization must repress, or aim to overcome; and suffering is not explained by civilization's failure to repress that fault. There is no such thing as Original Sin; and while some people are selfish, or quick to hate and to attack with violence, there is nothing in their habits that is universal in our species. Human nature is only what the civilizing forces have made of it. As we have seen, the human genome itself, no less than our languages and cultures, is what the civilizing forces have made of it, over many generations. So if someone is 'naturally' disposed to be cruel or selfish or cowardly or whatever, that is because the heady combination of history, environment, epigenetic inheritance, and that person's own free-willed choices, have made him that way. We may always have to deal with a certain number of criminals, sociopaths, and assholes. But if we do not see them as 'naturally born' that way, it might be easier to overcome their influence on the world.

Yet the belief still lingers, that evil exists in the world because we human beings are naturally predisposed to it. A popular modern version of this belief is called the 'deep roots theory of war', which supposedly explains the prevalence of war in human history by citing an innate aggressiveness in human nature. The theory is supported by some very influential anthropologists and political scientists. Steven Pinker, in his famous book *Better Angels of our Nature* (2012), assumed a Hobbsean view of people when he wrote that 'chronic raiding and feuding characterize life in a state of nature'.[343] The view was also endorsed by US President Barak Obama, in the speech he gave when he accepted the Nobel Peace Prize. 'War, in one form or another, appeared with the first man. At the dawn of history, its morality was not questioned; it was simply a fact, like drought or disease.' He treated this statement as a 'hard truth', adding that as President, 'I face the world as it is.'[344] To be fair, neither Obama nor Pinker nor any other supporter of the 'deep roots' theory of war celebrates this 'hard truth'. They want to see an end to war; they think if we understand our warlike nature better then we will overcome it. But the evidence against the theory is strong. I have already shown some of the evidence that civilization itself was founded on empathy and co-operation. What is more: lethal violence in hunter-gatherer communities tends to be rare, and tends to be perpetrated by single individuals and not by organized groups, and that most killings resulted not from Malthusian competition for resources, but instead from personal feelings like jealousy or revenge.[345] Studies of archaeological remains also support the view that war has never been especially common in human prehistory, and that it was a distinct cultural development which emerged only about 10,000 years ago.[346] The trouble with the 'deep roots' theory of war is that it appears to explain war while at the same time rendering us nearly powerless against it. Indeed, it leaves us only one strategy for dealing with it: we must be rescued by some political savior, 'a good guy with a gun'. It is the scientific analogue of Original Sin, which also appears to explain evil while rendering us powerless to resist it; we must be purified by an otherworldly savior and his designated earthly representatives. In either case, salvation comes at a price: moral and political obedience. This is nonsense. It is better to regard human nature as a malleable material. This position is better supported by the evidence. It's also a more ethically worthy aspiration: for to become better people, we have to see that becoming better is an achievable possibility.

Fifth: *You do not have a destiny.* I include this proposition only by way of introduction to the next; but it deserves a moment of reflection for its own merits. Each person is absolutely unique in the world: there will never be another person like you, ever again. From this obvious fact, it does not follow that there are any forces at work in history or in the soul which, *a priori*, pick out one person instead of another for any kind of greatness, nor for any kind of ignominy. Your spiritual books and teachers might tell you that you are an 'old soul' or an 'indigo child', or that you are awakened or ascended, or that some law of attraction will deliver health and prosperity if only you want it sincerely enough. These beliefs are false. It fits the case better to say you are completely unique, completely irreplaceable, completely different from all others – but so is everyone else, and therefore you are not necessarily marked out for unusual specialness. Some may feel that this proposition disenchants the world. It makes events appear accidental and random. Some may think it leaves them disempowered, or without a basis for their self-esteem. I think it restores an important element of human freedom in our lives. To choose one example of a destiny: some people believe that they have a 'soul mate', a person especially marked out to be their sexual partner, or to be another kind of important figure in their life: a business associate, a parent, a best friend, or even a pet dog. If you do have a soul mate, then you have no choice but to love her, or otherwise to work with her – even if she later turns out to be a terrible person. (In which case you might think you were mistaken about who your soul mate is. But that belief only preserves the illusion: it sets you up to be mistaken again and again.) If, instead, you do not have a soul mate, then you can make your own choices about who you want to love. The reality is that there are people out there who are well-matched and poorly-matched with you, for lots of different reasons and purposes. There is also a spectrum in between those positions, and lots of people filling every place along that spectrum. And if you find that someone loves you, that can make life all the more rich and delicious: for that person chose you on her own, and for her own reasons; and you may have earned her love for your own actual merits – and perhaps also for your flaws, too!

Sixth: *No past age was fully 'golden'. The future is never fully 'dark', nor fully 'bright'. There are no Promised Lands. There are no Chosen People. We are not living in the End Times.* The point of these statements is to dispel certain political and religious illusions, especially those concerned with the supposed manifest destiny of nations; hence my invocation of the Biblical terms 'Chosen People' and 'Promised Land'. It may be obvious that there were times in the past that were 'better', according to some metric, than times are now. There might be better times ahead of us in the future. But to imagine that there are supernatural forces at work leading us inevitably toward, or away from, 'better' times, is to fall into illusion. And this would be an obvious, non-controversial statement, if not for the fact that some leading American politicians, and some pseudo-Islamic terrorist organizations, do believe we are living in the 'end times.'[347] This is why some politicians support going to war in the Middle East, for example. It is also why some oppose the political effort to halt global warming.[348] If we are living in the End Times, we can just wait to let God clean up our mess for us. But if we are not living in the End Times, then we will have to clean up this mess on our own. This same point was raised by Dr. Rowan Williams, Archbishop of Canterbury, when he taught that God will not save us from global warming.[349] More: if we are not living in the End Times, then any political or economic forecast of 'doom and gloom' need not appear inevitable. It will appear more like a problem that we may have the power to prevent. If any people on earth are 'chosen', or if any land is 'promised' to them, then they are a people who chose each other,[350] and they are a people who promised to themselves the land in which they already dwell.

Like the previous proposition, this may seem to make the world appear less ordered, and less enchanted. However, the point is to encourage people to stand up and earn their specialness. If someone is a Toynbee-esque pioneer because that was her destiny, then there is no point in admiring her for it. She was fulfilling a predetermined plan; she did no more than what was expected of her. If, on the other hand, no one has a destiny, then those pioneers deliberately declined easier paths in life, and chose harder work. Those choices make them more worthy of praise. Their appearance in the world is less of an expectation and more of a surprise; I think that makes the world *more* enchanted, not less.

Furthermore, to individuals and societies who achieve some kind of greatness, this proposition may also serve as a warning against hubris. Successful men often come to believe that they are somehow magically protected, and so they will always be successful. But in reality, it's always possible for them to fail. As the Roman emperors used to have someone stand near them to whisper in their ear, 'Remember you're only human', so the

Toynbee-esque pioneers of our time may also need to be reminded that they, like everyone else, have no destiny. Let us add, finally, that if someone did not achieve greatness, we need not punish them for it. They were not declining a destiny; they still possess the intrinsic dignity that accords them the right not to suffer; and the simplest explanation for their 'failure' is likely to be that their opportunities for flourishing were denied them – such is the nature of the Ancient Great Wall.

Seventh: *The worship of the gods is not what matters.* This thought came to me almost twenty years ago. It was among the most liberating ever to cross my mind. It took me many years to grasp its significance, and many more to explore its implications. Presently, I've settled on an interpretation like this: the gods, if they exist, are not laws to obey; they are presences to be experienced. [351] In the process of reaching that interpretation I was forced to decide: if the worship of the gods isn't what matters, then what does? I found many answers. People and relationships matter. The earth matters. Life, yours and mine, matters. Art, music, culture, science, justice, knowledge, history, peace, and any other similar thing that enriches your experience of life and your relations with the world, also matter. The extent to which life is worth living matters. Death matters. And thinking about these things matters, too. The idea that devotion to a deity isn't important may seem like hubris. I see it as a new kind of spirituality. It's a spirituality of seriously exploring the highest and deepest questions that face humankind, and of finding answers by means of our own intelligence. It's a spirituality of seeking partners with whom to share that exploration. In that sense it is a humanist activity, but it is an activity that elevates one's humanity to the highest sphere. Suppose we discover that the gods do, in fact, exist: then you should befriend them, or ignore them, the same way you would anybody else; they are only the people who happen to live on the 'other side'. Suppose instead we discover indisputable proof that the gods do not exist: that discovery need not produce an existential crisis, for you were not relying on the gods to give your life meaning in the first place. And in either situation, the way is clear for a good and worthwhile human life, on this earth, for you and everyone close to you, for however long you live.

Having set aside some ideas that I'm very sure are false, the way is opened to investigate alternative ideas that are more likely to be true.

§ 37. Facing the Immensities

We have seen and dispelled some of the illusions that haunt us; or, if we haven't entirely dispelled them, we have loosened their power over us. There may be more illusions than those I've described, and thus we may need more progressive negations to test them. I invite readers to experiment with their own. Remember, the point of the exercise is not only to dispel our illusions; it's also to see what realities remain after the illusions are dispelled. Yet this meditation, and the ones that follow, will be more speculative and aspirational than the others, for I am looking into the future now. I'm looking for sources of optimism for the future of humanity, which are not illusions. I contemplate only a small number of positions here, knowing that there may be others; but these few seem simple enough, and I'm confident they pass the test of the progressive negation. By the way: I use the word *position* in a multifold sense here: first, as a pro-position, the opposite of a negation; second, as a tip of the hat to John Rawls and his 'original position'; third, as a posture or a pose to adopt, much like a fashion model might 'strike a pose' in a certain costume; and fourth, as a place on earth, upon which I declare, 'Here I stand. I cannot do otherwise. God help me.'

When I strip away the illusions of the permanent self, the virtuous prince, the higher and lower men, and the No Alternative, what remains? When I strip away the social roles I play, the pretence of knowing everything, the supposed faults in my original nature, the future I might be wishing for, and the commandments of the gods, what remains?

Some people may answer: nothing but loneliness, fear, and despair. The illusion of the permanent self gave me confidence in the future. The illusion of the virtuous prince made me feel safe. The illusion of the higher and lower men gave me a social role. The illusion of No Alternative gave me a sense of integrity and commitment. By stripping away these illusions, I also strip away those sources of confidence, safety, belonging. I might be left with nothing worth committing to, nothing for my integrity to hold, nothing to comfort me when I am lonely or afraid, and nothing to lift me from despair.

But I am left with more than that. I find that I ramble across the surface of an earth and through an expanse of cosmic spacetime so vast no one single person can comprehend all of it on her own, in a single lifetime. This ensures that the world will always be a realm of discovery and revelation. I find that every person I meet is another world in her own right. Every person comes to every encounter with another person her own history, experience, point of view, and the like, which is never a precise mirror image to anyone else's. My neighbor is so different from me, that she is not even my opposite: she defines herself in her terms, not in mine. It is a deep reality that we can never get all the way inside anyone else's head. And nor can I share more than a mere portion of my own heart and mind with others: however much of myself I can share, I can never share all. Other people are therefore always capable of the unexpected, always capable of surprise. Indeed, I cannot explore my own heart and mind to the bottom of their depths; when I land in some place or situation I've never encountered before, I might surprise myself. Stripped of my illusions, I remain a being of finite but nonetheless profound physical and mental powers. I may be mortal, but I can change the world, in big ways and in small, with the work of my hands, the sound of my voice, and the sight of my eyes.

Over the past few years, I have come to call deep realities like these *the immensities*.[352] The encounter with the immensities interests me, not only because the traditional accounts of the 'state of nature' mostly ignore them, but also because they appear to me as obviously unignorable, unavoidable, and demanding time, attention, and response. They are archetypal, non-negotiable, and perpetually recurring realities for human life on earth: solitude and loneliness; the intrinsic otherness of our neighbors; the magnificence of the earth; the passage of time and the finality of death. Each of them can appear to us in many faces; they can dwell behind any mask. They configure the real, the true, the good, and the beautiful; they are the only steady lamps in the wilderness; they are among 'the highest and deepest things' of which the study of philosophy and indeed the seeking of spirituality concerns itself. They are the events, experiences, and circumstances that are in some sense inevitable in every person's life, and which reveal something absolutely different from, and even greater than, the self. They are timeless, in the sense that our most distant ancestors, no less than ourselves, had to confront them. They tend to appear most clearly in situations where a choice is required, and you can see how your choices (or your refusal to choose) would produce irreversible consequences. They also appear when your usual way of thinking about things appears inadequate and some new way of thinking is called for. In this sense they are similar to what philosopher Karl Jaspers called 'limit situations,' and what William James called 'momentous choices'. Thus they call one's powers into question; they demand a response. Then, in the act of responding to them, your life is configured. You set yourself on a certain path, or into a certain way of being in the world, perhaps irreversibly, whether towards flourishing or towards bereftness. It falls to us to re-discover the immensities, in search of new and better sources of optimism and hope.

Stripped of my illusions, I encounter the immensities more

honestly, and I find that the world is more magical than the illusions made it out to be. For it is not the mysteriousness or the inscrutability of the world that makes it magical, but its never-ending discoverability. Facing the immensities like this left me open to loneliness and despair. Yet we must risk loneliness and despair, to have any chance of finding a source of optimism and hope that is not an illusion.

I find my optimism in the sunrise in the morning, the melting snows of spring, the flowers coming up from the darkness of earth, and the rich summer fruit on the trees. I find it in music and poetry and art, and in scientific adventurism, and the kindness of strangers. I find it while drinking fine wine on restaurant patios, in the old quarters of great cities, or in village gardens by the feet of green hills, or in the quiet solitude of my library. I find it when playing guitar with my friends; singing their songs, hearing them sing mine. I find it when I witness excellence in the arts: Shakespeare's plays, Beethoven's symphonies, Yeats' poems, Van Gogh's skies. I find it in the oceanic feeling of belonging to this earth and to this time in history. And I find it in people who delight in these things, as I do. In a park near my house, I see children from immigrant families who don't speak each other's languages nonetheless playing soccer and racing bicycles together, and having a wonderful time. At the college where I serve as professor, students and staff from nearly fifty different countries around the world study together, play games together, share their academic discoveries, and form friendships that some of them will keep for the rest of their lives. Perhaps most of all, I find my sense of hope and optimism in humanity's ability to change itself. We can enact deliberate plans – sometimes taking generations to reach fruition – to become the kind of people we want to be. Each generation passes its hopes and plans to the next generation; yet each generation soon acquires the power to break in some way from the plans of its predecessors, follow plans of its own, and pass those plans on to their successors. This hope is perhaps very faint, for the process is achingly slow, and there's no guarantee that any generation will take up and improve upon the best of what their predecessors bequeathed to them. Nevertheless, liberated from the Illusion of No Alternative, we can survey more possibilities for human life and human society. We can see all our practices as the product of human choices, past and present; we can then decide whether to keep them, change them, or discard them. We may, in so doing, render ourselves vulnerable again to loneliness, nihilism, and despair: the experiences that the illusions were erected to prevent. Yet with these unhappy possibilities comes the most wonderful kind of freedom: the chance to enter into a relationship with the people and the world around us which brings out the best in us.

§ 38. Songs from the Wood

I would like to meditate on those who sought an original relationship with the earth, because it is the immensity which, as we have seen, civilization has been pushing away from itself ever since people built the first house. So it should make for an interesting case study of what can be discovered when the illusions relating to our involvement in the immensities are stripped away. Did philosophers like Lao Tzu, Siddhartha Gautama, and Jean Jacques Rousseau, depart their cities not only because of what they disliked about their cities, but also because some immensity called to them from the wild?

Rousseau nearly said as much:

> I like to walk at my leisure, and halt when I please. The wandering life is what I like. To journey on foot, unhurried, in fine weather and in fine country, and to have something pleasant to look forward to at my goal, that is of all ways of life the one that suits me best. It is already clear what I mean by a fine country. Never does a plain, however beautiful it

may be, seem so in my eyes. I need torrents, rocks, firs, dark woods, mountains, steep roads to climb or descend, abysses beside me to make me afraid.[353]

French scholar Marcel Schneider attributed to Rousseau a new ecological religion that, '...saw God in the barbarity of the sun, in the passing clouds, and in the falling rain, sweet and pure.' [354] American eco-philosopher Gilbert LaFreniere showed how Rousseau's thought directly influenced virtually all the well-known early American nature writers including Henry David Thoreau, Nathaniel Hawthorne, George Perkins Marsh, John Muir, and Aldo Leopold.[355] LaFreniere also showed how Rousseau's early critics were wrong; Rousseau was not, as people like Voltaire said, advocating anti-progress. Rather, Rousseau wanted progress toward a human world with more empathy, co-operation, and happiness, such as that which existed in the (hypothetical) state of nature. However, as LaFreniere explains, 'This ideal could never be realized in a competitive, commercial, industrial society, but only in a rural, agrarian way of life which stressed the primacy of agriculture and the positive effects on human behavior of a life close to nature.' (LaFreniere, *ibid*, pg. 48)

People like Rousseau have been answering the call of the wild for centuries. We have already seen some of this in James C. Scott's study of Zomia, in upland southeast Asia. Among Americans and English-speakers in general, Thoreau's two-year experiment in quasi-solitary forest living is best known. A close second might be Chris McCandless, the young adventurer who went to live alone in the wildlands of Alaska, and whose life was the subject of a feature film (*Into the Wild*, 2007). I'd like to meditate on how the song from the wood was heard and answered by an entire community. So let's go to Germany around the end of the 19th century. Around that time, Germany was the most industrialized and population-dense nation in Europe. It was also the most polluted: historian William Rollins described the German landscape of the time as 'wounded', its rivers and streams as 'open-air sewers'; the overall situation was 'a man-made ecological disaster' caused by an 'overdose of progress'.[356] Most Germans of the time were convinced of the benefits and importance of technology, and so unable to fully acknowledge the problem. Yet a nascent environmentalist movement grew among the middle class, starting with local architectural preservation societies and housing reform initiatives, then growing to include landscape protection societies, gardening and bird watching clubs, and the like. It culminated in 1904 with the foundation of the *Bund Heimatschutz*, the 'League for Homeland Protection'. If the movement had a motto, it would be this: 'Learning to see, teaching to see; that is the goal of the Heimatschutz!'[357] The significance of this sentence appears when we remember that 'under a hegemony of capitalist-utilitarian thinking, people assessed the world surrounding them largely in the one-dimensional terms of finance.'[358] So the Heimatschutz was a political movement to protect landscapes from development, but also an *aesthetic* movement to help people see things differently than the way *Homo economicus* sees them. We could say the movement aimed for a transformation, not only of public policy, but also of consciousness.

Let's look closer at what prompted that transformation of consciousness. In 1880, polemicist Ernst Rudorff published 'On the Relationship of Modern Life to Nature', an essay that is now regarded as the central statement of the Heimatschutz movement. Here's a selection:

They are doing their best to make the pleasant and variegated countryside into a schematic plan – one that is as bare, clean-shorn, and regularly parceled-out as possible. Any tip of woods that juts out gets shaved away out of a love for the idea of a nice straight line; any meadow that stretches into a forest is planted up; even inside the forests they no longer tolerate any clearings or glades into which deer could run. Streams which have the bad habit of winding their way along a curved bed are now forced to flow straight ahead in ditches...[359]

Rudorff's legacy is somewhat mixed; he was an aristocrat who saw class divisions as 'necessary' and his policy goals involved little more than 'compensation for the necessary chasm between property-owners and non-property-owners'.[360] As it turned out, Rudorff's plan was mostly effective: most of the largest stretches of protected 'wild' lands in Europe were protected by the aristocracy, until some of those lands came under the jurisdiction of the state. (The land in Germany where I encountered the storm was at the time still owned by a local duke.) Nonetheless he clearly saw the stress and despair that industrial modernity often imposes on working class people's minds. For example, in the same essay he wrote of how modernity's own special version of the Ancient Great Wall, the property line, affects him:

> What an unbearable feeling: having to look upon the earth as a conglomeration of individual bits of property, having to consider the world blocked off with the exception of the public highway and those few spots that the mercy of others has been so good as to allot to me for my vacation! (Rudorff, *ibid.*)

To ease that stress, Rudorff thought that natural landscapes should be more accessible to people, protected from development, and in some cases protected from privatization. Some of his proposals were very specific: public and private co-ownership of landscapes of special beauty; an end to 'stream regulation'; transition zones between forest, field, and meadow had to be preserved; new hedgerows had to be planted when old ones were removed; and trees had to be protected: '...not only in order to promote the picturesqueness of the landscape but at the same time in order to take steps to maintain the bird population.'[361]

For some people, however, these modest and achievable goals were not enough. Various small anti-modernist and counter-culture movements appeared, the earliest of which were the *Wandervogel* groups (the 'free birds'), who appeared around 1895. As described by folklorist and participant-observer Gordon Kennedy, the *Wandervogel* movement began as small groups of high school students from Berlin who went on countryside hikes in their free time. These hikes started as weekend trips but grew longer, eventually up to an entire month in one go (just as Rousseau used to do). They established semi-permanent camps for large gatherings 'around the equinox fire of the ancient Germans', which they learned about by reading Tacitus' *Germanica*. Most of the *Wandervogeler* were teenagers: they dressed in ragged clothes, spoke their own versions of medieval peasant languages, and were often loud and deliberately offensive. They wanted nothing to do with middle class life, which they saw as 'superficial, coarse, complacent, gluttonous, materialistic, industrialized, technocratic, and pathetic' – notwithstanding that many of them came from middle-class families. Their communities were 'anti-bourgeois and Teutonic pagan in character... They took long hikes in the country where they sang their own versions of Goliardic songs, and camped under primitive conditions. Both sexes swam nude together in lakes and rivers.'[362] As the members grew older they joined adult groups including the *Liebensreform* (life-reform) movement, and the *Naturmenschen* (natural men, or nature boys), who were the long-haired beard-and-sandals hippies of their time. These adult groups had various degrees of overlap in membership and ideology, but in general they advocated alternative and 'natural' lifestyles as a *medical* antidote to the physical and psychological ills of industrial modernity. To this end they promoted the curative powers of vegetarian or raw-foods diets, abstinence from alcohol, nudism and naked sunbathing, and pure water.

Socially, they experimented with communism, anarchism, sexual liberty, and the worship of female pagan deities.[363] A kind of naturist retreat centre was established near Ascona, Switzerland, in the year 1900, which attracted eco-lifestyle seekers and spiritual nonconformists from all over Europe. Kennedy described it as a place where 'life-experiments were in vogue: surrealism, modern dance, Dada, paganism, feminism, pacifism, psychoanalysis, nature cure.'[364]

What eventually became of all these back-to-nature communities? Kennedy made some large claims about the reach of their influence, mostly based on strong but anecdotal evidence. He wrote that Ascona was visited by many of the period's most famous writers including Hermann Hesse, Carl Jung, Isadora Duncan, D.H. Lawrence, and Franz Kafka. It's also asserted that eden ahbez, an American proto-hippy and the composer of *Nature Boy*, the song recorded and made famous by Nat King Cole,[365] was mentored by a German-born draft-dodging émigré and naturmenschen named Bill Pester. The lyrics of *Nature Boy* could be treated as a wisdom-text of the movement, or for that matter as a gospel for any people who want to live simply, freely, and without interference from the absurdities of civilization:

> The greatest thing you'll ever learn
> Is just to love, and be loved in return.

This is precisely the kind of consciousness-transforming proposition that tends to emerge from the honest encounter with the immensities – but only when we approach the immensities in a certain way (and we will see more about that point later). As an aside: many people say ahbez' song was autobiographical. I think he was singing about his mentor, who certainly was 'a very strange enchanted boy' who 'wandered very far, over land and sea'. But I digress.

Over the next decade, many more nature boys, especially

including several medical doctors who had converted to naturopathy, moved from Germany to California. Kennedy asserts these immigrants became the nucleus of inspiration for California's 'hippies' a generation later – even to the point of instilling a preference for driving the Volkswagen bus.[366] The end of the *Bund Heimatschutz* is better documented, but not nearly as happy. For a while the organization successfully influenced regional and national policy, for instance in 1902 they influenced the state to forbid billboard advertisements in landscapes and city neighborhoods of outstanding beauty. However, by 1914 the organization became 'an unwieldy welter of different-sized regional and local groups with respectively different needs'; infighting and a narrowing of vision eventually led one of its leaders to declare that the movement had failed.[367] Moreover: some of the language used by the movement, especially the language of homeland, German-ness, and the *Volk*, which began as a perfectly innocent vocabulary for continuities in art and culture, was absorbed by the nationalist-racial militancy that today we associate with Nazism. At least in its beginnings, as Rollins makes clear, the movement had strong class-leveling and anti-capitalist principles in its world view – nothing could be further from the NSDAP platform. That said, some of the Heimatshutz leaders did eventually go on to become card-carrying Nazis.[368] The association is hard to shake off, even now, some eighty years later. While attending a conference in the Ruhr valley, I met a man who told me German environmentalists were among the smartest and most committed in the world. But he felt an urgent need to distance himself from 'the blood-and-soil people'. 'They talk like us but all they really care about is race,' he said.

Kennedy's description of the retreat centre at Ascona reads uncannily similar to the neo-pagan community as I encountered it in the 1990s. For most of that decade I attended several annual neo-pagan camping festivals, where I met all kinds of strange and wonderful people: crystal healers, goddess prophets, trance dancers, rebel academics, full-time nudists, polyamorous Crowley-worshipping sex magicians, tree-hugging eco-freaks – beautiful misfits, all of them. By day, people attended workshops and rituals, feasted and drank together, skinny-dipped in the lake, and discussed spiritual or philosophical matters of increasing weirdness. By night we gathered around a fire for dancing and drumming and love-making until dawn. It was an excellent education in practical empathy for people whose lives were radically different from that of the insulated, small-town, middle-class, conservative fishbowl in which I grew up. (I loved my hometown, but I also knew what it was. And I later learned the pagan community has its own version of the Illusion of the Higher and Lower Men. But that's another story.) Of special relevance to this meditation: I recall a day at WiccanFest when I was walking by the admin office as a car drove into the campground. The driver leaned out his window and shouted to everyone in the commons: 'Civilization is still over-rated!' A joke, to be sure; yet memorably ironic. For this man was driving a nice car, and had returned from a town-run where he purchased some camping supplies including a bag of ice – on a very hot high-summer day. Civilization had benefitted him in a dozen highly visible ways, in the last hour alone. Yet the joke was also an expression of the same dissatisfaction with civilization's mainstream values, and the same preference for a 'natural' way of life, exemplified a century ago by the Naturmenschen.

I wanted to know what the present-day naturmenschen think of civilization, and whether that joke from twenty years ago still holds. So I did some 'field research'. I sought out and interviewed ex-urbanites, off-the-grid homesteaders, and residents of small towns or islands, far from major cities. I asked them several questions including: What does the word 'civilization' mean to you? Has moving to an off-grid way of life (or planning or wishing to live that way) changed the way you think about things? Of the replies I received, I chose these to reprint here, as they exemplify the others, and seem to me well-expressed.

Here's one answer, from a friend of mine who lived mostly off-grid on Quadra Island BC, and on Rathlin Island, Ireland, for many years:

Twice in my life I have lived in very remote communities where I learned to become self-sufficient. Growing and gathering my own food was important, as was the barter system. Recycling, composting, and water storage became part of the daily routine. Media entertainment was difficult to come by due to frequent power outages so books, board games, and community participation were the main sources of entertainment: music on the beach or a community hall or people's homes for one example. Because travel could be difficult re-using items, sewing, knitting etc. were skills that were important. Living off-the-grid not only gave me purpose but was surprisingly less stressful than living in the city. One interesting thing that happened was that, when living that way, one becomes highly attuned with the cycles of nature, the signs and symbols of the birds and animals and meteorological events. Different ways to tell if a big storm was coming in so that one could prepare by making sure there was enough water and food for cooking in the house. When there is no power for days on end a house can be very, very quiet. It's amazing how one's brain and body suddenly develop anxiety when all the power comes back on. I don't know if it is the hum or the electricity itself, but it is tangible. I believe I was much healthier living out of the city. I think I learned how to be mindful, patient and grateful when living off grid. I was certainly able to focus better then than now. Moving back to the city has left me a little scatterbrained, behind in my obligations (especially to friends! Even though they are patient), with disrupted sleep patterns, and a quiet sense of desperation as I feel though I am falling farther behind. It's a bit alarming coming back into a world where media seems to control our thoughts and desires. Living off-grid creates a sense of focus, purpose, and curiosity about the world and how we fit in it. (S. Iles, artist)

Here's another reply, from one of my friends here in Bohemia, who says she lives partially off the grid and at a distance from major cities because:

I hate the economics and politics of power companies. At a distance: for sanity's sake. For beauty. Because I like silence and my own company a lot of the time (i.e.: classic Romanticism). And because I believe the skills people cultivate away from the center ought to be kept alive. They tend to cycle back into both fashion and necessity. (M. Reidinger, anthropologist)

I admire all these ideas and experiences. Yet I can see at least one critical problem here: it's annoyingly difficult to persuade people to appreciate the beauty of the song from the wood, if they can't already hear it. Here's an informant who described some of the problems that arise when people leave their cities without really leaving their 'city' way of thinking and living.

If people flee from the cities but try to keep living their city lives away from the urban grid, they risk hurting both the cities and the uncivilized places to which they flee. If, instead of walking or riding public transit every day to work, they now drive, they are not really striking a blow at our unjust civilization, but are undermining its ability to adjust (to make cities less car dependent). If too many people find it easy to move to the country because they can easily drive to work, the country fills up with city people who are not really devoted to

the communities they move to. And people in those communities who might have depended on public transportation
suffer as rural bus and train lines are cut and more and more
people drive. This phenomenon has radically transformed the
Czech and Slovak countryside in particular over the last 25
years. Transit accessibility has greatly diminished just as more
and more people are drawn to a rural idyll that they are not
actually prepared to live in. The villages are filled with people
who spend little time in the villages, and those who don't
drive, especially the older residents of those villages, suffer
from worsening transit services. I understand that living in
this limited, problematic world requires compromises; no one
lives exactly the life she or he would hold to be ideal. But for
me it is a fundamental principle that I would not live
anywhere that required me to transport myself by car. I think
that this is essential both to maintaining the communal and
cultural life of these places far from civilization, and to
enabling civilizational centers to develop ways for large
concentrations of people to live together. (J.G. Feinberg,
anthropologist)

One of my friends in Bohemia described to me an occasion when
the mayor of the region invited two executives from a Canadian
gold mining company, to see the land from the local lookout
tower – the same tower I had nicknamed the philosopher's
research station. The mayor wanted to impress the executives
with the beauty of the land, and the wrongness of damaging that
beauty with their mining project. Instead, the executives saw the
land as *Homo economicus* would see it. They pointed toward directions where train tracks could be built to supply their mines, and
hills where additional mines could be dug. At the height of
Germany's Heimatschutz movement, and everywhere in the
developed world today, only a small fraction of the people who
go into the woods for fun, such as hikers, fishers, cyclists,

hunters, and so on, will get politically involved in efforts to legally protect the same landscapes on which they enjoy those activities.[369]

That someone doesn't 'get it' is a tragedy, but that tragedy doesn't by itself make someone a bad person. For instance, a person who doesn't hear the song from the wood might instead hear the call of a different immensity: the bright lights and exciting sounds of the city, for instance, or the silence and darkness of interstellar space. The greater tragedy would be someone who can't hear the call of the immensity from any direction at all.

Another great tragedy might emerge from those who do hear the song from the wood, and in their eagerness to rush close to its source they destroy that source. Alison Hawthorne Deming, the American scientist and poet, had a similar concern for the impacts of eco-tourism. In 1996 she was sent by a tourism magazine to several remote islands in the Sea of Cortez to write about her experiences there. One of her observations is that ecotourism can give to visitors a sense of 'our own innocence as reflected in a foreign place', and that it can support local economies without requiring the industrial harvesting of forests or other resources; an indubitably good principle. But it can also do other kinds of harm to the areas visited, in both their ecologies and their human communities. As she wrote:

> Mass tourism, no matter what the intention, may hasten environmental degradation by adding further stress to natural resources, wildlife, and cultural integrity...huge resorts plunked down on the beach displacing local people; cruise ships dumping waste offshore; safari vans rushing cheetahs for photos; hordes of camera-toting invaders gawking and snapping shutters at tribal people as if at Mickey and Minnie Mouse.[370]

To find the kind of life-affirming insight that the encounter with the immensity can offer when stripped of its illusions, such as the insight of ahbez' beautiful song, space must be given to the immensity to let it unfold in its own way; and in addition, you have to approach the immensity a certain way. I have alluded to that point already; I will explore it more deeply in the next meditation.

§ 39. Responding to the Immensities

Some people do not experience wonder and love when they look upon the beauty of the earth. Instead they experience something like fear, or discomfort, or selfish opportunism, or placid indifference. It is similar for other immensities: some feel burdened or disgusted when they meet new people; some feel twitchy and despondent when alone. There has to be something in the person who stands before the immensity, which empowers that person to transform the experience so that they 'get it'. So, my solution to the third root question shall have to include its own model of its civilized person. However, recalling a problem I had identified earlier about such models, I shall eventually need to ask: could my model avoid embroiling itself in the politics of identity? But let's build our model up, before we burn it down.

The branch of philosophy that investigates the ethics of character and identity is called virtue ethics; I sometimes prefer to call it areteology, that is, a rational account (*logos*) of what is excellent (*arete*) in human affairs. Different cultures or different individual philosophers may have their different lists of virtues, but they all normally have something like the following logic in common. Every person wants, among other things, to live a fulfilling and happy life. To succeed in the pursuit of a fulfilling and happy life you must install certain consistent habits, certain ways of thinking and seeing and living, certain ways of being in the world, which are indicative of excellence; these habits are called the virtues. The differences between cultures and individual thinkers tend to be differences in what a fulfilling life looks like, and differing lists of what virtues are needed to achieve that life. That general idea, which gets its earliest philosophical treatment from Plato and Aristotle and (in a different way) from Confucius, has undergone a kind of renaissance in 20th century philosophy, mostly initiated by a circle of feminist philosophers from Oxford who emerged after the second world war: including Elizabeth Anscombe, Phillipa Foot, and Iris Murdoch. But enough of the history lesson. What we are here to discover is whether the logic of virtue can help us 'get it' when we are confronted with the immensities of reality – not only the song from the wood, but the call of other immensities too: arts and culture, urban life, solitude and loneliness, even death.

The most important virtue that someone must possess for this purpose, is the ability to affirm the basic proposition that life and the flourishing of life are ethically desirable and good. I suppose this is more like a logical commitment, and less like a 'virtue' as described above. But it seems clear to me that without it, no other virtues could be possible. For one reason: life and being alive are the necessary pre-condition for having and pursuing anything else that may be of value to you: art and beauty, wealth and prosperity, knowledge, justice, happiness, and even the opportunity to criticize the ethical desirability of life.[371] For another reason: its corresponding negation would be a 'death-affirming' proposition that offers no moral resistance to murder and suicide. Death-affirming forces like those, left unchecked, would make life and flourishing impossible for everyone, except perhaps the lucky or powerful few. We thus see how the life-affirming proposition passes the test of the progressive negation, and the death-affirming proposition fails it. For reasons like these, the ethical desirability of life should appear logically self-evident.

This deep commitment to the goodness and worthiness of life is enough to enable someone confronted by the immensities to say, as a matter of hypothesis, that there's something interesting and valuable happening. But it may not be enough to help someone actually *see* that something. That is the place where the virtues step in. Here I treat the virtues as ways of *responding* to the immensities, ways of being in the world that bring out the best in you when tested by the immensities. To express it another way: the virtues are the ways of being in the world that elicit from the encounter with the immensities the things that make life desirable and good. Here I treat the good life itself, the *eudaimonia* that Aristotle said everyone wants, as the life in which you consistently and habitually respond to the call of the immensity in a way that affirms the goodness of life and that brings out the best in you and in everyone involved. The word 'respond', by the way, comes from the Greek root word *sponde,* meaning 'to make a drink offering, to make a treaty, to pour a libation'.[372] Thus to re-spond is to complement that offering with another offering of your own; from there, we get the idea of *responsibility*, which is the ability-to-respond to an ethical calling.

So, what are those virtues?

To the immensity of the earth: the virtues are those ways of being in the world that enable you to look upon the earth, in all its beauty and its danger, yet feel no need to own it all, nor to destroy it; but instead, to find it satisfying enough just to explore it, to play with it, to *know* it. To the immensity of the earth, I therefore propose the virtues of *wonder*: including imagination, creativity, open-mindedness, aesthetic taste, and curiosity. This need not exclude the practical *use* of the earth, for instance in farming or even terraforming. But it calls for such practices to be conducted in careful (as in full-of-care), sustainable, and co-operative ways; just as loving another person doesn't exclude materially benefitting from that person, so long as that person materially benefits from you, too. It might be countered that much of the earth is dangerous: predatory animals, infectious deadly diseases, rough seas and high winds, and the like. We could even consider the vacuum of outer space: an environment intrinsically hostile to life as we know it. We should not want to open ourselves to needless danger. To this I would like to reply: the dangers of the earth are part of its beauty, as we have seen in the discussion of the sublime. And the work involved in protecting oneself from those dangers can stimulate the same sense of wonder as the world's safer spectacles.

To the immensity of interpersonal otherness and the differences between people: the virtues are those ways of being that enable you to look upon your neighbor, however strange and different she may be, and feel no need to make her conform to your demands, nor a need to send her away (such as, to her death). Instead, the virtues look upon your neighbor and they see another realm of discovery. They enable you to see another *earth*, in a manner of speaking: your neighbor's different eyes are another way of looking upon the earth; and with your neighbor by your side, maybe with your lover's hands clasped in yours, you have another way to explore it. So the same sense of discovery and wonder can emerge from meeting a person. To the immensity of interpersonal otherness, I propose the virtues of *humanity*: including the feminist ethics of care, the 'heroic' virtues of courage, friendship, and generosity; the 'Seven Grandfathers' of Wisdom, Truth, Humility, Bravery, Honesty, Love, and Respect.[373]

It might be countered that some of the people to whom you open yourself like this might turn out to be terrible people: greedy, violent, irrational, incapable of empathy. Surely a sound ethical theory would not leave good people vulnerable to freeloaders and sociopaths. To this I would like to reply: the only sure way to avoid such terrible people is to live entirely alone. For reasons already described, no one can live that way. The risk of running into such terrible people is the 'price', so to speak, for running into good and beautiful people. That the good occasionally come to harm from the bad is part of the tragedy of things; the risk of despair that no civilization can fully remove from life. But it is not, by itself, enough of a reason to run away and never speak to anyone again.

The point of the call of the immensity is not to measure who 'deserves' your virtuous treatment, or why. (That is the logic of deontology.) It is, rather, a matter of what you are ethically called to do. So, what are you ethically called to do? In the logic of areteology, you are called to live a flourishing and worthwhile human life. (This position is obviously consistent with the need to protect yourself from environmental dangers, and terrible people.) It is a basic axiom of areteology, going all the way back to Aristotle, that the virtues must benefit the possessor, or else they are not truly virtues. Now, virtues like generosity, hospitality, empathy, respect, and the like, may appear as if they only benefit other people, or that they cost the person who performs them. But they also benefit the possessor, in that they are the 'price' of admission into your neighbor's world. Acts of kindness and compassion are carriers of your presence; they are like ways of saying, 'I am here – is anyone else out there?' And they are the best ways to express one's presence with a realistic hope of hearing the answer: 'Yes, I am here too,' a sacred 'Yes' that carries its own message of generosity and compassion.

To the immensity of solitude, and of death: the virtues are those ways of being in the world that allow you to feel no need to avoid loneliness and death at any cost, however destructive to yourself or others. Instead, they allow you to find in your solitude a foundation of self-awareness and integrity. In a similar way, the virtues allow you to look upon your own coming death, and feel no fear. Instead, the virtues allow you to inscribe a satisfying exclamation-mark upon the story of your life, which others thereafter may read and so remember you. They allow you to choose your life deliberately, rather than merely continue it; and that choice can make life all the more fresh and succulent. To the immensities of loneliness and death, I propose the virtues of *integrity*: including reason, consistency, dignity, Socratic wisdom, acknowledged vulnerability, forgiveness, mercy, the will to establish a legacy, and the will to let go.

In this schematic of virtue, I think I have found another cause for hope. It is in the prospect of a greater depth of life-experience that can appear when I am willing to let go of my illusions, willing to risk harm and despair, in pursuit of a more honest relationship with reality. That may be the best way to find the sacred; it may be the way to find the best partners in the search for the highest and deepest things.

There may be more ways to respond to the immensities than these ways examined here. I have almost certainly not exhausted the possibilities. I present this list as only the result of my own experiments in living my life. But my own experiment is still ongoing. I am only 42 years old; I may have more than half my life still ahead of me.

I am aware that my argument here, and the experiences in my life which I regard as evidence in its favor, might not persuade the whole world to agree with me. Human nature, being so malleable, will occasionally produce people who remain spiritually unmoved by moonrises over seashores, unmoved by mountains, unmoved by the laughter of happy children, unmoved by the Ode to Joy. Indeed there will always be a few people who prefer the comforting illusions over a potentially heart-breaking reality. The usual way philosophers reply to this counter-argument is to say we can judge that such un-moved people are somehow 'un-virtuous'; they also often say there are better dimensions of happiness and human flourishing that the unvirtuous person misses (and which he has no idea that he misses). But, most importantly, nearly all the historic philosophers who examined the virtues assigned enormous importance to education. People must be exposed at an early age to the right kind of influences, and trained in the wisest ways to understand the world and solve problems. Plato famously argued that the leadership class of his ideal society had to be highly educated in both mind and body, from a very early age. Confucius wrote that a person who lacked education would be 'obscured' by ignorance, heartlessness, violence, and recklessness. (Analects 17:8) Mencius, a Chinese philosopher in the tradition of Confucius, wrote that people without education are not fully human: 'According to the way of man, if they are well fed, warmly clothed, and comfortably lodged but without education, they will become almost like animals.' (*Book of Mencius*, 3A:4)[374] The education system in which I serve as professor, the Cégep system of Quebec, includes humanist and philosophical education for the explicit purpose of teaching moral and cultural values. As noted in a report for Cégep Vanier College on history and purposes of its humanities program: 'The Core programs are designed to help each student develop to a higher level in his basic skills of reading, thinking, writing, and speaking; to initiate critical reflection on his – and his society's – intellectual, artistic, moral, social, and political values; to promote a deep insight into the human condition both past and present.'[375] Similarly the Parent Report (1964), which effectively created the Cégep system, stressed the importance of philosophy for young people's intellectual and moral development: '...so that they [the students] may be aware of the major problems confronting mankind and encouraged to develop their reasoning ability. Time spent thinking is not wasted; it liberates man spiritually, gives him the intellectual courage to withstand undue pressures and to outdo himself...'[376] Education is clearly one of the civilizing forces, in the sense that it is a force-at-work that treats human nature as a material to work upon.

Yet education is also a battlefield. Knowing the influence it can have, especially over the young, various factions in a society who want their values and their way of life affirmed will therefore take deep interest in what students are taught and how the teachers teach it. We have already seen the example of

Canada's residential school system for Aboriginal children; the system that deliberately aimed 'to kill the Indian in the child'.[377] The treatment of education as a battleground also explains, as another example, the persistent and often angry resistance to the Province of Ontario's proposed changes to sex education for primary schoolchildren. The proposed changes included frank discussions of gender identity, sexual consent, and masturbation. A survey found that about one-sixth of Ontario parents considered removing their children from public schools, so as to ensure their children did not receive that curriculum.[378] I think my worry still stands: that some species of identity politics is likely to appear around any model of the civilized person, no matter how virtuous that person may be. (This is another place where the risk of despair appears; the characteristic *wabi-sabi* of my philosophy.) But I think this is not a reason to entirely abandon the effort of crafting it. People need not agree with each other on every precise point in order to live alongside each other in peace. It is sufficient for people to agree that their disagreements can be resolved by negotiation, and that no one needs to resort to violent force. Especially in matters of education, thinking must replace killing.

As an aside: each of the main moral theories in Western philosophy has a problem like this. For deontology, it's obedience and authority; for utilitarianism, it's the sacrifice of the few for the needs of the many; for areteology and virtue, it's identity politics. But I digress.

At any rate, political engagement does not really begin with individual virtue. It begins at the place where the individual and her virtue meets others, usually (although not exclusively) in a public realm. It begins with people encountering each other, discovering shared or differing identities, and common or competing interests. The individual, in her solitude, prepares what she will bring to the meeting: but her preparation doesn't become a civilizing force until the meeting takes place. (It can also be a political matter if someone is excluded from the meeting, for instance because she is physically disabled and unable to attend, or because she has been shunted out of the Ancient Great Wall and so not allowed to attend.) So there are important questions here about how to translate these virtues into political praxis. It is easy to enact laws and build institutions that punish people for doing harm to each other; it's much more difficult, some say impossible, to enact laws and build institutions that reward people for helping each other and bettering themselves. In the next meditation, I will imagine ways to translate these personal discoveries into public praxis; but I apologize in advance if these suggestions appear hard to implement, insufficiently argued, or incomplete.

I am near the end of these meditations – yet still at the beginning of my work!

§ 40. The Deliberate Civilization

Everyone already knows, and probably already lives by, some such template of civilization. History has bequeathed many examples to us:

- The Tzedekah (cf. Isaiah 58:6-8), The Ten Commandments, the Pirke Avot (Judaism)
- The Lord's Prayer, the Beatitudes, the Golden Rule (Christianity)
- The Five Pillars of Submission: faith, prayer, charity, fasting, and pilgrimage (Islam)
- The Four Classical Virtues: courage, prudence, temperance, justice (Plato)
- The Five Relations: ruler and minister, parent and child, husband and wife, elder brother to younger brother, and friends (Confucianism)
- The Eightfold Path: right views, right intention, right speech, right action, right livelihood, right effort, right

mindfulness, right concentration (Buddhism)
- The Social Contract (Jean Jacques Rousseau)
- The Invisible Hand (Adam Smith)
- The Critique of the Gotha Program: 'From each according to his ability; to each according to his needs.' (Karl Marx)[379]
- The thirty principles of the Universal Declaration of Human Rights
- The New Deal (Franklin Roosevelt)
- The Great Society (Lyndon B. Johnson)
- The ten central capabilities of the Capability Approach to economic justice (Amartya Sen, Martha Nussbaum)
- The Leap Manifesto (Naomi Klein, Avi Lewis)

Each of these, as I see them, are occasions in history where people proposed and experimented with a new way to respond to the immensities. One thing they all have in common is that they are *deliberate* attempts to direct the civilizing forces in order to improve the quality of people's lives – albeit according to different pictures of what an improved quality of life might look like.

In the same spirit, I propose the creation of *the deliberate civilization*, by which I mean a society that deploys its civilizing forces (social, cultural, economic, political, religious, and so on) in the service of creating social and political and geo-spacial environments well-suited for individual and collective human flourishing. The deliberate civilization is not necessarily concerned with maximizing energy capture, nor with maximizing wealth, nor maximizing dominance over the environment. It is concerned with what Aristotle called *eudaimonia*, flourishing, and 'the good life'; it is concerned with exploring, furthering, and expanding the possibilities for excellence (*arete, gong-fu,* etc.) in human affairs. The deliberate civilization might have a place for piety and order, as in the old feudal societies of Western history; it might have a place for competitiveness and productivity, as in the neoliberal world view of *Homo economicus*. But above those values, the driving virtues of the deliberate civilization shall be the virtues of humanity, integrity, and wonder; and most of all *curiosity*: that is, curiosity about the world around us, about each other, what more and what else our possibilities for life may be, and especially about what more and what else it can mean to be human.

To help make a society like that actually appear in this world, the civilizing forces must be deployed such that, as far as possible:

- The illusions which interfere with any person's relationship with reality (i.e. the immensities) are rooted out;
- No one is abandoned to an environment likely to draw out the worst in her;
- Everyone is welcomed into an environment likely to draw out the best in her;
- There can be many models of what is best (or worst) in us, and many kinds of environments which can bring out the best (or the worst) in us; these are determined by the insights and decisions that emerge from the general conversation in each community.

These principles are easily applicable to any plane of social relations where the civilizing forces are visibly deployed, big picture and small. So, it obviously includes things that governments can do, from international relations to local municipalities. But it also includes things that private enterprises, religious organizations, social clubs, families, and friendship circles can do.

It might seem that there is some vagueness and relativism in my proposal here. To explain why I think it is not so vague, or rather why that vagueness is not a problem, I should state what I mean by *the general conversation*. From the fact that people are always intrinsically unlike each other in some small way (an immensity itself), I can agree that everyone will have their own experience of the immensities, and their own idea of how best to respond to them. But there is nothing relative about the immensities themselves: they are the gates of objective reality before which everyone stands. They surround every person in every direction; they configure each person's history and identity when she responds to them in situations demanding irreversible choices. It is only in the matter of how to respond to the immensities where there might be differences of opinion. The general conversation is the instrument by which differences of opinion can be resolved into definite plans of action. It stands in the place of what Rousseau called 'the general will', and in the place of what Adam Smith called 'the higgling and bargaining of the market...which, though not exact, is sufficient for carrying out the business.'[380] It is the ongoing and universally inclusive public debate about any and all questions of public interest – a civilizing force in its own way. Its most visible statements are made when we vote. Yet the conversation can take place anywhere two or more people can discuss public questions with each other and put various answers to the test of their actual lives. So it can take place in courts of law, in places of worship, and at bargaining tables between labor unions and employers. It can take place in coffee shops, on city buses, on radio call-in shows, in speeches by politicians or celebrities, on computer networks, in books and movies and theatres, and stand-up comedy shows. Its only limiting requirements are those of any other rational debate. For instance it requires people to abstain from lies and insults and aggression, and to avoid logical fallacies. It requires getting all the relevant facts straight, openness to negotiation and compromise, and an acknowledgement that the best ideas are not necessarily one's own. It also requires participants to decide among themselves how best to deal with people who exploit or dominate the conversation unfairly. So where a critic might see vagueness, a participant may find intellectual freedom.

The deliberate civilization is thus a society that *deliberates* – that is, a society in which thinking and talking has replaced fighting and killing as the primary means to create change. If there are doubts about the relative merits of one social plan over another, or uncertainties about what really is in the interest of the community as a whole, those doubts and uncertainties can be resolved into practical and testable answers by the debating and negotiating of parties in the conversation. It might be objected that this is unrealistic because people will always cheat and lie to each other. In reply, I should like to ask you if you really want to live in a world populated by such nasty people, or if you want to see yourself as such a nasty person. The moment you answer me with thoughtfulness instead of with insults and violence, the conversation will have begun.

As I contemplate principles like these, it immediately occurs to me that many of the things we need to do to create the deliberate civilization are things people are already doing. And this is another source of optimism and hope. For example:

- Free or accessibly-priced public education from primary school to college and university, such as that which exists in almost every country in Europe, and in most of Asia.
- Universal public health care, such as that which exists in every developed nation in the world (except the United States).
- Accessibly-priced ($8/day), publicly regulated and professionally delivered early childhood care and education, such as that which exists in the Canadian province of Quebec.
- Statistical reporting of Gross Domestic Happiness instead of Gross Domestic Product, as is done in the Kingdom of Bhutan.
- Evidence-based government policy research instead of

ideology-based policy.

- Farmer's markets; local arts, foods, and handicrafts markets.
- Concerts, theatre performances, gallery shows, music and culture festivals, and street buskers.
- Outdoor kindergartens, such as those that are common in rural areas of Germany.
- Exercise of consumer sovereignty; buying from retailers or companies whose policies and practices meet high standards for ethics and community service.
- Divestment from fossil fuels; investment in renewable nonpolluting energy sources such as solar power.
- Voting for candidates and parties that represent ethically progressive platforms. Proportional representation, so that each party's share of seats in parliament more closely reflects each party's share of the popular vote. (I am a fan of the Single Transferrable Vote system used in Ireland and other European countries, but there are other versions.)
- Attending public rallies, joining letter-writing campaigns, lobbying politicians and media professionals, hosting fundraising events, and other forms of targeted publicity. Remember, political activism is not joining a club, nor is it clicking a button on a website; activism is *doing something*.
- Dinner parties in the style of the classical Greek symposium: where the guests are expected to bring prepared presentations of music and poetry and short philosophical lectures – and rebuttals! In an age when commercial media is veritably designed to make people uncomfortable (so that they will consume the advertised product) or fearful (so that they will vote for the hawkish politician), an evening of nothing more than good food and good conversation with good people, who are flesh-and-blood present around you and not merely linked through a computer network, can be a surprisingly subversive and

empowering occasion.

- Rewilding projects. 'Rewilding' means withdrawing farms, depopulated urban areas, and the like, so that nature can reclaim those areas. Rewilding protects ecological functions like water and air reclamation, and makes surrounding inhabited areas less vulnerable to natural disasters such as landslides and floods, and the general effects of climate change.[381] There are rewilding projects in many places around the world, notably along the length of Europe's former 'Iron Curtain'. Some rewilding projects are especially large, such as a rewilded 10,000-acre artificial island in the Netherlands. The largest rewilding project in Europe is a 27,000-acre area of county Mayo, Ireland.[382] Rewilding projects require a mostly hands-off approach to the selected areas, although they sometimes allow minimally-invasive ecological management and resource use, such as hunting, forest gardening and forest grazing, hedgerow maintenance, tourism, and education.
- Dark Sky Preserves: areas that are kept free of light pollution, so that we may still look up, as Vitruvius imagined our distant ancestors looked up and so became human. Urban light pollution is now so strong that one-third of the human race cannot see the Milky Way. Most city-dwellers have now never known a truly starry sky in all their lives: and as another consequence of urban light pollution, their eyes have mostly lost the ability to adjust to darkness.[383]
- Sustainable Compact Cities. The idea here, pioneered by internationally-renowned architect Richard Rogers, is to build densely populated yet socially diverse cities where businesses and residences stand near or together with cultural installations like theatres, cafes, parks, and public squares; where public transit is efficient and well-designed, so there is almost no need for a private car; and

where 'communities are focused around neighbour-hoods'.[384] As Rogers describes them:

Cities should be about the people they shelter, about face-to-face contact, about condensing the ferment of human activity, about generating and expressing local culture... Proximity, the provision of good public space, the presence of natural landscape and the exploitation of new urban technology can radically improve the quality of air and of life in the dense city. Another benefit of compactness is that the countryside itself is protected from the encroachment of urban development. (*ibid* pg. 40)

- Social businesses. This is a model of semi-capitalist enterprise, described by Nobel-prizewinning economist Muhammad Yunis. The idea is to bring together two of humanity's strongest psychological drives, profit-seeking self-interest and community-oriented altruism, such that both of them drive the enterprise together. A social business seeks profit for its owners, but also seeks to improve certain social conditions related to the interests of the business in the areas where it operates. It invests its profits in ways that promote those social goals. For example, a rice mill company in Sierra Leone, Mountain Lion Agriculture, created an 'In-Kind Input Loan Program' so that the farmers it works with won't take on any debts. The company sells seed, fertilizer, and pesticides, and rents equipment to the farmers, 'on a strictly cost basis (i.e. no interest)'. The company also buys the harvested rice from the same farmers, to sell to distributors and the public.[385]
- Various equality rules to help defeat the illusion of the Higher and Lower Men. Employment equity laws are the best known examples of these; though they are rare in the private sector, they tend to be the norm in unionized

public-sector fields. But there are other kinds of rules which aim at a similar target. For example, some Canadian companies have corporate policies that prevent the company's highest paid employees from receiving more than ten times the income of the lowest paid employee. At most other companies that do not have this policy, the average ratio of highest-paid to lowest-paid is more like 122-to-one.[386]

- Internet neutrality: the requirement that all internet servers treat all data passing through their networks equally, such that users can access any website they want, and barriers like paywalls or 'throttling' cannot make it artificially easier to reach some websites and harder to reach others.

Almost all of those examples are things that belong to what philosopher John McMurtry called *the civil commons*: 'Society's organized and community-funded capacity of universally accessible resources to provide for the life preservation and growth of society's members and their environmental life-host.'[387] Its highest manifestation, McMurtry says, is democratic government; yet it is not the same as government, nor is it a state function. Beginning in the historical village commons before the enclosures (and the clearances), it also includes public education, public arts and broadcasting, religious rituals, health care, sports fields, old age pensions, city plans, sidewalks and footpaths, the atmosphere of the earth, the air we breathe, women's shelters, municipal sewers and garbage collection, parks and gardens, and human language itself.[388] The creation of a deliberate civilization, it seems to me, will require (among other things) the preservation, the sound management, and perhaps the expansion, of the civil commons, as the foundation upon which every person's capacity for curiosity and excellence can be engaged as deeply as her individual potential allows.

Let me consider some last-minute objections. It may be argued that the deliberate civilization, because it would have to marshal its forces in this deliberate way, must somehow be unfree. For instance, Herbert Spencer argued that 'all socialism involves slavery' and that 'it matters not whether [the slave's] master is a single person or a society.'[389] About fifty years later Friedrich Hayek made a similar point: 'Although the professed aim of [economic] planning would be that man should cease to be a mere means, in fact – since it would be impossible to take account in the plan of individual likes and dislikes – the individual would more than ever become a mere means, to be used by the authority in the service of such abstractions as 'the social welfare' or the 'good of the community'.'[390] What these writers did not see was the way in which their anti-government and free-market ideology was as much a social program as the communist ideology that they opposed. Nor did they see how individuals among the lower economic ranks of society would have to sacrifice their lives to the demands of *Homo economicus,* as surely as any feudal serf had to sacrifice himself to his lord, and as surely as any urban proletariat in a Soviet system had to sacrifice himself to the Communist party. But that is, perhaps, only a *tu quoque* point. The stronger reply to Hayek and Spencer's objection is that their argument is a case of the illusion of No Alternative. If the state can 'enslave' people in its efforts to improve them, as they believed, still it is clear that landlords and industrialists and bankers can enslave people too. Their way of enslaving people is rather more insidious, as it is wrapped in the illusions of freedom and democracy. McMurtry, in his discussion of the civil commons, regarded the distinction between individual rights and community rights as a false opposition: 'The individual's right to the resources of life – health care, learning, clean air and water, and so on – is grounded in the community's ability to provide them.'[391] Individual initiative is obviously necessary for personal flourishing, yet numerous public resources are equally necessary, if not more so: resources like air and water, schools, roads and other infrastructure, patent offices, police services and law courts, national central banks, government funded science research, and so on; indeed individuals might be unable to fully prosper without them. Since the civil commons is as much cultural as it is political, we might also invoke Charles Taylor's discussion of the *horizon of meaning*, that is, the cultural background from which individual choices acquire their meaning, and without which individual choices lose their meaning. As Taylor says:

> Even the sense that the significance of my life comes from its being chosen – the case where authenticity is actually grounded on self-determining freedom – depends on the understanding that *independent of my will* there is something noble, courageous, and hence significant in [the act of] giving shape to my own life.[392]

To put Taylor's argument another way: I can affirm that I am an individual; but the *significance* of my individuality depends upon its standing out from a horizon of meaning. And that horizon is something I share with others. This horizon is made of our shared language, history, art, music, philosophy, foodways, religion, politics, family life, romantic love – all the multifold relationships in which we are involved. Of course, this may invoke the age-old problem of where to draw the boundary between the public and the private, and exactly how much of an individual's time (or money) a society may demand. I see that as something each community can decide for itself in the course of the general conversation.

It might be argued that expanding the civil commons would be too expensive. However, the dispelling of the illusion of the virtuous prince revealed a deep and ready source of revenue: the money that corrupt businessmen and politicians conceal from the tax authorities. Tax evasion by the super-wealthy is estimated to cost the governments of the world about $200 billion per year.[393] The true scope of tax evasion is probably impossible to fix precisely, but the revelations of the Panama Papers imply that the true figure is much higher than the figure quoted here. There are other ways to require cheaters and freeloaders to contribute their fair share:

- Ending government subsidies to producers of nonrenewable and high-polluting energy, such as fossil fuels.
- Carbon taxes for other high-polluting industries.
- Financial transaction taxes, such as the 0.1% 'Tobin' tax on foreign currency conversions.
- Increase public royalties for resource extraction works.

Finally, it might be objected that the deliberate civilization is a kind of unrealistic utopia. It won't make *everyone* happier; it won't make *all* environments into Gardens of Eden or Lands of Youth. To this I think the best reply is to say: the deliberate civilization is a dynamic and experimental society, not a theoretically planned and 'perfect' one in the style of Plato's Republic or Augustine's City of God. It does not point the way to a Promised Land, because it holds that there is no such thing. Instead, it aims for more achievable and modest goals, mainly to do with improving the quality and delivery of public goods. It can also be replied that a worthwhile and flourishing human life is not necessarily a life with no sadness. If despair cannot be eradicated, still it does not follow that we cannot have hope at the same time. It seems to me that false hope is worse than no hope at all, and that the hope that can come when we are willing to risk despair is better than the hope that comes from illusion.

The world in which we presently live is a world where too many people, by design of the civilizing forces, never find the good in them. At this moment, the world's next great scientist, great inventor, great poet, great leader, may be laboring beneath the burden of poverty, chronic illness, illiteracy, racism, sexism, homophobia, and religious bigotry. In a deliberate civilization, fewer of those obstacles will stand in her way. It may be argued that the next tyrant, or serial killer, or military dictator, may also be prevented by poverty from becoming a larger-scale villain. It is my hope that the deliberate civilization will have fewer terrible people to contend with, because it will deliberately resist the environments from which terrible people tend to spring. Our problem is not a failure to turn our utopian dreams into realities. Our problem is that most of our utopian dreams were only mirages, propped up to protect ourselves from despair; and that protection came with too terrible a price in ruined lives and needless deaths. Indeed, there may be a moral demand for something like the deliberate civilization. For the precariats and the oppressed of the world should not have to wait for the lucky accident of a naturally generous benefactor who assumes power in the state or in the private sector or in religion. They do not deserve to suffer. Neither do you. We should all use every instrument at our disposal, in government, industry, arts and culture, and interpersonal relations, to deliberately build a better world, right now, for as many people as we can. If that thought is not now self-evident, then all these meditations shall have ended in failure.

I arise from my seat by this lake, and thank its waters. I have decided to turn around and rejoin the city. Yet before I reach the city, I shall stop with some friends for the night; they've built a fire in the back garden, they're roasting some food over it, and they've brought their drums and guitars. Tomorrow I will go out again and do what I can to make the world a better place, for me and for everyone around me. But tonight I will eat and drink, make music, and tell stories, all with my people, beneath these stars. Despite all the world's absurdities and illusions, and all their terrible consequences, there are always, nevertheless, things of beauty to be found. I have decided to be the kind of person who can hear its call. In all these late nights and long distance adventures, I have found these four lamps to light the way:

- First, the discovery that human nature is sufficiently malleable that human society and culture can change, even if it can change only very slowly, and even if it is supposed that some individuals cannot change;
- Second, civilization itself emerged as we taught ourselves empathy and co-operation and compassion, and it continues to be partially sustained by those values;
- Third, although we may be left with despair when we cast away our illusions, so we are also left with a chance to find greater depths of life than we could find any other way;
- Fourth and finally, yet perhaps most importantly, many of the things we need to do to bring about a better world are things we are already doing.

On the scale of the big picture, we may not see a deliberate civilization of the kind I describe for many generations. For these things take time; indeed they can take centuries. I do not say that a better world is already on the way; that, too, would be a mirage. I wish to say instead that a better world is *possible* – no destiny prevents it, for we do not have a destiny – but we shall have to work for it. On the scale of the small picture, we can create the deliberate civilization right here and now. It appears in the same moment, and in the same place, any two or more people come together, endeavor to dispel their illusions, and speak to each other honestly and lovingly. In so doing, they create for each other a chance to pursue a good and worthwhile human life on earth.

Quod erat demonstrandum. Ergo bibamus.

End Notes

1   Myers, *Circles of Meaning, Labyrinths of Fear* (O Books, 2012), pg. 27. Please pardon the hubris of quoting my own books.

2   Rupert Jones, 'Punk Rock Brand', *The Guardian*, 9th June 2015.

3   Richard Norton-Taylor, 'Terror trial collapses after fears of deep embarrassment to security services', *The Guardian*, 1st June 2015.

4   '9 people killed in shooting at black church in Charleston, SC' Thomson Reuters/CBC News, 17th June 2015.

5   Daniel Schwartz, 'Q&A: The FBI's role in 'manufacturing' terrorism', *CBC News*, 3rd May 2013

6   Statistics Canada: CANSIM, table 102-0551.

7   Durkheim, *Suicide*, (London: Routledge/The Free Press, 1951) pg. 175-186. Also, c.f. Armstrong, *An Outline of Sociology as Applied to Medicine*, 3rd edition, (London: Wright, 1989) pg. 28-9.

8   Jamie Strashin, 'Rob Ford: A mess of contradictions whose fans were quick to forgive', *CBC News*, 23 March 2016; Robyn Doolittle, 'Police investigated crack video while Rob Ford in rehab, new documents reveal', *The Globe and Mail*, 24th September 2014; Ann Hui, 'Rob Ford's racial slurs violated city council's code of conduct, report finds', *The Globe and Mail*, 26th March 2015.

9   Schumpeter, 'Death and transfiguration: The golden age of the Western corporation may be coming to an end', *The Economist*, 19th September 2015.

10   Emma Bath, 'World's population to reach 11.2 billion by end of the century, UN says', Reuters/The Globe and Mail, 29 July 2015; United Nations, Department of Economic and Social Affairs, Population Division (2015). *World Population Prospects: The 2015 Revision, Key Findings and Advance Tables*,

Working Paper No. ESA/P/WP.241.

11 British cabinet minister Iain Duncan Smith, for example, argued that the state's child benefit should not extend past a family's second child, in order 'to help behavioral change'. (Rowena Mason, 'Child benefit may be limited to two children, says Iain Duncan Smith', *The Guardian*, 14th December 2014.) 'Behavioral change' is a weasel-word for punishing poor people for having too many children. It's a trope that goes all the way back to the time of author Charles Dickens, whose character Ebenezer Scrooge suggests that the poor and destitute of London should die 'and decrease the surplus population'.

12 Michele Chandler, 'It's About Forty Years Until the Oil Runs Out', *Insights*, Stanford University School of Business, 1st January 2008.

13 Damian Carrington, 'Four billion people face severe water scarcity, new study finds', *The Guardian*, 12th February 2016.

14 *The Global Risks Report*, 11th Edition. (Geneva: World Economic Forum, 2016), pg. 6.

15 Motesharrei, Rivas, and Kalnay: 'Human and Nature Dynamics (HANDY) Modeling Inequality and Use of Resources in the Collapse or Sustainability of Societies', *Ecological Economics* Vol. 101, May 2014, pp.90-102.

16 Dana Flavelle, 'Canada's inequality growing: StatsCan', *The Toronto Star*, 11th September 2014.

17 Larry Elliott, 'Richest 62 people as wealthy as half of world's population, says Oxfam', *The Guardian*, 18th January 2016.

18 IPCC, 'Summary for Policymakers' in: *Climate Change 2013: The Physical Science Basis* (Cambridge University Press, 2013), pg. 17, emphasis original. The phrase 'extremely likely' is used in the text as a technical term for the scientist's level of confidence in the conclusion.

19 IPCC, 'Summary for Policy Makers' in *Climate Change 2014: Impacts, Adaptation, and Vulnerability.* (Cambridge University

Press, 2014) pg. 13.

20   Glenn Scherer, 'Climate Science Predictions Prove Too Conservative', *Scientific American*, 6th December 2012.

21   Williams, Zalasweiwicz, Haff, et.al.: 'The Anthropocene Biosphere', *The Anthropocene Review*, Vol. 2, No. 3, December 2015.

22   Waters, Zalasweiwicz, Summerhays, et.al. 'The Anthropocene is functionally and stratigraphically distinct from the Holocene', *Science/AAAS*, Vol. 351, iss. 6269, 8th January 2016.

23   Lanzi and Dellnic/OECD Environment Directorate, *The Economic Consequences of Outdoor Air Pollution*, (Paris: OECD Publishing, 9th June 2016), pp. 14-15.

24   Motesharrei, Rivas, and Kalnay, *ibid*.

25   Tim Adams, 'Artificial Intelligence: 'We're like children playing with a bomb'', *The Guardian*, 12th June 2016.

26   'Killer robot arms race? Hawking, Musk and renewed rhetoric on rise of the machines', *The Globe and Mail/The Canadian Press*, 28th July 2015.

27   Stephen Erlanger, 'Are Western Values Losing Their Sway?', *The New York Times/Sunday Review*, 12th September 2015.

28   Niall Fergusson, 'Episode Six: Work'. *Civilization: is the West History?* (London UK: Channel 4, 2011).

29   Truth and Reconciliation Commission of Canada: *Honouring the Truth, Reconciling for the Future: Summary of the Final Report*, (National Centre for Truth and Reconciliation/ University of Manitoba, 2015), pg. 27.

30   *ibid.* pg. 49.

31   Truth and Reconciliation Commission of Canada: *Honouring the Truth, Reconciling for the Future: Summary of the Final Report*, (National Centre for Truth and Reconciliation/ University of Manitoba, 2015), pg. 1.

32   Shepard B. Clough, 'The Rise and Fall of Civilizations: How economic development affects the culture of nations',

(McGraw-Hill, 1951), pg. 2-3.

33 Felipe Fernández-Armesto, *Civilizations*, (Toronto: Key Porter, 2000), pg. 3.

34 Spencer, 'Progress: Its Law and Cause', *The Westminster Review*, Vol. 67 (1857).

35 c.f. Ian Morris, *The Measure of Civilisation*, (London UK: Profile Books, 2013), pg. 7-8.

36 Arnold Toynbee, 'The Genesis of Civilizations', *A Study of History*, Abridged edition by D.C. Somervell, (NY: Dell, 1946), Vol. 1, Sec. 2.iv.1, pg. 68. Emphasis his.

37 Toynbee, *ibid*, pg. 102.

38 Kroeber, *Configurations of Cultural Growth*, (Berkeley: University of California Press, 1944) pg. 7, 10.

39 Clark, *Civilisation*, pg. 122.

40 *Ibid*. pg. 21.

41 *Ibid*, pg. 119.

42 Marcus Wohlsen, 'Larry Page Lays Out His Plans For Your Future', *Wired Magazine*, 19th March 2014.

43 Danielle and Andy Mayoras, contributors, 'Mark Zuckerberg and His Charitable Plan Should Be Followed, Not Criticized' *Forbes Magazine*, 9th December 2015.

44 Gibbon, *The Decline and Fall of the Roman Empire*, (Chicago: Encyclopedia Britannica/Great Books of the Western World, 1952), Vol. 2, pg. 591.

45 Steven Strauss/Alternet, '8 striking parallels between the U.S. and the Roman Empire' *Salon*, 26 December 2012.

46 C.F. Atkinson, trans. Oswald Spengler, *The Decline of the West*, (London: George Allen & Unwin, 1980), Vol. 1, pg. 24

47 D.K. Simonton, 'Kroeber's cultural configurations, Sorokin's cultural mentalities, and generational time-series analysis: A quantitative paradigm for the comparative study of civilizations' *Comparative Civilizations Review*, 49, pp.96-108.

48 Clough, *The Rise and Fall of Civilization: How economic development affects the culture of nations* (McGraw Hill, 1951).

49   C.f. Christopher Scarre & Brian Fagan, *Ancient Civilizations*, (Longman, 1997), pg. 6-7.

50   From the instruction manual accompanying *Civilization 3: Game of the Year Edition* (Infogames Interactive, 2002), pp. 5-6, 18. Note: I cite Meier here, not as the author of the manual (since that information isn't given), but as the product's chief developer.

51   Morris, *Why the West Rules – For Now*, (McLelland & Stewart, 2011) pg. 83.

52   Morris, *Why the West Rules – For Now*, pg. 143-4.

53   Nikolai Kardashev, 'Transmission of Information by Extraterrestrial Civilizations', *Soviet Astronomy*, Vol. 8, No.2, Sept-Oct 1964, p. 217.

54   Fernandez-Armesto, *ibid*, pg. 24.

55   Coomaraswamy, 'What is Civilisation?' cited in *What is Civilisation? And Other Essays* (Ipswich, UK: Golgonooza Press, 1989), pg. 8.

56   Perry, *Western Civilization: A Brief History* 10th edition, (Boston: Wadsworth, 2013) pg. 7.

57   Huntington, 'A Clash of Civilisations?' *Foreign Affairs*, Summer 1993.

58   Kroeber, *Style and Civilizations*, (University of California Press, 1957).

59   N. Elias, *The Civilizing Process* Revised edition, (Blackwell: 2000), pg. 7. Emphasis added.

60   Clark, *Civilisation*, (London: BBC, 1969), pg. 1.

61   Philip Bagby, *Culture and History*, (University of California Press, 1958-1963), pg. 163.

62   Robert Park and Ernest Burgess, *The City: Suggestions for the Study of Human Nature in the Urban Environment*, (Chicago: University of Chicago Press, 1925), pg. 1.

63   Fernandez-Armesto, pg. 23.

64   Harries, *The Ethical Function of Architecture*, (Cambridge, Mass, USA: MIT Press, 2000), pg. 106.

65 Maya Rhodan, 'UN: Number of City-Dwellers to Double by 2050', *Time Magazine* 9th December 2013; Edith M. Lederer, 'UN predicts near doubling of city dwellers by 2050' *Associated Press*, 10th December 2013.

66 Ian Johnson, 'China's Great Uprooting: Moving 250 Million into Cities' *The New York Times*, 15th June 2013.

67 Gorman, Steve. 'Scientists study huge plastic patch in Pacific', *Reuters*, 4th August 2009.

68 Ryan, P. G.; Moore, C. J.; Van Franeker, J. A.; Moloney, C. L. (2009). 'Monitoring the abundance of plastic debris in the marine environment', *Philosophical Transactions of the Royal Society B: Biological Sciences* 364 (1526): 1999–2012.

69 'Canadians produce more garbage than anyone else', *CBC News*, 17th January 2013.

70 The elder Mirabeau; cited in Elias, *The Civilizing Process*, pg. 34.

71 Elias, *The Civilizing Process*, pg. 34.

72 Elias, *ibid*, pg.32.

73 Cf. Pierre Bourdeau, *Distinction: A Social Critique of the Judgment of Taste,* (London: Routledge, 1984), pg. 41.

74 Cf. Stephen Angle, *Sagehood: The Contemporary Significance of Neo-Confucian Philosophy,* (OUP, 2009) pg. 141.

75 Newman, *Foundations of Religious Tolerance,* (University of Toronto Press, 1982), pg. 65.

76 Vitruvius, *The Ten Books of Architecture,* trans. Morris Hickey Morgan, (New York: Dover, 1960), book 2, ch. 1,1, pg. 38.

77 Lecky, *History of European Morals*, Vol. 1, pg. 162.

78 Semper, 'The Basic Elements of Architecture', cited in Wolfgang Herrmann, *Gottfried Semper: In Search of Architecture,* (Cambridge: MIT Press, 1989), pg. 98.

79 Frank Lloyd Wright, *The Natural House,* (NY: New American Library, 1970) pg. 32. Emphasis his.

80 Vitruvius, *ibid*, pg. 39.

81 *Ibid* pg. 39-40.

82   Cited in Andrew Howley, 'The Ancient Past as a Window to the Future' *Report on the Dialogue of Civilization conference, Guatemala*, National Geographic Society, 1st May 2013.

83   Felipe Fernandez-Arnesto, *Civilizations,* (Toronto: Key Porter, 2000), pg. 5.

84   'Oh deer! Frenzied fawn runs rampant at N.B. legislature', *CBC News*, 31 May 2007; 'Stubborn goat 'arrested' after refusing to leave Saskatchewan Tim Hortons', *CTV News*, 28 September 2015; 'Dramatic cougar chase in Victoria ends with tranquilizer dart', *Canadian Press/Globe and Mail*, 5th October 2015.

85   His Holiness Pope Francis: *Encyclical Letter* Laudato Si' *of the Holy Father Francis on Care for Our Common Home*, (Vatican City: Libreria Editrice Vaticana, 2015), § 2.

86   R.E. Turner, *The Great Cultural Traditions, The Foundations of Civilization, Vol. 1: The Ancient Cities* (New York: McGraw Hill, 1941).

87   Libanius, *Orations*, § 25.

88   R.D. McCrie, *A History of Security*, in chapter 2 of Gill, ed. *The Handbook of Security* (Palgrave MacMillan, 2014), pg. 23-4.

89   Richard Rogers, *Cities for a Small Planet* (London: Faber & Faber, 1997), pp. 11-14.

90   Cited in Warren Belasco, *Food: The Key Concepts* (NY: Berg, 2008) pg. 18.

91   Gibbon, *Decline*, book 2, pg. 33.

92   For these word-origin stories I relied on *The Shorter Oxford English Dictionary: On Historical Principles* (Oxford UK: Clarendon Press, 1984).

93   Arnold Toynbee, 'The Genesis of Civilizations', *A Study of History*, II.B, pg. 192.

94   Huntington, *The Clash of Civilizations*, pg. 41.

95   Fernandez-Armesto, 'Civilization', pg. 3.

96   Locke, *Second Treatise of Government*, V.26.

97   cited in Morley, *Rousseau* Vol. 1, (London: Chapman and Hall, 1873) pg. 314.

98   Elias, *The Civilizing Process*, pg. 47.

99   C.f. Ronald Hutton, *The Triumph of the Moon* (Oxford University Press, 1999) pg. 4.

100 OED, Vol. 2, pg. 1493.

101 Alistair McBay, 'Scottish evangelists identify Paganism as one of the 'biggest threats to Western civilization'. News blog of the National Secular Society (of the UK), 16th November 2015.

102 Tacitus, *Agricola*, § 21 (pg. 73).

103 Francis, Jones, & Smith, *Origins: Canadian History to Confederation*, 3rd edition (Harcourt Brace, 1996) pg. 25.

104 McLuhan, *Touch the Earth*, pg. 23.

105 McLuhan, *Touch the Earth*, pg. 45.

106 Cited in B.G. Hoffman, 'The Historical Ethnography of the Micmac of the Sixteenth and Seventeenth Centuries', Thesis, University of California, 1955, pg. 591.

107 Daniel Paul, *We Were Not The Savages*, 3rd Edition (Halifax: Fernwood, 2006) pg. 38.

108 Plutarch, 'Pericles', in *The Rise and Fall of Athens: Nine Greek Lives*, trans. Ian Scott-Kilvert, (London: Penguin, 1960), pg. 178.

109 Plutarch, *ibid* pg. 172, 182-3.

110 Wallace, *The White Roots of Peace*, pg. 11.

111 Wallace, *ibid*, pg. 14.

112 Wallace, *ibid*, pg. 41.

113 *Njal's Saga*, trans. R. Cook, (London: Penguin, 2001), §70, pg. 117.

114 Njal's Saga, §97, pg. 165.

115 L. W. King, trans. *The Code of Hammurabi*, (Kessinger Publishing, 2004), pg. 1, emphasis added.

116 Elizabeth Gray, trans. *Cath Maige Tuired*, (Dublin: Irish texts society) pg. 53, §107.

117 Cited in Seán O Tuathail, *The Excellence of Ancient Word*; see also Elizabeth Gray, trans. *Cath Maige Tuired: The Second Battle of Mag Tuired*, (Dublin: Irish Texts Society, 1982), § 66, pg. 71.

118 Holbech, *Système sociale*, (London: 1774), pg. 113, 162.

119 Schweitzer, *ibid*, pg. 36, emphasis added.

120 *Ibid.* pp. 37-8.

121 Plutarch, *Plutarch's Morals. Translated from the Greek by Several Hands. Corrected and Revised by William W. Goodwin, with an Introduction by Ralph Waldo Emerson*, 5 Volumes, (Boston: Little, Brown, and Co., 1878). Vol. 2., pg. 464.

122 William Edward Hartpole Lecky, *History of European Morals: From Augustus to Charlemagne*, 3rd ed., Vol. 1, (London: Longmans, Green, & Co, 1886), pg. 100-101. Emphasis added.

123 Aldo Leopold, 'The Land Ethic', cited in Botzler and Armstrong, *Environmental Ethics: Divergence and Convergence*, 2nd edition, (Boston: McGraw Hill, 1998), pg. 412.

124 Strachey, trans. Freud, *Civilization and its Discontents*, (New York: Norton, 2010), pg. 63.

125 Leo Strauss, 'German Nihilism', *Interpretation*, Spring 1999, Vol. 26, No. 3, pg. 365.

126 Newman, *Foundations of Religious Tolerance*, pg. 70-1.

127 Michael Shuman, *Confucius: And the World He Created*, (New York NY: Basic Books, 2015) pg. 13.

128 This is, I admit, a point of dispute. Confucius' own teachings tend to be agnostic on most questions about human nature. It's Mencius, his most important student and interpreter, who makes the case for humanity's good-heartedness. But I digress.

129 Cited in Chomsky, *Necessary Illusions*, (Concord, Ontario: Anansi Press. 1989), pg. 113.

130 US Secretary of State John Kerry: *Remarks at a Lighting*

Ceremony, Paris France, November 16th, 2015. Text retrieved from US Department of State web site: www.state.gov.

131 Jeremy Diamond, 'Donald Trump: Ban all Muslim travel to U.S.' *CNN Politics*, 8th December 2015.

132 Oliver Sachgau, "White Students Union' posters spark outrage' *The Toronto Star*, 14th September 2015; Liam Casey, 'Toronto universities take down fliers promoting white students' union' *The Globe and Mail*, 14th September 2015.

133 Lucas Powers, 'Conservatives pledge funds, tip line to combat 'barbaric cultural practices" *CBC News*, 2nd October 2015.

134 Ashley Csanady, "Barbaric Cultural Practices' bill to criminalize forced marriage, tackle 'honour killings' passes final vote', *The National Post*, 17th June 2015.

135 Les Perreaux, 'Quebec legislature pleads for calm after Muslim woman attacked', *The Globe and Mail*, 1st October 2015; John Barber, 'Veil debate becomes big issue in Canada election, putting Conservatives into lead', *The Guardian*, 1st October 2015; Colin Perkel, 'Incidents prompt Ottawa police to urge Muslim women to report abuse', *The Globe and Mail*, 16th October 2015.

136 Julie Béchard, Penny Becklumb, Sandra Elgersma, 'Legislative Summary of Bill C-24' Parliament of Canada: Library of Parliament Research Publications, 5th March 2014, Revised 8th July 2014.

137 'Every individual is equal before and under the law and has the right to the equal protection and equal benefit of the law without discrimination and, in particular, without discrimination based on race, national or ethnic origin, color, religion, sex, age or mental or physical disability.' Constitution Act, 1982: Canadian Charter of Rights and Freedoms, 15(1).

138 David Berger, Philip Berger, Tzeporah Berman, and Mitchell Goldberg, 'New law makes Canadian Jews second-class

citizens', *The Toronto Star*, 14th October 2015.

139   Tom Parry, 'Liberals move to overhaul rules on revoking, granting citizenship', *CBC News*, 25 February 2016.

140   Gibbon, *Decline*, book 2, pg. 49.

141   Sigmund Freud, *Civilization and its Discontents*, pg. 98, 99.

142   Coomaraswamy, 'What is Civilisation?', pg. 2.

143   Rig Veda, x.90.1,11-12.

144   Coomaraswamy, 'What is Civilisation?', pg. 5.

145   Augustine, *City of God*, book XIX, chap. 13.

146   *Ibid*. ch. 15.

147   OED entry on 'Profane', Vol. 2, pg. 1679-80.

148   Coomaraswamy, 'What is Civilisation?', pg. 9.

149   Coomaraswamy, 'What is Civilisation?', pg. 7.

150   Clark, *Civilisation*, pg. 154.

151   Vitruvius, *ibid*, pg. 40.

152   R. Humphries, trans. Lucretius, *De Rerum Natura* (Indiana University Press, 1968).

153   'Competition of riches, honour, command, or other power, inclineth to contention, enmity, and war: because the way of one competitor, to the attaining of his desire, is to kill, subdue, supplant, or repel the other.' Hobbes, *Leviathan*, 11.

154   'When he rises up, the mighty are terrified; they retreat before his thrashing. The sword that reaches him has no effect, nor does the spear or the dart or the javelin. Iron he treats like straw and bronze like rotten wood... Nothing on earth is his equal: a creature without fear. He looks down on all that are haughty; he is king over all that are proud.' Job 41:25-34.

155   J.M. Cohen, trans. Rousseau, *Confessions*, (London: Penguin, 1954), pg. 19.

156   Rousseau, *Confessions*, pg. 327.

157   Franklin Philip, trans. Rousseau, *Discourse on Inequality*, (OUP, 1994), pg. 24.

158   Here's the original French: 'Ils parlaient de l'homme

sauvage, et ils peignaient l'homme civil.' Jean-Marie Tremblay, presenter: Jean-Jacques Rousseau, *Discours sur l'origine et les fondements de l'inégalité parmi les hommes*. Classics of Social Sciences collection, Cégep de Chicoutimi/Bibliothèque de l'Université du Québec à Chicoutimi, pp. 9, 19.

159 Rousseau, *ibid*, pg. 55.

160 c.f. Rousseau, *The Social Contract*, book 1, chapter 6.

161 M. Cranston, trans. Rousseau, *The Social Contract* ,(London: Penguin, 1968), book 1, chapter 7, (pg. 64-5)

162 Hobbes, *Leviathan*, ch. 13, pg. 85.

163 Rousseau, *Discourse on Inequality*, pg. 61.

164 Locke, *Second Treatise of Government*, chap. 5, § 41.

165 Francis, Jones, Smith, *Origins* pg. 7-16; see also, *Report on Plans and Priorities* (Ottawa: Indian and Northern Affairs Canada, 2007/2008), pg. 9.

166 Paul, *We Were Not The Savages*, pg. 21.

167 c.f. Paul, *We Were Not The Savages*, pp. 10-30.

168 McLuhan, *Touch the Earth*, pg. 39.

169 c.f. Bringhurst, 'The Audible Light in the Eyes', *The Tree of Meaning*, pp. 83-4.

170 Fernandez-Arnesto, pg. 23.

171 'Book blames reserves for natives' plight', *Halifax Chronicle-Herald*, 17th April 2000.

172 Paul, *We Were Not The Savages*, pg. 367.

173 Paul, *We Were Not The Savages*, pg. 10.

174 Coomaraswamy, 'What is Civilisation?', pg. 7.

175 Clark, *Civilisation*, pg. 21.

176 Entry on 'Nature' in *The Shorter OED*, Vol. 2, pg. 1387.

177 Reardon, Sara. 'Poverty shrinks brains from birth', *Nature*, 30 March 2015.

178 Reardon, Sara. 'Poverty linked to epigenetic changes and mental illness', *Nature*, 24 May 2016. See also: Noble, Houston, Brito, et.al., 'Family income, parental education

and brain structure in children and adolescents', *Nature Neuroscience*, Vol. 18 No.5, May 2015, pp. 773-780.

179 Robert Cieri, Steven Churchill, et.al.: 'Craniofacial Feminization, Social Tolerance, and the Origins of Behavioral Modernity' *Current Anthropology*, Vol. 55, No.4, (August 2014), pp.419-443. The acronyms MSA/MP refer to 'Middle Stone Age/Middle Paleolithic'; LSA/UP refers to 'Later Stone Age/Upper Paleolithic'.

180 Susan Rosser (prof. of human biology at the University of Edinburgh), 'We've learned to read our genes. Now we need to start writing them', *The Guardian*, 5th June 2016; cf. Boeke, Church, Hessel, et.al.: 'The Genome Project –Write' *Science* 2nd June 2016, 10.11.26.

181 'Indeed terror is in all cases whatsoever, either more openly or latently, the ruling principle of the sublime.' Burke, *A Philosophical Enquiry into the Origin of our Ideas of the Sublime and Beautiful* (NY: Dover, 2008 [first published 1759]) pg. 39.

182 'The law is like religious faith. If God exists, there is no need to believe in Him. If people do believe in Him, this is because the self-evidence of his existence has passed away.' Chris Turner (trans.) Baudrillard, *The Illusion of the End*, (Stanford University Press, 1994), pg. 80.

183 Dana Hamplová, 'Are Czechs the least religious of all?', *The Guardian*, 24th June 2010.

184 Source: Wing-Tsit Chan, *A Source Book in Chinese Philosophy*, (New Jersey USA: Princeton University Press, 1963), pp. 139-176.

185 'The Global Religious Landscape', *The Pew Forum on Religion and Public Life*, Pew Research Centre, 18 December 2012.

186 Adam Smith, *The Wealth of Nations*, Book 1, ch 2.

187 'John Stuart Mill, 'On the Definition of Political Economy, and on the Method of Investigation Proper to It,' in *Essays on Some Unsettled Questions of Political Economy*, 2nd edition (London: Longmans, Green, Reader, and Dyer, 1874) v.38.

188 For a deeper treatment of this close identification between rationality and self-interest, see John McMurtry, 'I am Rational, Therefore I Self-Maximize' in McMurtry, *Unequal Freedoms* (Toronto: Garamond, 1998), pp. 127-132.

189 Rawls, *A Theory of Justice*, Revised edition, (OUP 1999), pp. 111, 123-5.

190 Friedrich Hayek, *The Road to Serfdom* (University of Chicago Press, 2007), pg. 86.

191 *Strategic Regional Plan to Improve Health and Social Services*, Cree Board of Health and Social Services, 24th September 2004, pg. 20, emphasis added.

192 Guy Standing, 'The Precariat – The New Dangerous Class', *Policy Network*, 24th May 2011; and Guy Standing, 'A New Class: Canada neglects the precariat at its peril', *The Globe and Mail*, 13th June 2015.

193 Sarah Kendzior, 'Why Young Americans are Give Up On Capitalism', *Foreign Policy*, 16th June 2016; Jordan Weissman, 'Our Low Wage Recovery', *The Atlantic*, 31st August 2012; Bertrand Marotte, 'Almost half of workers are living paycheque to paycheque, survey finds', *The Globe and Mail*, 9 September 2015.

194 Justin Li, 'Transgender bathroom rights, access a hot U.S. political topic', *CBC News*, 12 April 2016; Marisa Taylor, 'The growing trend of transgender 'bathroom bully' bills', *Al Jazeera America*, 1st April 2015.

195 Matt Kwong, 'North Carolina's transgender bathroom law: 5 personal stories about HB2's impact', *CBC News*, 8th May 2016.

196 Sam Brodey and Julia Lurie, 'Get Ready for the Conservative Assault on Where Transgender Americans Pee', *Mother Jones*, 9th March 2015.

197 Zach Stafford, 'Transgender homicide rate hits historic high in US, says new report' *The Guardian*, 13th November 2015; see also 'Addressing Anti-Transgender Violence', TPOCC

Human Rights Campaign, 2015.

198 Gail Bederman, 'Manliness and Civilization', (University of Chicago Press, 2008) pg. 2.

199 Cited in Bederman, *ibid*, pg. 3.

200 Nicola Slawson, 'Jo Cox murder suspect 'told police he was political activist'' *The Guardian*, 18th June 2016; Daniel Boffey and Nicola Slawson, 'Jo Cox murder accused gives name as 'death to traitors, freedom for Britain'', *The Guardian*, 18th June 2016.

201 Jamie Doward, 'Anders Behring Breivik: motives of a mass murderer', *The Guardian*, 23rd July 2011.

202 Marx, 'Estranged Labour', in *Economic and Political Manuscripts of 1844*, (Prometheus, 1988), §XXII, pg. 71.

203 Rawls' version of the experiment, the Original Position and the Veil of Ignorance, 'corresponds to the state of nature in the traditional theory of the social contract'; however he adds that the Original Position 'is not, of course, an actual historical state of affairs', rather is 'a purely hypothetical situation characterized so as to lead to a certain conception of justice'. Rawls, *A Theory of Justice*, Revised edition, (OUP, 1999), pg. 11.

204 To which it could be argued: isn't autonomous reason an 'organized law or formality'? To which I answer: the standard accounts of the 'state of nature' experiment didn't treat it that way. Rather, they treated reason as a natural capacity of individuals and their intelligence, and not as a state of affairs between two or more individuals.

205 M. Dyble, G.D. Salali, et.al.: 'Sex equality can explain the unique social structure of hunter-gatherer bands', *Science*, 15 May 2015; Vol. 348, Iss. 6236, pp. 796-798. Also: 'Stonehenge burials show 'surprising degree' of gender equality', *BBC News*, 3rd February 2016.

206 I'm acknowledging the 'original affluent society' theory of anthropologist Marshall Sahlins, Jared Diamond, and

others. Cf: Marshall Sahlins, *Stone Age Economics*, (Chicago: Aldine, 1972). Also: Jared Diamond, 'The Worst Mistake in the History of the Human Race', *Discover Magazine*, May 1987, pp. 64-66.

207 Sahlins, 'The Original Affluent Society', cited in Sahlins, *Culture in Practice: Selected Essays*, (NY: Zone Books, 2005) pg. 124.

208 I'm also acknowledging critics of the 'original affluence society' theory. For instance: David Kaplan, 'The Darker Side of the 'Original Affluent Society'', *Journal of Anthropological Research*, Vol. 56, No. 3, (autumn 2000), pp. 301-324.

209 'Society is indeed a contract...a partnership not only between those who are living, but between those who are living, those who are dead, and those who are to be born. Each contract of each particular state is but a clause in the great primæval contract of eternal society, linking the lower with the higher natures, connecting the visible and invisible world, according to a fixed compact sanctioned by the inviolable oath which holds all physical and all moral natures, each in their appointed place.' Edmund Burke, *Reflections on the French Revolution*, (Harvard Classics, 1909 [first published 1790]), §165.

210 I acknowledge the groundwork laid here by philosophers like Martha Nussbaum and Cornell West, and the 'Black Lives Matter' political movement.

211 Rubenstein & Kealey (2010), 'Cooperation, Conflict, and the Evolution of Complex Animal Societies', *Nature Education Knowledge*, 30(10):78.

212 Richardson & Boyd, 'Cultural Inheritance and Evolutionary Ecology', in Smith & Winterhalder, eds. *Evolutionary Ecology and Human Behaviour*, (London: Aldine Transaction, 2009), pg. 83.

213 Stewart & Plotkin, 'Small groups and long memories

promote cooperation', *Scientific Reports*, 6 (2016), 1st June 2016. C.f. also: Katherine Unger Baillie, 'Cooperation emerges when groups are small and memories are long, study finds', *Phys.org*, 1st June 2016.

214 Gilman, *Women and Economics*, (Boston: Small, Maynard, & Co. 1898). ch. VII.

215 Gilman, *ibid*, ch. IV.

216 Wrangham, Jones, Laden, Pilbeam and Conklin-Brittain. 'The Raw and the Stolen: Cooking and the Ecology of Human Origins', *Current Anthropology*, Vol. 40, No.5, December 1999. Also: Gavrilets, 'Human origins and the transition from promiscuity to pair-bonding' *Proceedings of the National Academy of Sciences of the USA*, 19th June 2012; 109(25): 9923-9928. Also: Chapais, Bernard, *Primeval Kinship: How Pair-Bonding Gave Birth To Human Society*, (Harvard University Press, 2008), pp. 157-184.

217 Spiro Kostof, *A History of Architecture: Settings and Rituals* (OUP, 1985) pp. 21-23.

218 T. Ferguson & J. Tamburello, 'The Natural Environment as a Spiritual Resource: A Theory of Regional variation in Religious Adherence', *Sociology of Religion: A Quarterly Review*, Vol. 76, No.3 (Autumn 2015), pp. 295-314.

219 Harries, *The Ethical Function of Architecture*, pg. 138.

220 OED entry on 'Temple', Vol. 2, pg. 2258.

221 Ricoeur, *Figuring the Sacred*, (Fortress Press, 1995), pg. 50.

222 Stephen Pollington, *The Mead Hall*, (Frithgarth, Norfolk, UK: Anglo-Saxon Books, 2003) pg. 115.

223 Harries, *ibid*, pg. 140.

224 Though this argument is mostly inspired by philosophers like Heidegger, some psychologists are catching on. C.f. Proulx, Todorov, Aiken, & de Sousa, 'Where am I? Who am I? The Relation Between Spatial Cognition, Social Cognition and Individual Differences in the Built Environment', *Frontiers in Psychology*, 11th February 2016.

225 Joseph Campbell, *The Power of Myth*, (New York: Anchor/Doubleday, 1988), pg. 118-9.

226 P. Gregory, trans. René Girard, *Violence and the Sacred*, (Baltimore: Johns Hopkins University Press, 1977), pg, 31. Emphasis added.

227 Ibid. pg. 30-1, 37.

228 Deborah C Mooney, J.G. O'Gorman. 'Construct Validity of the Revised Collett-Lester Fear of Death and Dying Scale', *Omega Journal of Death and Dying*, 43 (October 2001), pp.157-173. Also: Trinda Power & Steven Smith. 'Predictors of Fear of Death and Self-Mortality: An Atlantic Canadian Perspective', *Death Studies*, Vol. 32, Iss. 3 (2008).

229 Fritsche, Jonas, Fischer, et.al.: 'Mortality salience and the desire for offspring', *Journal of Experimental Social Psychology*, Vol. 43, Iss. 5 (Sept. 2007), pp. 753-762.

230 Greenberg, Kosloff, Solomon, et.al.: 'Toward Understanding the Fame Game: The Effect of Mortality Salience on the Appeal of Fame', *Self and Identity*, Vol. 9, Iss. 1 (2010), pp. 1-18.

231 Jong, Halberstadt, & Bluemke. 'Foxhole atheism, revisited: The effects of mortality salience on explicit and implicit religious belief', *Journal of Experimental Social Psychology*, Vol. 48, Iss. 5 (Sept. 2012), pp. 983-989.

232 'The way people think about thinking changes the way they pay attention to the unusual experiences associated with sleep and awareness, and that as a result, people will have different spiritual experiences, as well as different patterns of psychiatric experience.' Tanya Luhrmann, cited in Clifton B. Parker, 'Hallucinatory 'voices' shaped by local culture, Stanford anthropologist says' Stanford University: *Stanford Report*, 16th July 2014.

233 Stephen Cave, *Immortality: The Quest to Live Forever and How it Drives Civilization*, (New York: Crown, 2012) pp. 3-6.

234 This is mainly because infant mortality is enormously lower

than ever before in the history of the world. But it is also the case that life expectancy for those in middle age (40-60) is much longer than ever before. C.f. Yves Decady and Lawson Greenberg, *Health at a Glance: Ninety years of change in life expectancy*. Statistics Canada, Catalogue no. 82-624-X (July 2014).

235 Shimelmitz, Kuhn, Jelinek, et.al.: "Fire at will': The emergence of habitual fire use 350,000 years ago', *Journal of Human Evolution*, Vol. 77, December 2014, pp. 196-203.

236 P. Skoglund, 'Ancient wolf genome reveals an early divergence of domestic dog ancestors and admixture into high-latitude breeds', *Current Biology* 25(11), 2015, pp. 1515-1519.

237 Frantz, Mullin, Pionnier-Capitan, et.al.: 'Genomic and archeological evidence suggest a dual origin of domestic dogs', *Science*, 3rd June 2016, Vol. 352, Iss. 6290, pp. 1228-1231.

238 Michael Charles, 'East of Eden?' in S. Colledge & J. Conolly, eds., *The Origins and Spread of Domestic Plants in Southwest Asia and Europe* (University College London/Left Coast Press, 2007), pg. 40-8.

239 Molina, Sikora, Garud, et.al.: 'Molecular evidence for a singular evolutionary origin of domesticated rice', *Proceedings of the National Academy of Sciences*, 108 (20): 8351. Also: Huang, Kurata, Wei, et.al.: 'A map of rice genome variation reveals the origin of cultivated rice', *Nature*, 490 (October 2012), pp. 497-501.

240 J.F. Doebley, 'The genetics of maize evolution', *Annual Review of Genetics*, iss. 28, (2004), pp. 37-59. Also: 'Wild grass became maize crop more than 8,700 years ago', *National Science Foundation/AAAS: EurekaAlert public release*, 23rd March 2009.

241 Mintz, *Sweetness and Power: The place of sugar in modern history*, (Penguin, 1985), pg. 19-20.

242 Schoenwetter, James. 'Pollen records of Guila Naquitz

Cave', *American Antiquity/Society for American Archaeology*, 39(2), April 1974, pp. 292-303.

243 McTavish, Decker, Schnabel, et.al.: 'New World cattle show ancestry from multiple independent domestication events', *Proceedings of the National Academy of Sciences of the USA*, 110(15) (April 2013), pp. E1398-E1406.

244 Giuffra, Kijas, Amarger, et.al.: 'The origin of the domestic pig: independent domestication and subsequent introgression', *Genetics*, 154(4), April 2000, pp. 1785-1791.

245 Outram, Stear, Bendrey, et.al.: 'The earliest Horse Harnessing and Milking', *Science/AAAS*, Vol. 323, Iss. 5919 (March 2009), pp. 1332-1335.

246 Mary Matossian, *Shaping World History: Breakthroughs in Ecology, Technology, Science, and Politics* (Routledge, 1997) pg. 43.

247 Zink & Lieberman, 'Impact of meat and Lower Paleolithic food processing techniques on chewing in humans', *Nature*, 10.1038. March 2016.

248 J. L. Buck, *Land Utilization in China*, (U of Chicago Press, Chicago, IL, 1935).

249 James C. Scott, 'The Art of Not Being Governed: An Anarchist History of Upland Southeast Asia', (Yale University Press, 2009), pg. 41.

250 Talheim, Zhang, Oishi, et.al.: 'Large-Scale Psychological Differences Within China Explained by Rice Versus Wheat Agriculture', *Science/AAAS*, Vol. 344, Iss. 6184 (May 2014), pp. 603-608. A comment piece later argued that the difference should not be between rice and wheat, but rather rice and non-rice grain products: Shihu Hu and Zhiguo Yuan, 'Commentary', *Frontiers in Psychology*, 2015; 6: 489.

251 Arendt, 'On Violence' in *Crises in the Republic*, (Harcourt Brace and Company, 1972), pg. 143.

252 Following Locke here, who wrote that the basic problem of life in the state of nature was unfairness of punishments:

people are lenient to their friends and excessively harsh to their enemies.

253 Stephen Pollington, *The Mead Hall,* (Frithgarth, Norfolk, UK: Anglo-Saxon Books, 2003), pg. 182.

254 Marvin Harris, 'Our Kind: Who We Are, Where We Came From, and Where We Are Going', (Harper Perennial, 1989), pg. 394.

255 James Scott, *The Art of Not Being Governed,* (Yale University Press, 2009), pg. 8.

256 L. W. King (trans.) *The Code of Hammurabi,* (Kessinger Publishing, 2004), pg. 1.

257 Gregory, *Gods and Fighting Men,* pg. 76.

258 Macalister, trans. *Lebor Gabála Érenn,* Book V, 1956, p27.

259 Julius Caesar, *The Conquest of Gaul,* VI. 18, pg. 142.

260 George Bull (trans.) Niccolo Machiavelli, *The Prince,* (Penguin, 2003), pg. 57-8.

261 Nelson, Moore, Olivetti, & Scott, 'General and Personal Mortality Salience and Nationalistic Bias', *Personality and Social Psychology Bulletin,* Vol. 23, No.8 (August 1997), pp. 884-892.

262 Greenberg, Pyszczynski, Solomon, et.al.: 'Evidence for terror management theory II: The effects of mortality salience on reactions to those who threaten or bolster the cultural worldview', *Journal of Personality and Social Psychology,* Vol. 58(2), Feb. 1990, pp. 308-318. See also: Schimel, Simon, Greenberg, et.al.: 'Stereotypes and terror management: Evidence that mortality salience enhances stereotypic thinking and preferences', *Journal of Personality and Social Psychology,* Vol.77(5), Nov, 1999, pp. 905-926.

263 'Two Decades of Terror Management Theory: A Meta-Analysis of Mortality Salience Research'., *Personality and Social Psychology Review,* 14, May 2010, pp. 155-195.

264 Dana Milbank, 'Donald Trump is a bigot and a racist', *The Washington Post,* 1st December 2015.

265 Jeff Guo, 'Death predicts whether people vote for Donald Trump', *The Washington Post*, 4th March 2016.

266 Harris, 'Our Kind', pg. 393.

267 Cited in Belasco, *Food: The Key Concepts*, (NY: Berg, 2008), pg. 79.

268 Douglas Fischer, "Dark Money' Funds Climate Change Denial Effort', *Scientific American*, 23 December 2013. C.f. also: Brulle, 'Institutionalizing delay: foundation funding and the creation of U.S. climate change counter-movement organizations', *Climate Change*, 21 December 2013. (DOI 10.1007/s10584-013-1018-7).

269 Barret, Speth, Eastham, et.al.: 'Impact of the Volkswagen emissions control defeat device on US public health', *Environmental Research Letters*, Vol.10, No.11, (28th October 2015)

270 Bertel Schmitt, 'How Volkswagen Really Blew It: It Was China, Not Dieselgate', *Forbes*, 29th January 2016; Bertel Schmitt, 'So Much for Dieselgate: Outselling Toyota, Volkswagen is World's Largest Automaker in First 4 Months' *Forbes*, 30th May 2016.

271 'Panama Papers: Leaks spur global investigations', *BBC News*, 4th April 2016.

272 Neil Macdonald, 'Panama Papers taunt the masses with more proof that game is rigged' *CBC News*, 5th April 2016.

273 Erlanger, Castle, & Gladstone, 'Iceland's Prime Minister Steps Down Amid Panama Papers Scandal', *The New York Times*, 5th April 2016.

274 Jane Mayer, 'Covert Operation: The billionaire brothers who are waging a war against Obama', *The New Yorker*, 30th August 2010.

275 Bill McKibben, 'The Koch Brothers' New Brand', *The New York Review of Books*, 10th March 2016.

276 Freire, *Pedagogy of the Oppressed*, (Continuum, 1996), pg. 39.

277 Freire, *ibid*, pp. 78, 89. A translator's footnote explains how,

in English, 'the terms 'live' and 'exist' have assumed implications opposite to their etymological origins. As used here,
'live' is the more basic term, implying only survival; 'exist'
implies a deeper involvement in the process of 'becoming'',
ibid pg. 79, fn. 14.

278 Freire, *ibid* pg. 120-1.

279 *Ibid.* pg. 138.

280 *Ibid.* pg. 40, 41.

281 Cited in Hersh, *ibid.*

282 William Pfaff, 'The Long Reach of Leo Strauss', *International Herald Tribune*, May 15, 2003.

283 Strauss, *Natural Right and History*, pg. 309.

284 Strauss, *ibid*, pg. 310-1. Phrases in scarequotes are where Strauss quotes Burke.

285 Strauss, *ibid*, pg. 311.

286 Seymour Hersh, 'Selective Intelligence', *The New Yorker*, 12th May 2003. A number of Strauss' other doctoral students also found senior appointments in Bush's administration. Paul Wolfowitz, for instance, was Bush's deputy defense secretary.

287 Gary J. Schmitt & Abram Shulsky, 'Leo Strauss and the World of Intelligence (By Which We Do Not Mean *Nous*)' cited in Deutsch & Murley, eds. *Leo Strauss, the Straussians, and the American Regime* (Oxford UK: Rowman & Littlefield, 1999) pp. 410, 411.

288 'Persecution, then, gives rise to a peculiar technique of writing, and therewith to a peculiar type of literature, in which the truth about all crucial things is presented exclu-sively between the lines. That literature is addressed, not to all readers, but to trustworthy and intelligent readers only.' Strauss, 'Persecution and the Art of Writing.' *Social Research*, 8:1/4 (1941), pg. 491.

289 Abram Shulsky & Gary Schmitt, *Silent Warfare: Understanding the World of Intelligence*, 3rd edition

(Washington: Potomac Books, 2002), pg. 176.

290 Cited in Hersh, *ibid*.

291 Myers, 'Circles of Meaning, Labyrinths of Fear', (O Books, 2012), pp. 335-345; Myers, et. al., 'Clear and Present Thinking' (Northwest Passage Books, 2013), pp. 39-45.

292 Aubrey de Sélincourt (trans.) and A.R. Burn (rev.), Herodotus, *Histories*, 3:39. (Penguin, 1972), pg. 219-220.

293 All fragments of Heraclitus are cited in Charles Kahn, *The Art and Thought of Heraclitus*, (Cambridge University Press, 1979), pg. 45.

294 Cited in Curd & McKirahan, *A Presocratics Reader: Selected Fragments and Testimonia*, (Indianapolis: Hackett, 1996), pg. 46.

295 Curd & McKirahan, *Ibid*, pg. 48. Italics added for clarity.

296 Freud, *The Future of an Illusion*, pg. 31.

297 Strachey, trans. Freud, *Civilization and its Discontents*, (New York: Norton, 2010), pg. 24.

298 Margaret Thatcher, former PM of Britain, interview on 23 September 1987, cited in Douglas Keay, *Women's Own*, 31 October 1987.

299 David Ricardo, *The Principles of Political Economy and Taxation*, (London: J.M. Dent & Sons, 1965), pg. 63. Emphasis added.

300 Lasalle, *Offenes Antwortschreiben* (1863); c.f. Gray, Alexander, *The Socialist Tradition: Moses to Lenin*, (Longmans, Green and Co., 1946-7), p. 336.

301 Herbert Spencer, *Social Statics, Or, The Conditions of Human Happiness Specified, And the First of them Developed*, (New York: Appleton, 1883), Ch. XXV 'Poor Laws', §6, pg. 355-6. Emphasis added.

302 Spencer, *ibid*, Ch. XXV §6, pp. 352-3.

303 'Every species of animals naturally multiplies in proportion to the means of their subsistence, and no species can ever multiply beyond it. But in civilised society it is only among

the inferior ranks of people that the scantiness of subsistence can set limits to the further multiplication of the human species; and it can do so in no other way than by destroying a great part of the children which their fruitful marriages produce.' Smith, *The Wealth of Nations*, Book 1, ch. 8 'Of the Wages of Labour', §39.

304   Spencer, *ibid*, Ch. XXV §5, pp. 351.

305   Spencer, *ibid*, Ch. XXV §5, pp. 352.

306   c.f. Spencer, *ibid*, pp. 45, 54, 55, 107, 175, Also, his related motto 'No other arrangement of things can be imagined/is conceivable' appears at pp. 76 & 414. For further discussion of Spencer's elimination of choice from his description of the path to happiness: see Iain Stewart, 'Positivist Natural Law in Spencer's Social Darwinism' in *Challenges to Law at the End of the 20th Century: Legal Systems and Legal Science*. (Proceedings of the 17th World Congress of the International Association for Philosophy of Law and Social Philosophy, June 16-21, 1995, Vol. IV). To wit: 'He [Spencer] does not say anything like, 'if there is a cosmic evolutionary path X, then it is a natural law that Y'; rather, he tells us that there jolly well is X, and, if we do not recognize its requirements Y, we are unfit to live.' Pg. 85.

307   Valentina Pop, 'Schaeuble: Greece has 'no alternative' to austerity', *EU Observer*, 14 January 2013.

308   Gideon Rachman, 'No Alternative to Austerity', *Financial Times*, 30 April 2012.

309   Ostry, Loungani, and Furceri, 'Neoliberalism: Oversold?' *Finance & Development: The Quarterly Magazine of the IMF*. Vol. 53, No. 2, June 2016, pp. 38-41. This essay does not represent IMF policy, but it is interesting to see it appear in an IMF publication since it speaks against the fiscal neoliberalism that the IMF has championed since the 1980s.

310   Hayek, *The Road to Serfdom*, pg. 100.

311   John Mason, 'Leo Strauss and the Noble Lie: The Neo-Cons

at War' *Logos*, 3:2, Spring 2004.

312 Strauss, 'German Nihilism'. *ibid*, pg. 365.

313 Strauss, *ibid*, pg. 369. Emphasis his.

314 Strauss, *Natural History and Right*, 7th impression (University of Chicago Press, 1971), pg. 5.

315 Strauss, *ibid*, pg. 6.

316 Daniel Drezner, 'Why the post-truth political era might be around for a while', *The Washington Post*, 16th June 2016; Jonathan Freedland, 'Post-truth politicians such as Donald Trump and Boris Johnson are no joke', *The Guardian*, 13th May 2016.

317 'Federal scientists closely monitored during polar conference', *CBC News*, 24th April 2012.

318 Vann Newkirk II, 'Political violence in the era of Trump', *The Atlantic*, 3rd June 2016.

319 NASA Near Earth Object Program, 'NEO Groups', from NASA's web site at neo.jpl.nasa.gov/neo/groups.html, accessed 18th June 2015.

320 Hannah Osborne, 'Stephen Hawking: Space Travel is 'Life Insurance' for the Survival of Human Race', *International Business News, UK edition*, 22 September 2014. Also: see D. Shukman, 'Hawking: Humans at risk of lethal 'own goal'', *BBC News* 19th January 2016.

321 Elien Blue Becque, 'Elon Musk Wants To Die On Mars' *Vanity Fair*, 10th March 2013.

322 NASA Near Earth Object Program, 'Target Earth', from NASA's web site at neo.jpl.nasa.gov/neo/target.html, accessed 18th June 2015.

323 Richard Oppel, Jr., 'Taping of Farm Cruelty is Becoming the Crime', *The New York Times*, 6th April 2013.

324 Staff reporters: 'Where do milk, eggs, and bacon come from? One in three youths don't know', *The Telegraph*, 14th June 2012.

325 Joyce Carol Oates, *Food Mysteries*, cited in Daniel Halpern

(ed), *Not For Bread Alone* (Hopwell NJ, USA: Ecco Press 1993) pg. 25.

326 James Strachey, trans. Sigmund Freud, *The Future of an Illusion*, (New York: Norton, 1961) pg. 7.

327 Mike Winter, 'Reflections on the Vancouver riots and the fragility of civilization', *Vancouver Observer*, 28th June 2011.

328 Cited in 'To Leave Your Mark: Selections from the Writings of Alfred Jospe' (Hoboken, NJ, USA: KTAV Publishing House, 2000) pg. 245.

329 Spencer, *The Man Versus the State* (Caldwell, Idaho, USA: Caxton Printers, 1968 [first published 1892]), pg. 52.

330 Bex Warner, trans. Thucydides, *The Peloponnesian War*, (Penguin 1954) 3.3.82-85, pg. 208, 211.

331 K. Jensen, A. Vaish, M.F.H. Schmidt, 'The emergence of human prosociality: aligning with others through feelings, concerns, and norms' *Frontiers in Psychology*, 5:822, 29th July 2014.

332 Common Cause Foundation, 'Perceptions Matter: The Common Cause UK Values Survey', (London UK: Common Cause Foundation, 2016), pp. 17, 21.

333 David Bell, 'Donations for Fort McMurray fire evacuees overwhelm volunteers', *CBC News*, 8th May 2016.

334 Stephen Hudak, 'Blood banks at capacity, donors urged to return in coming days', *Orlando Sentinel*, 12th June 2016.

335 Derek Tsang, 'Fewer wars, fewer people dying in wars now than in quite some time, Glenn Beck writer claims', *Politifact.com*, 21st July 2016; Steven Pinker, 'Guess what? More people are living in peace now. Just look at the numbers', *The Guardian*, 20th March 2015; Steven Pinker and Andrew Mack, 'The World Is Not Falling Apart', *Slate Magazine*, 22nd December 2014.

336 Scott Atran, *Talking to the Enemy: Faith, Brotherhood, and the (Un)Making of Terrorists* (New York: Ecco/Harper Collins, 2010), pg. 107.

337 Jonathan Glover, *Humanity: A Moral History of the Twentieth Century*, (Yale University Press, 1999), pg. 404.

338 Glover, *ibid*, pg. 24.

339 Cited in Manning and Beimler, 'The Emissary', *Star Trek: The Next Generation*, airdate (stardate?), 24th June 1989.

340 Victor Malarek, 'Killer's letter blames feminists', *The Globe and Mail*, 8th December 1989, pg. A7.

341 Lois Beckett, 'Orlando night club attack is deadliest US mass shooting in modern history', *The Guardian*, 12 June 2016.

342 Liam Stack, 'Before Orlando Shooting, an Anti-Gay Massacre in New Orleans was Largely Forgotten' *The New York Times*, 14th June 2016.

343 Pinker, *Better Angels of our Nature*, Reprint edition, (Penguin, 2012), pg. xxiv. For Pinker's treatment of Hobbes' view of human nature, see pg. 31.

344 Barak Obama, 'Remarks by the President at the Acceptance of the Nobel Peace Prize', (The White House, Office of the Press Secretary, 10th December 2009.)

345 Fry and Soderberg, 'Lethal aggression in Mobile Forager Bands and Implications for the Origins of War', *Science* (AAAS), Vol. 341, Iss. 6143 19th July 2013.

346 R. Brian Ferguson, 'The Birth of War', *Natural History*, July/August 2003, pg. 30. See also Ferguson, 'The Prehistory of War and Peace in Europe and the Near East', in Douglas Fry, ed. *War, Peace, and Human Nature*, (OUP 2013) pp. 191-240.

347 Sam Harris, 'Sam Harris on Sarah Palin and Elitism', *Newsweek*, 19th September 2008; Graeme Wood, 'What ISIS Really Wants', *The Atlantic*, March 2015.

348 Emma Green, 'Half of Americans Think Climate Change is a Sign of the Apocalypse', *The Atlantic*, 2nd November 2014.

349 'God 'will not give happy ending'', *BBC News*, 26th march 2009.

350 I am grateful to my friend Jordan Stratford (who also

happens to be a Gnostic priest) for this re-visioning of the notion of a 'chosen people'.

351 c.f. Myers, *Circles of Meaning, Labyrinths of Fear*, (Moon Books, 2012), pg. 457. C.f. 'Fear of the Lord' in *ibid*, pp. 437-445. Apologies for quoting myself.

352 The idea of immensity, as a concept in virtue ethics, was first published in my book *The Other Side of Virtue*, (O Books, 2008), pp. 154-170. That text described three immensities: the earth, interpersonal otherness, and death. A fourth, loneliness, was briefly mentioned in that text, and then developed more fully in *Loneliness and Revelation*, (O Books, 2010). I have endeavored to explain the argument here in such a way that the reader doesn't have to consult the earlier texts.

353 Rousseau, *The Confessions*, (London: Penguin, 1954), pg. 167.

354 Marcel Schneider, *Jean-Jacques Rousseau et l'Espoir Écologiste*, (Paris: Editions Pygmalion, 1978), pg. 26.

355 Gilbert LaFreniere, 'Rousseau and the European Roots of Environmentalism', *Environmental History Review*, Vol.14, No.4 (winter 1990) pp. 41-72.

356 William Rollins, *A Greener Vision of Home: Cultural Politics and Environmental Reform in the German Heimatschutz Movement, 1904-1918* (Ann Arbor: University of Michigan Press, 1997) pg. 1.

357 *Leuchtende Stunden*, cited in Rollins, *ibid*, pg. 155.

358 Rollins, *ibid*, pg. 155.

359 Rudorff, 'On the Relationship of Modern Life to Nature', cited in Rollins, *ibid*, pg. 74.

360 Rollins, *ibidi*, pg. 75.

361 Cited in Rollins, *ibid*, pg. 78.

362 Gordon Kennedy, ed. *Children of the Sun: A Pictoral Anthology From Germany to California, 1883-1949.* (Ojai, CA, USA: Nivara Press, 1998), pg. 69-70.

363 Kennedy, *ibid*, pp. 56-9; see also Rollins, *ibid*, pg. 73.

364 Kennedy, *ibid*, pg. 60.

356 Burt Folkart, 'Eden Ahbez: Wrote Hit Song 'Nature Boy'', *Los Angeles Times*, 11th March 1995.

366 Kennedy, *ibid*, pg. 182.

367 Rollins, *ibid*, pg. 101.

368 Rollins, *ibid*, pg. 80, 15-16.

369 c.f. Rollins, *ibid*, pg. 73.

370 Alison Hawthorne Deming, *The Edges of the Civilized World: Tourism and the hunger for wild places* 1st edition, (Minneapolis, MN: Milkweed Editions, 2007), pg. 148. Deming's essay first appeared in *Orion* Magazine, 15(2), 1996.

371 I acknowledge a similar argument made by philosophers John McMurtry, in *Unequal Freedoms*, and by Immanuel Kant, in *Groundwork to the Metaphysics of Morals*.

372 C.f. Belasco, *Food: The Key Concepts*, pg. 79.

373 Re: the heroic virtues: cf. Myers, *The Earth, The Gods, and The Soul: A History of Pagan Philosophy*, (Moon Books, 2013), pg. 257. Re: the classical virtues; cf. Plato, *The Republic*, 428b-462b. Re: the Seven Grandfathers: Willie Bruce, *Peacemaking Circles: An Aboriginal Best Practice*, (Ottawa: Aboriginal Employees Network/NRCAN, October 2006).

374 Quotes from Mencius and Confucius cited in Wing-Tsit Chan, *A Source Book in Chinese Philosophy*, (Princeton University Press, 1963) pg. 69.

375 'Humanities and General Education', Vanier College Report, 1974.

376 Government of Quebec, *Report of the Royal Commission of Enquiry on Education* ('The Parent Report'), 1964, Vol. III, ch. xxiv.

377 'Honouring the Truth, Reconciling for the Future', *Truth and Reconciliation Commission of Canada*, pg. 131-2.

378 Ashley Csanady, 'One in six Ontario parents considered pulling kids from school over new sex-ed curriculum: poll',

National Post, 3rd June 2016.

379 Marx, 'Critique of the Gotha Program', cited in Tucker, ed. *The Marx-Engels Reader* (New York: Norton, 1972) pg. 388.

380 Adam Smith, *The Wealth of Nations*, I.5.4.

381 Tracy McVeigh, 'Make way for the lynx and the bear as 'rewilding' projects gather pace across Britain', *The Guardian*, 3rd may 2015.

382 Elizabeth Kolbert, 'Recall of the wild', *The New Yorker*, 24th December 2012. Anik See, 'Rewilding projects aim to turn back the clock on environment', *CBC News*, 23 November 2014; Lenny Antonelli, 'Ireland's big rewilding project is first of its kind in Western Europe', *Earth Island Journal*, 16th October 2013.

383 Michelle Donahue, '80 Percent of Americans Can't See the Milky Way Anymore', *National Geographic*, 10th June 2016; Nicola Davis, 'Milky Way no longer visible to one-third of humanity, light pollution atlas shows', *The Guardian*, 10th June 2016.

384 Rogers, *Cities for a Small Planet*, pg. 33.

385 Information retrieved from the Mountain Lion Agriculture website, mlbr.org, June 2016. I am also grateful to Alex Zieba and Jason Dudek, two of the company directors, for personally describing the business model to me.

386 Tavia Grant, 'How one company levels the pay slope of executives and workers', *The Globe and Mail*, 16th November 2013. That company is Lee Valley Tools.

387 John McMurtry, *Unequal Freedoms: The Global Market as an Ethical System*, (Toronto: Garamond, 1998), pg. 24.

388 *Ibid* pg. 371; see also McMurtry, *The Cancer Stage of Capitalism*, (London: Pluto Press, 1999), pg. 206-7.

389 Spencer, *The Man Versus The State*, pg. 41-2.

390 Hayek, *The Road to Serfdom* (University of Chicago Press, 2007 [first published 1944]), pg. 130.

391 McMurtry, *Unequal Freedoms*, pg. 25.

392 Charles Taylor, *The Malaise of Modernity*, (Concord, Ontario, Canada: Anansi Press, 1991), pg. 37-9.

393 Gabrial Zucman, *The Hidden Wealth of Nations*, (University of Chicago Press, 2015).

Moon Books

PAGANISM & SHAMANISM

What is Paganism? A religion, a spirituality, an alternative belief system, nature worship? You can find support for all these definitions (and many more) in dictionaries, encyclopaedias, and text books of religion, but subscribe to any one and the truth will evade you. Above all Paganism is a creative pursuit, an encounter with reality, an exploration of meaning and an expression of the soul. Druids, Heathens, Wiccans and others, all contribute their insights and literary riches to the Pagan tradition. Moon Books invites you to begin or to deepen your own encounter, right here, right now. If you have enjoyed this book, why not tell other readers by posting a review on your preferred book site. Recent bestsellers from Moon Books are:

Journey to the Dark Goddess
How to Return to Your Soul
Jane Meredith
Discover the powerful secrets of the Dark Goddess and transform your depression, grief and pain into healing and integration.
Paperback: 978-1-84694-677-6 ebook: 978-1-78099-223-5

Shamanic Reiki
Expanded Ways of Working with Universal Life Force Energy
Llyn Roberts, Robert Levy
Shamanism and Reiki are each powerful ways of healing;
together, their power multiplies. *Shamanic Reiki* introduces
techniques to help healers and Reiki practitioners tap ancient
healing wisdom.
Paperback: 978-1-84694-037-8 ebook: 978-1-84694-650-9

Pagan Portals – The Awen Alone
Walking the Path of the Solitary Druid
Joanna van der Hoeven
An introductory guide for the solitary Druid, *The Awen Alone*
will accompany you as you explore, and seek out your own
place within the natural world.
Paperback: 978-1-78279-547-6 ebook: 978-1-78279-546-9

A Kitchen Witch's World of Magical Herbs & Plants
Rachel Patterson
A journey into the magical world of herbs and plants, filled with
magical uses, folklore, history and practical magic. By popular
writer, blogger and kitchen witch, Tansy Firedragon.
Paperback: 978-1-78279-621-3 ebook: 978-1-78279-620-6

Medicine for the Soul
The Complete Book of Shamanic Healing
Ross Heaven
All you will ever need to know about shamanic healing and
how to become your own shaman...
Paperback: 978-1-78099-419-2 ebook: 978-1-78099-420-8

Shapeshifting into Higher Consciousness
Heal and Transform Yourself and Our World with Ancient
Shamanic and Modern Methods
Llyn Roberts
Ancient and modern methods that you can use every day
to transform yourself and make a positive difference in the
world.
Paperback: 978-1-84694-843-5 ebook: 978-1-84694-844-2

Readers of ebooks can buy or view any of these
bestsellers by clicking on the live link in the title. Most
titles are published in paperback and as an ebook.
Paperbacks are available in traditional bookshops. Both
print and ebook formats are available online.

Find more titles and sign up to our readers' newsletter at
http://www.johnhuntpublishing.com/paganism
Follow us on Facebook at
https://www.facebook.com/MoonBooks
and Twitter at https://twitter.com/MoonBooksJHP